NICHO

ORDNANCE SURVEY
GUIDE TO THE
WATERWAYS

1: SOUTH

Nicholson

An Imprint of HarperCollins*Publishers*

Also available in this series:

Nicholson/Ordnance Survey Guide to the Waterways 2. Central
Nicholson/Ordnance Survey Guide to the Waterways 3. North
Nicholson/Ordnance Survey Guide to the River Thames
Nicholson/Ordnance Survey Inland Waterways Map of Great Britain

*The indication of a towpath in this book does
not necessarily imply a public right of way. If you
are in any doubt, check before you proceed with
the latest published Ordnance Survey Map.*
Pathfinder Series (2½ in to 1 mile scale or
1:25 000). These OS walker and rambler maps show the
countryside in great detail, including rights
of way in England and Wales.
Landranger Series (1¼ in to 1 mile scale or
1:50 000). This OS series covers the country
in 204 sheets and is ideal for detailed
exploring by car or on foot.

First published in 1983 by
Nicholson
77-85 Fulham Palace Road
Hammersmith, London W6 8JB
and
Ordnance Survey
Romsey Road, Maybush
Southampton S09 4DH

7th edition 1995

© Text, Nicholson 1995

Nicholson
An Imprint of HarperCollins*Publishers*

The series editor gratefully acknowledges the help
given by British Waterways and their staff. Thanks
is also due to CAMRA representatives and branch
members for their help in recommending real ale pubs.

Cover photograph: Derek Pratt

Great care has been taken throughout this book
to be accurate, but the publishers cannot accept
any responsibility for any errors which appear
or their consequences.

Printed by The Edinburgh Press Ltd.

Ordnance Survey ISBN 0319 00347 7
Nicholson ISBN 07028 2257 5

83/7/89

INTRODUCTION

The canals and navigable rivers of Britain were built as a system of new trade routes at a time when roads were virtually non-existent. After their boom period in the late 18th and early 19th centuries, they gradually declined in the face of fierce competition from the new railway companies, and large-scale commercial carrying ended by the time of the Second World War, when many of the routes had slipped into decay and ruin. It is true that in a few areas goods continue to be carried profitably to this day, but for the majority of canals it was the new traffic of pleasure boats that provided the impetus for rescue and restoration.

There is something for everyone in the canals: engineering feats like aqueducts, tunnels and flights of locks (all of which amazed a world that had seen nothing like it since Roman times); the brightly decorated narrowboats which used to throng the waterways; the wealth of birds, animals and plants on canal banks; the mellow, unpretentious architecture of canalside buildings like pubs, stables, lock cottages and warehouses; and the sheer beauty and quiet isolation that is a feature of so many canals.

So use this book to discover the waterways for yourself; it is one of four volumes covering the South, Centre and North of England and Wales; and the rivers Thames and Wey, and the Basingstoke Canal. A full-colour Nicholson/Ordnance Survey *Inland Waterways Map* is also available to help you plan your route.

Telephone dialling codes

When using dialling codes listed in this book, a '1' should be inserted following the initial '0'.
For example, 0636 becomes 01636.

The following cities now have entirely new codes:

Leeds:	was 0532	becomes **01132**
Sheffield:	was 0742	becomes **01142**
Nottingham:	was 0602	becomes **01159**
Leicester:	was 0533	becomes **01162**
Bristol:	was 0272	becomes **01179**

CONTENTS

Waterways Map showing Nicholson Guide Areas

━━━ Waterways covered in this guide
━━━ Waterways covered in other guides in the series
━━━ Other Waterways
- - - - Waterways unnavigable at present time

Ripon
Ripon Canal
York
River Ouse
Leeds
Aire & Calder Navigation
Navigation
Pocklington Canal
Selby Canal
Selby
Market Weighton Canal
River Hull
Hull
Castleford
Wakefield
Goole
Sheffield & South Yorkshire Navigation
Stainforth
Keadby
River Don
River Trent
River Anceholme
North Sea
Doncaster
River Idle
West Stockwith
Rotherham
Gainsborough
Sheffield
Worksop
Torksey
Chesterfield Canal
Fossdyke & Witham Navigations
River Trent
Lincoln
Newark
Erewash Canal
Gunthorpe
Boston
Trent & Mersey Canal
Nottingham
Kings Lynn
Burton upon Trent
Grand Union Canal
River Soar
Wisbech
Loughborough
Tamworth
Coventry Canal
Ashby Canal
Leicester
Peterborough
River Nene
Grand Union Canal Leicester Section
Foxton
Marston Junction
Rugby
Market Harborough
Welford
River Nene
Oxford Canal
Coventry
Crick
Kingswood Junc
Norton Junction
River Great Ouse
Bedford Rivers
Grand Union Canal
Napton Junction
Braunston Turn
Gayton Junction
Cambridge
Stratford-upon-Avon
Northampton
River Cam
Stoke Bruerne
Cosgrove
Banbury
Grand Union Canal
Oxford Canal
Leighton Buzzard
Marsworth
Bishops Stortford
Thrupp
Aylesbury
Hertford
River Stort
Oxford
Berkhamstead
Watford
Lee Navigation
LONDON
River Thames
Slough
River Thames
Crofton
Hungerford
Reading
Canal
Newbury
Aldershot
Basingstoke Canal
River Medway
Chatham
Guildford
River Wey
Maidstone

HOW TO USE THIS GUIDE

The maps are drawn at a scale of 2 inches to 1 mile. Adjacent to each map section is a description of the countryside and places of interest together with a commentary on the course of the canal or river. Details of the boatyards and pubs marked are also given, adjacent to each map, and are arranged in order from the top of the page to the bottom.

Symbols and abbreviations used in the text:

Ⓑ	Boatyard or boatyard services
Ⓡ	Refuse disposal
Ⓢ	Sewage or 'Elsan' disposal
Ⓦ	Water
Ⓟ	Petrol
Ⓓ	Diesel
Ⓔ	Electric boat recharging
🍺	Public house
✗	Restaurant
❗	Licensed to sell alcohol
L	Open for lunch
D	Open for dinner
EC	Early closing
MD	Market day
BW	British Waterways
IWA	Inland Waterways Association
NT	National Trust

Symbols used on maps:

Ⓑ	Boats or boatyard services
🍺	Public houses
R	Refuse disposal
S	Sewage or 'Elsan' disposal point
W	Water point

28 8' 8"	Locks, with number and 'rise'. The symbol points uphill.
	Staircase locks.
197	Bridge and its number. Many are named.
	Pipe bridge.
	Tunnel - often described in the text.
	Aqueduct - often described in the text.
	Winding hole - turning point for boats longer than ordinary width of the canal (it's pronounced as in the wind that blows). Canal junctions are also good places to 'wind'.
	Weir.

Towing Path

Scale and north point
The strip maps are drawn at 2 inches to 1 mile. North is indicated on each map.

Navigational notes
These appear where necessary to point out potential hazards, navigational limits or other vital information.

Boatyards
Services listed are those usually available; do not, however, expect a hire base to stop what they are doing on fleet 'turn around' day (usually Saturday) to help you - *they will be extremely busy.* Any other day you are sure to be made to feel welcome. Remember also that moorings get filled very quickly, so do not assume that there will be space for your boat. Always ask.

A feature of these guides is the 'milestone' which appears on every map thus:

This performs many useful functions. It reminds you of your direction of travel - in this example **up** the page is towards Napton, **down** the page is towards Oxford; it denotes distances and indicates the number of locks between the milestone and strategic points (usually junctions) along the waterway - in this example, Napton is 22¼ miles (M) with 22 locks (L) from the 'milestone', and Oxford is 27 miles and 17 locks from the milestone. By deducting the miles and locks on one milestone from those on the next, distances from page to page can be accurately estimated. Using the 'lock-miles' system (see **Planning a cruise,** page 13) the time your journey will take can be calculated, and with a little experience based on your speed of travel and lock operation, your own time formula can be arrived at.

Where this device occurs on a map it simply means that the actual route of the waterway would not fit neatly onto the page, so the cartographer has 'bent' the map, using two north points. The navigator on the water, or the walker on the bank, will notice nothing amiss. Distances in this book should be measured along the thick blue line only, not including these gaps.

LOCKS AND THEIR USE

The different locks and their attendant machinery are a source of endless fascination for all waterway users. Understanding why they are there and the principle upon which they work will help you in their use.

A lock is a device for transporting craft from a higher water level to a lower level, or vice versa, for example when a canal crosses a range of hills. It consists of a box with gates at each end, and a separate means of letting water in at the top (higher level) and out at

the bottom (lower level). This is controlled by paddles. These paddles may simply open and shut holes in the gates (gate paddles), or they may open and shut underground culverts (ground paddles). A windlass (carried on the boat) is used to wind the paddles open and shut. Whilst locks differ in detail, the following instructions will apply in the case of the vast majority of *narrow* canal locks. Some extra points regarding wide locks are covered later.

lock gate with paddle mechanism

How to go through a lock

PRELIMINARIES
Stop the boat well outside the lock and secure it. If members of your crew can get off the boat before the lock (at the narrow point under a bridge for example) and run ahead to prepare the lock, this will save time.

GOING UP IN A LOCK (LOCKING UP)

Lock empty - ie water at lower level

Open bottom gates(s)
Drive boat in
Close gate(s)
Check bottom paddles closed
Keep boat near to the bottom of lock
Open top paddles to fill lock
Open top gate(s) when lock is full
Drive boat out
Close top gate(s)
Close up paddles

Lock full - ie water at higher level

Check top gate(s) and paddles closed
Open bottom paddles to drain lock
Open bottom gate(s)
Drive boat in
Close bottom gate(s) and paddles
Keep boat near to the bottom of lock
Open top paddles to fill lock
Open top gate(s) when lock is full
Drive boat out
Close top gate(s)
Close top paddles

GOING DOWN IN A LOCK (LOCKING DOWN)

Lock full – ie water at higher level

Open top gate(s)
Drive boat in
Close top gate(s)
Check top paddles closed
Keep boat near to the bottom of lock
Open bottom paddles to empty lock
Open bottom gate(s)
Drive boat out
Close bottom gates and paddles

Lock empty – ie water at lower level

Check bottom gate(s) and paddles closed
Open top paddles to fill lock
Open gate(s)
Drive boat in
Close top gate(s) and paddles
Keep boat near to the bottom of lock
Open bottom paddles to empty lock
Open bottom gate(s)
Drive boat out
Close bottom gate(s) and paddles

If you have to drain or fill a lock in order to enter it, make sure there is no boat approaching that could usefully use the lock before you. Always try to conserve water, which is being continually passed down the canal from its summit and thus requires constant replenishment at a higher level.

SOME GENERAL DO'S AND DON'TS AT LOCKS

Do not leave your windlass slotted onto the paddle spindle - if something slips it could be thrown off and cause injury.

Always leave all gates and paddles closed when you leave, but look out for notices which may give other instructions for the proper operation of a particular lock.

Always wind the paddles down - letting them drop is bad practice, and causes damage.

Beware of protrusions in the side walls of the lock chamber that may damage the boat, and don't use fenders in narrow locks - they may jam.

When opening and closing lock gates, keep to the landward side of the balance beam.

Don't rush around at locks, especially in wet weather, when the sides are slippery. Never jump across partly opened gates.

Always make the safety of the crew and boat your prime concern and remember that if things do start to go wrong, you can stop everything by closing the paddles.

There is no reason why your children, wearing buoyancy aids and properly supervised, should not help at locks - it is all part of the fun, after all - but impress upon them the potential dangers, and establish some common-sense rules. You have no authority over other people's children, and their participation should be discouraged. Great difficulties could ensue should they be injured in any way.

Beware of fierce top gate paddles, especially in wide locks.

Don't leave your windlass behind; hundreds are lost this way each year.

WIDE LOCKS

Taking a narrowboat (7ft beam) through a wide lock (14ft) can present special difficulties, especially when locking up. If all the top paddles were to be opened fully at the same time, the boat would be buffeted considerably. The diagram below illustrates one method of ensuring a smooth passage. The stern line held ashore will provide added security.

Locking up in a wide lock
(a suggested technique)

1 secure the bow line to a bollard or ring like this, leading BACK from the bows

2 open paddles same side as boat FIRST

3 this will create a circulation of water in the lock that will hold the boat tight on the bow line and hard against the side of the lock

4 gently open remaining paddles so as not to disrupt the circulation already established

STAIRCASE LOCKS

Where the top gates of one lock are the bottom gates of the next. Usually there is a board nearby giving operating instructions - read it carefully and make sure you understand it before you start. And remember: in a narrow staircase you can't pass a boat coming the other way.

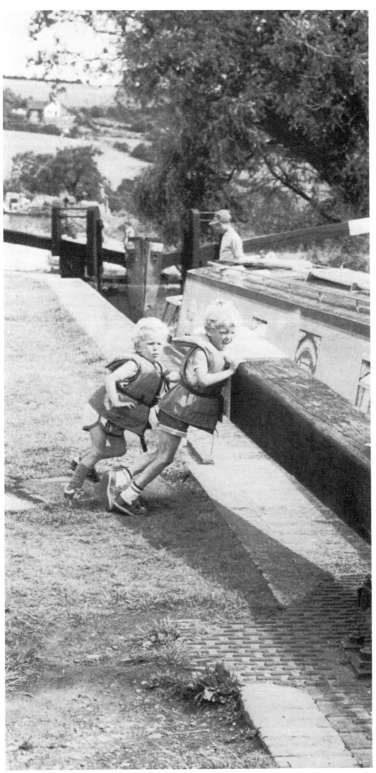

Even young children can help, if properly supervised, but you must make sure life jackets are worn all the time when near the water. *David Perrott.*

GENERAL CRUISING INFORMATION

The majority of the waterways covered in this book are controlled by British Waterways. All craft using BW canals must be licensed and those using BW rivers must be registered. Charges are based on the length of the boat and a canal craft licence covers all the navigable waterways under BW's control. Permits for permanent mooring on the canals are also issued by BW. Apply in each case to the British Waterways Offices listed on page 203 or to:

Customer Services
British Waterways
Willow Grange
Church Road
Watford,
WD1 3QA
Telephone: 0923 226422

Other river navigation authorities relevant to this book are mentioned where appropriate.

Getting afloat

There is no better way of discovering the joys of canals than by getting afloat. The best thing is to hire a boat for a week or a fortnight from one of the boatyards on the canals (each boatyard has an entry in the text, and most of them offer craft for hire; brochures may be easily obtained from such boatyards). Or, go on one of the trip boats for a couple of hours, or longer. The notes on page 13 will help you plan a cruise.

General cruising

Most canals are saucer-shaped in section and so are deepest in the middle. Very few have more than 3-4ft of water and many have much less. Try to keep to the middle of the channel except on bends, where the deepest water is on the *outside* of the bend. When you meet another boat, the rule is to keep to the right, slow down, and aim to miss the approaching boat by a couple of yards: do not steer right over to the bank or you will most likely run aground. The deeper the draught of the boat, the more important it is to keep in the middle of the deep water, and so this must be considered when passing other boats. If you meet a loaded working boat, keep right out of the way. Working boats should always be given precedence, for their time is money. If you meet a boat being towed from the bank, pass it on the outside rather than intercept the towing line. When overtaking, keep the other boat on your starboard, or right, side.

Speed

There is a general speed limit of 4 mph on most British Waterways canals. This is not just an arbitrary limit: there is no need to go any faster, and in many cases it is impossible to cruise even at this speed. Canals were not built for motor boats, and so the banks are easily damaged by excessive wash and turbulence. Erosion of the banks makes the canal more shallow, which in turn makes running aground a more frequent occurrence. So keep to the limits and try not to aggravate the situation. It is easy to see when a boat is creating excessive turbulence by looking at the wash - if it is 'breaking' or causing large waves, you are going too fast and should slow down.

Slow down also when passing moored craft, engineering works and anglers.

Slow down when there is a lot of floating rubbish on the water: old planks and plastic bags may mean underwater obstacles that can damage a boat or its propeller if hit hard. Try to drift over obvious obstructions in neutral.

Slow down when approaching blind corners, narrow bridges and junctions.

Running aground

Running aground is a not uncommon event, but is rarely serious, as the canal bed is usually soft. If you run aground, try first of all to pull the boat off by gently reversing the engine. If this fails, use the pole as a lever against the bank or some solid object, in combination with a tow rope being pulled from the bank. Do not keep revving the engine in reverse if it is obviously having no effect. Another way is to get your crew to rock the boat from side to side while using the pole or mooring lines. If all else fails, lighten your load; make all the crew leave the boat except the helmsman, and then it will often float off quite easily.

Remember that if you run aground once, it is likely to happen again as it indicates a particularly shallow stretch - or that you are out of the channel. If you are continually bumping the bottom in a shallow stretch, it may be that you are going too fast, causing the boat to 'dig in' at the back. Going slower may make things more comfortable.

In a town you may run aground on sunken rubbish; this is most likely to occur near bridges and housing estates. Use the same methods, but be very careful as these hard objects can easily damage your boat or propeller.

Remember that winding holes are often silted up - do not go further in than you have to.

Mooring

All boats carry metal stakes and a mallet. These are used for mooring when there are no rings or bollards in sight, which is usually the case. Generally speaking you may moor anywhere to BW property but there are certain basic rules. Avoid mooring anywhere that could cause an obstruction to other boats; do not moor on a bend, in a winding hole or a narrow stretch, do not moor abreast boats already moored. Never moor in a lock, and do not be tempted to tie up in a tunnel or under a bridge if it is raining. Pick a stretch where there is a reasonable depth of water at the bank, otherwise the boat may bump and scrape the canal bed - an unpleasant sensation if you are trying to sleep. For reasons of peace and quiet and privacy it is best to moor away from main roads and railway lines.

Never stretch your mooring lines across the towpath; you may trip someone up and face a claim for damages.

There is no need to show a riding light at night, except on major rivers and busy commercial canals.

Beware of mooring at unrecognised sites in cities - you may attract the unwelcome attention of vandals.

So long as you are sensible and keep to the rules, mooring can be a pleasant gesture of individuality.

Knots

A simple and easy way of securing a rope to a bollard or mooring stake is to use a couple of round turns and a half hitch or two made with a loop and pulled tight. This can be released quickly by pulling the loose end, which will have been left tidly coiled.

When leaving a mooring, coil all the ropes up again. They will then be out of the way, but ready if needed in a hurry. Many a sailor has fallen overboard after tripping on an uncoiled rope.

Fixed bridges

At most bridges the canal becomes very narrow, a means of saving building costs developed by the engineers. As a result, careful navigation is called for if you are to avoid hitting either the bridge sides with the hull, or the arch with the cabin top. As when entering a lock, the best way to tackle 'bridgeholes' is to slow down well in advance and aim to go straight through, keeping a steady course. Adjustments should be kept to a minimum for it is easy to start the boat zig-zagging, which will inevitably end in a collision. One technique is to gauge the width of the approaching bridgehole relative to the width of the boat, and then watch one side only, aiming to miss that side by a small margin - say 6in; the smaller you can make the margin, the less chance you have of hitting the other side of the bridge. If you do hit the bridge sides when going slowly it is not likely

to do much damage; it will merely strengthen your resolve to do better next time.

Moveable bridges

Swing and lift bridges are an attractive feature of some canals and cannot be ignored as they often rest only 2 or 3ft above the water. They are moved by being swivelled horizontally, or raised vertically. Operation is usually manual, although some have gearing to ease the movement. There are one or two mechanised versions; these have clear instructions at control points. Before operating any bridge make sure that approaching road traffic is aware of your intention to open the bridge. Use protective barriers if there are any and remember to close the bridge again after you.

Some lift bridges are *very unstable,* and could close while your boat is passing underneath, with disastrous consequences. For this reason it is prudent to have your strongest (or heaviest) crew member hold it open until the boat is clear. Many swing bridges are very heavy to operate, and require two strong people to move them. Keep your crew off the sides of the boat when you are negotiating narrow bridges - they could easily be knocked off and seriously injured.

Tunnels

Many people consider a canal incomplete without one or two tunnels, and certainly they are an exciting feature of any trip. Nearly all are easy to navigate, although there are a few basic rules:

Make sure you boat has a good headlight in working order and *always* use it.

If it is a narrow tunnel (ie 7ft) make sure there is no boat coming the other way *before* you enter. Craft of 7ft beam can pass in some wide tunnels - slow right down when you meet to lessen the almost inevitable bump.

In most tunnels the roof drips constantly, especially under ventilation shafts. Put on a raincoat and some form of hat before going in.

A notice on the tunnel portal will give its length, in yards, and will say whether unpowered craft are permitted to use it.

Where there are restrictions on time of entry, and one-way systems, these must be adhered to. To meet head on half way through a long narrow tunnel would create great difficulties.

Safety

Often the gap between a canal craft and tunnel walls or bridges is very narrow, and it is possible for crew members to get crushed while underway. Ensure that everyone is safely inboard when negotiating these hazards.

Care of the engine

Canal boats are generally powered by either diesel, petrol or two-stroke engines. If you have a hire craft, the boatyard will give you instructions for your daily maintenance, which will no doubt include some or all of the following:

Every day before starting off, you should:

Check the oil level in the engine.
Check the fuel level in the tank.

If your engine is water-cooled, check that the filter near the intake is clean and weedfree.

Otherwise the engine will over-heat, which could cause serious damage.

Check the level of distilled water in the battery, and ensure that it is charging correctly.

Lubricate any parts of the engine, gearbox or steering that need daily attention.

Check that the propeller is free of weeds, wire, plastic bags and any other rubbish. The propeller and the water filter should be checked whenever there is any suspicion of obstruction or overheating - which may mean several times a day.

· Pump the bilges every day.

If there is a stern gland greaser, screw it down a turn at the end of each day's cruising.

When navigating in shallow water, keep in mind the exposed position of the propeller. If you hit any underwater obstruction put the engine into neutral immediately. When running over any large floating object put the engine into neutral and wait for the object to appear astern before re-engaging the drive.

Fuel

Petrol engines and petrol/oil outboards are catered for by some boatyards and all road-side fuel stations. Running out is inconvenient; remember you may have to walk several miles carrying a heavy can.

Diesel-powered craft, and narrowboats, in particular, can usually cruise for over two weeks before needing to be refilled. Those using diesel-powered hire craft rarely need to be concerned about fuel. Those with their own boats, however, should bear in mind that boatyards are few and far between on some parts of the network, and should a diesel-powered boat run out of fuel, the system will need to be bled before the engine can run again. Most boatyards sell marine diesel (indicated Ⓓ in the text), which is cheaper than the road fuel.

Electrically powered boats

These are becoming increasingly popular on the inland waterways, in view of their quietness and lack of environmental pollution. Indicated Ⓔ under the **BOATYARD** heading are those establishments known to offer recharging facilities - polite enquiry by electric boat users will certainly reveal more. If you are lucky enough to be using this form of power, please note the following:

All boats using this information are assumed to have a battery charger on board and 50 metres of cable fitted with standard 13 amp terminals.

It is essential for the safety of the boater, the owner of the supply and the general public that a proper residual current circuit breaker (RCD) be carried by the boat and fitted between the boat's cable and the supply unless the supply is already so protected. The RCD must be tested for correct operation before battery charging starts.

Water

Fresh water taps occur irregularly along the canals, usually at boatyards, BW depots, or by lock cottages. These are marked on the maps in the guide. Ensure that there is a long water hose on the boat (BW taps have a ½-inch slip-on hose connection). Fill up every day.

Lavatories

Some canal boats are fitted with chemical lavatories which must only be emptied at one of the sewage disposal points marked on the map Ⓢ (for which you will need a BW key) or located at boatyards. Many boats now have pump-out toilets, which must be emptied with a special machine - usually at boatyards and indicated in the text. This symbol at the canalside indicates just such a 'pump-out station' (although not all boatyards with the facility display it). Expect to have to pay.

Some BW depots and boatyards have lavatories for the use of boat crews; again, you may need your BW key.

Litter

Keep all rubbish until you can dispose of it at a refuse disposal point, indicated Ⓡ on the map, or at a boatyard equipped to deal with it. Do not throw anything over the side.

By-laws

Although no-one needs a 'driving licence' to navigate a boat, boat users should remember that they have certain responsibilities to others on the waterways and should abide by the Waterways Code (available from BW offices). Prospective navigators are advised to obtain a copy of the by-laws relevant to the waterways on which they are to travel.

FREEPHONE CANALS

Ring 100 and ask the operator for this service if you are confronted with an emergency out of office hours. Vodaphone and Cellnet users should ring 0384 240948.

Stoppages

Although BW and other navigation authorities plan their maintenance for the winter months, it often becomes necessary to carry out repairs during the cruising season. Many of the structures on the canal system are beginning to show their age (especially the tunnels) and repairs are a lengthy and costly affair, sometimes resulting in stoppages lasting many years. A long dry spell can lower water levels and restrict lock operation, and a canal embankment can, of course, breach at any time.

To avoid disappointment it is wise to check that your planned route is clear before you set off, and that there are no time restrictions on locks that may upset your schedule. Those using hire craft may be able to get this information from their boatyard, although some are surprisingly lax. It is best to check for yourself by ringing the BW Area Offices (listed at the end of this book) or the relevant navigation authority. News of any last minute stoppages is available on 'Canalphone', as a recorded message. Ring 0923 201401 for the North and Midlands, or 0923 201402 for the South and Midlands. Check before you go.

PLANNING A CRUISE

It is wise when planning a cruise to establish a means of calculating the time it takes to travel any given length of canal. This ensures that you can reliably work out whether you will reach a shop or pub before closing time. And of course for those who have hired their boat, it is vital to return to the starting point on time.

The time taken to navigate any canal depends, of course, on the average cruising speed of your boat and the amount of time it takes to negotiate the locks along the way. Remember that there is in any case an overall legal speed limit of 4 mph on all canals. In practice, 3 mph is a realistic canal cruising speed for most boats and 3 mph is the maximum which can be achieved on shallow canals, such as the Peak Forest.

To the uninitiated, 3 mph may sound an unbearably slow rate of progress through the countryside; but a few hours of gentle cruising on a fine day is usually enough to convert most people to this pace. For only by proceeding at walking pace can you appreciate the peace and beauty of the countryside, watch the bird life, and see the scurry of voles, rats and other creatures as they suddenly notice the slowly approaching boat.

The length of time taken to work through a lock depends on several things: whether the lock is full or empty, wide or narrow, deep or shallow. It depends on the number and size of the paddles that control the sluices, on the presence or otherwise of other boats near the lock, and of course on the number and competence of the boat crew. Most people take between 10-20 minutes on average to work through a typical lock - or, to put it another way, they may take as long to get through a lock as they would have taken to travel another mile at 3 mph. Herein lies a basis for a simple method of estimating time required to travel along a given length of canal: take the number of miles to be travelled and add the number of locks to be negotiated on the way. This gives the number of 'lock-miles'. Divide this by three, and the result is the approximate length of time it will take, in hours. Thus if you intend to travel 30 miles, and there are 12 locks along the way, the calculation is as follows: 30 + 12 divided by 3 (mph) = 14 hours, assuming your average cruising speed to be 3 mph and assuming you take about 20 minutes to get through each lock (if they are all narrow locks in good condition then you may well better this time). The length

of your journey and the number of locks can easily be calculated using the 'milestones' that appear on every map in this series of guides. To refine the system, simply tailor it more closely to the actual cruising speed of your boat and the efficiency of your lock-operating technique.

An excellent fortnight's trip, for example, would be the circuit formed by the River Soar and Trent & Mersey, Coventry, Oxford and Grand Union (Leicester section) canals. This is 152 miles and 100 locks long (about 84 hours' cruising time), and takes you through some of the very best parts of Leicestershire. You will see the Foxton staircase locks, Braunston Tunnel, the delightful canal village of Shardlow and have time to explore the lock-free Ashby Canal (22 miles long - 2 days there and back) or the meandering course of the unspoilt Market Harborough arm, 5 miles long.

For just a one-week holiday, a good round trip with plenty of contrasts could encompass the Staffs & Worcs north of Aldersley Junction, the Trent & Mersey from Great Haywood to Fradley, the Coventry to Fazeley Junction, the Birmingham & Fazeley to Farmers Bridge and returning along the Birmingham Canal Main Line. With 75 miles and 79 narrow locks, this should take no more than 50 hours' cruising time. You will enjoy the old locks and bridges of the Staffs & Worcs as it follows the pretty valleys of the rivers Penk and Sow, culminating at Tixall Wide. After a visit to Shugborough Hall you continue past the eccentric footbridge at Drayton Manor before starting the long climb to Farmers Bridge. There's a choice of routes on the Birmingham Canal Main Line to complete the circuit.

These are just two examples of the many circular cruising routes available - a glance at the planning map on pages 4 and 5 will reveal many more. Of course, there is also much to be said for a straight out and back cruise - it will all look different when you are coming the other way, and you can arrange to re-visit that favourite pub again. The whole secret is to *allow plenty of time*, for shopping, for exploring and for gentle cruising. Many a holiday has been spoilt by becoming a race against time. The most comprehensive source of information for planning a waterways cruise is Nicholson's *The Ordnance Survey Inland Waterways Map of Great Britain*.

See also 'Stoppages' in the **General Cruising Information** section.

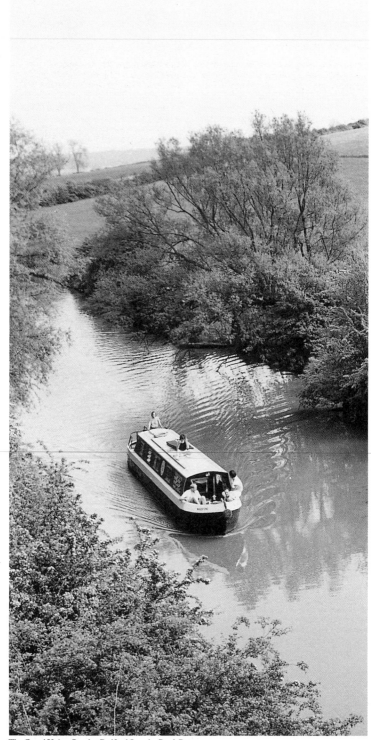

The Grand Union Canal at Radford Semele. *Derek Pratt.*

RIVER AVON

Maximum dimensions

Length: 70'
Beam: 13' 6"
Draught: 3' 6"
Headroom: 8' (at normal levels)

Lower Avon Navigation Trust
(Tewkesbury to Evesham Lock)
Mill Wharf, Mill Lane, Wyre Piddle,
Pershore, Worcs. Tel: (0386) 552517

Upper Avon Navigation Trust
(Evesham Lock to Alveston Sluice)
Avon House, Harvington, Evesham, Worcs.
Tel: (0386) 870526.

Mileage

Avon Lock, TEWKESBURY to:
Pershore Lock: 14 ½
Evesham Lock: 25 ¾
Bidford Bridge: 32 ¾
Tramway Bridge, STRATFORD: 42 ¼
Alveston Sluice: 45 ½

Locks: 17

Rising at Welford on the Leicestershire and Northampton boundary and joining the River Severn at Tewkesbury, the River Avon was first made navigable to Stratford by William Sandys of Fladbury during the period 1636-39, with plans to extend eventually to Warwick.

In 1717 the ownership of the river was split into the Upper and Lower Avon, the dividing line being Workman Bridge, Evesham; following several changes in ownership, the Upper river was purchased by the Great Western Railway in 1863. By refusing tolls they avoided the obligation to maintain the river and as a result within 10 years it was in a ruinous state. In 1875 all traffic on the Upper Avon had ceased.

Although deteriorating gradually, the Lower Avon did remain navigable to Pershore until it was bought, for £1500, by C. D. Barwell in 1950. At this time the Lower Avon Navigation Trust was formed and restoration began, with navigation being restored to the Bridge Inn, Offenham by June 1964. In July of that year, the southern section of the Stratford-on-Avon Canal from Kingswood Junction to Stratford was also re-opened, making the restoration of the Upper Avon the next logical step. But with no right of access to the river, a non-effective navigation authority, all but two of the weirs collapsed and the locks in complete ruin, it seemed an all but impossible task.

Under the leadership of David Hutchings MBE the Upper Avon Navigation Trust was formed in 1965, and in 1969 work began. An appeal was made to raise £300,000 and eventually over a third of this sum was given by one anonymous donor. Despite enormous difficulties, the Upper river was officially opened by HM Queen Elizabeth the Queen Mother on 1 June 1974. A truly magnificent achievement for private initiative and volunteer labour.

Cruising on the Avon

This is a river navigation, and as such can present problems to those more accustomed to the still waters of the canals. Just 36 hours of summer rain can put sufficient 'fresh' water into the river to make passage hazardous – the 'pull' upstream of the weirs increases, cross-currents below the weirs become fierce and the water 'piles up' as it rushes through narrow bridge-holes. *When this happens, all boats must moor up out of the main stream and wait for the level to return to normal.* If you are in any doubt, phone your hire company or seek expert advice.

All the locks on the river are wide locks, and those on the Upper Avon demonstrate considerable ingenuity in the recycling of gates and paddle gear from other canals and rivers – as a consequence some of the locks are difficult to operate, and require a good deal of physical strength. Do not believe that a cruise on this part of the river will necessarily be restful.

Finally, those accustomed to the cosy informality and 'go as you please' atmosphere of the narrow canals will not be impressed by the plethora of 'Private' and 'No Mooring' notices. Many landowners and local authorities have yet to come to terms with the river, especially the Upper river, as a navigation, and boaters can begin to feel distinctly unloved. Many villages are sited back from the river, away from the floods, and the scenery is generally that of quiet water-meadows with prolific bird life. However, those who plan their journey carefully and avoid the crowded summer peak period will find much to enjoy.

The Lower and Upper Navigation Trusts are charities operated almost entirely by volunteers. Boat crews can help them to keep down their costs by observing their rules and requests. They should also be acquainted with the relevant by-laws, and ensure that their craft is equipped with such items as an anchor made off to a chain and warp, a bow fender and so on.

Remember also:

Power gives way to sail.

Maximum speed – Lower Avon 6 mph, Upper Avon 4 mph.

Watch out for anglers, and slow down.

Keep off private land.

Keep well away from weirs and slow down when approaching locks and blind corners.

Moor only at recognised sites, moor economically, and be prepared to 'breast up' (moor side by side) where this does not obstruct traffic. Moorings are *very* limited and marked [M] on the maps.

Tewkesbury

The River Avon joins the Severn some 600 yards upstream past Healing's Mill, which still receives grain by barge from time to time, is the attractive Avon Lock, mechanised and with a resident lock keeper (0684 292129). Continuing upstream through the narrow navigation arch of King John's Bridge, built circa 1200 and widened in 1964, the river widens, passing a marina on its way into open farmland and water-meadows, a reach extensively used by the local sailing clubs. There is no longer a ferry at Twyning, and moorings are limited to those of the attractive Fleet Inn, where a lane beside the pub leads to the small village.

Navigational note
Craft entering the Avon from the Severn should be wary of a shallow spit projecting south west from the north bank at the junction of the two rivers. When approaching from upstream on the Severn, do not cut the corner but steer close to the south side of the junction. Craft leaving the Avon and wishing to proceed upstream on the Severn should not turn north until Mythe Bridge can be seen in its entirety.
Craft navigating between the Severn and the Avon Lock should steer a course close to the Town Quay and Healing's Mill, thus avoiding the mudbank opposite. Note that Avon Lock is operated by a resident lock keeper – do not disturb him outside his usual operating times, which are posted by the lock. Keep your craft clear of the lock wall nearest the lock house, as there are three metal bosses that stand proud of the wall, and may catch your boat when ascending or descending.
When entering the Avon from the lock, and when passing through the centre arch of King John's Bridge, visibility is restricted, and great care should be taken.

Tewkesbury
Glos. EC Thur. MD Wed, Sat. All services. A historic town at the junction of the rivers Avon and Severn, with many attractive and ancient buildings to see, chief among these being, of course, the Abbey. One of the more unusual aspects of Tewkesbury is the great number of tiny alleys leading off the main street that is the backbone of the town. These alleys yield tempting views of discreet cottages, gardens, back walls and private yards. One of these – Baptist Chapel Court – leads to the old chapel, built around 1655. This tiny, simple building and its little burial ground reflect well the modest aspirations of the minority Baptist movement. There are many other buildings of great interest throughout Tewkesbury, chiefly of the timbered variety, with overhanging gables. Some have curious names like 'House of the Nodding Gables' and 'Ancient Drudge'. There is also a liberal scattering of historic pubs, notably the Hop Pole Inn (associated with Dickens' *Pickwick Papers*) and the Bell hotel, an Elizabethan building which was Abel Fletcher's home in the book *John Halifax, Gentleman.*
Tewkesbury Abbey This superb building is cathedral-like in proportions and is generally reckoned to be one of the finest Norman churches in the country. It is contemporary with Gloucester Cathedral, and has the same type of vast cylindrical arches the length of the nave. This massive scale is repeated throughout the building: the beautifully decorated central tower, 46ft square and over 130ft high, is the largest Norman tower in existence. The recessed arch that frames the mighty west window is over 60ft high. The Abbey's interior is no less splendid than the exterior, and contains interesting monuments, notably the Despencer and Beauchamp tombs. The Abbey, which was completed in about 1120, was part of a Benedictine monastery until this was threatened with dissolution by King Henry VIII in 1539. The townspeople bought the Abbey – for £453 – to save it from demolition, and it became the town's parish church.

The Abbey Cottages Church Street. The most unusual buildings in Tewkesbury must surely be the row of medieval shops near the Abbey. These 25 cottages were rescued from dereliction and threatened demolition when it was realised that they are unique in this country. As built, in about 1450, they were made of wattle and daub in a heavy timber framework. The ground floor consisted of trodden earth, the windows had no glass, and there was no chimney in the roof – the smoke from the fireplace escaped through a hole under the eaves. The shutters covering the big window facing the street folded down to form a shop counter. One of the houses has been restored to this original state and may be visited: the others have been modified to provide pleasantly discreet modern houses. This restoration won a Civic Trust award.
Tewkesbury Museum Barton Street. A small museum in a delightfully irregular timber-framed house. Displays of local history, costumes and furniture. Also a large model of the Battle of Tewkesbury. *Open weekdays during the summer.*
Barton Fair takes place in Tewkesbury every *10 October* except when that date falls on a Sunday. One of the oldest fairs in the country, it used to be held at the monastery gate.
Tewkesbury Steam Fair and Organ Festival every *July*, in the meadows by the Avon. This is becoming an important event on steam enthusiasts' calendars, attracting increasing numbers of cherished traction engines, steam rollers and miscellaneous fairground machinery every year.
Battle of Tewkesbury 4 May 1471 The last decisive battle in the Wars of the Roses, fought to the south of the town, where the Lancastrians, under Queen Margaret's commanders Somerset, Wenlock and Devonshire were defeated by Edward IV's Yorkists under Edward, Gloucester and Hastings.
Tourist Information Centre 64 Barton Street, Tewkesbury (0684) 295027.

BOATYARDS

Ⓑ **The Tewkesbury Yacht Marina** Bredon Road, Tewkesbury (0684 293737).
Ⓡ Ⓢ Ⓦ Ⓟ Ⓓ Ⓔ Pump-out, gas, overnight mooring, long-term mooring, winter storage, slipway, gantry, chandlery, books and maps, boat sales, engine repairs, toilets, showers.
Ⓑ **Telestar Pleasure Cruisers** 185 Queen's Road, Tewkesbury (0684 294088). On the Mill Avon by Abbey Mill. Cruiser hire, day boat hire. BW & Avon licences.

MOORING

See also Boatyards and Pubs. Overnight moorings on Mill Avon by Healing's Mill (fee).

PUBS AND RESTAURANTS

There are many pubs and hotels in Tewkesbury, including:
🍺 **Bell** Church Street. 12thC inn opposite the Abbey.
🍺 **Berkeley Arms** Church Street. 17thC.
🍺 **Olde Black Bear** High Street. Said to be the oldest inn in Gloucestershire.
🍺 **Riverside** On the Mill Avon. Mooring by arrangement.
🍺✕ **Royal Hop Pole Hotel** On the Mill Avon near Abbey Mill (0684 293236). Lunch and dinner, mooring by arrangement.
🍺 **Fleet Inn** Twyning. Riverside with gardens, overnight mooring by arrangement.
🍺 **Village Inn** Twyning.

River Avon at Tewkesbury. *Derek Pratt.*

Bredon

A ½ mile above Twyning, the M5 motorway crosses the flood plain on a high embankment, beyond which is the village of Bredon, where the fine 14thC Tithe Barn can be seen from the river. There are many moored cruisers and tidy gardens making the river-front attractive and interesting. The river is wide to Strensham Lock, and is used extensively by the unusually named Severn Sailing Club. Below the lock a pipe bridge carries the Coventry Water Main over the navigation, and beyond this the weir spills into the river, creating a very strong cross current when there is 'fresh' water in the river. The lock is operated by a resident lock keeper (0386 750355) who lives in the old Mill House. A limited number of moorings are available by arrangement with him, and you may buy an ice cream here. The river now starts to meander around Eckington village, passing under a railway bridge carrying the main Exeter to Newcastle-upon-Tyne line before reaching Eckington Bridge, a many-arched and irregular 16thC structure, still in good condition.

Bredon
Hereford & Worcs. PO, stores. A substantial and attractive village with many fine timbered buildings. Close to the river is a 14thC Tithe Barn (National Trust), 124ft long and once one of the best preserved in the country, where grain – paid as taxes to the church – was once stored. Severely damaged by fire, it has now been rebuilt. The Church of St Giles has a vaulted Norman porch, and dates from c1180 – it was mentioned by John Masefield in 'All the land from Ludlow Town to Bredon Church's spire'. Bredon Hill, which dominates the river for several miles, rises to 961ft some 3 miles to the north east – it is said that eight or more counties can be seen from its summit on a fine day. On the southern slope is an 18thC castellated folly, Bell's Castle, and on the top is a 2ndC BC hill fort containing Parson's Folly, a prominent tower built late 18thC. The hill was celebrated in A. E. Housman's *A Shropshire Lad*.

Strensham
Hereford & Worcs. Birthplace of Samuel Butler (1612-1680), verse satirist and secretary to Judge Thomas Jeffrey, who lived in the 16thC house by the well-sited Church of St Phillip and St James, which has a painted gallery and two fine brasses of the Russells, once the Lords of the Manor. The key is kept at the farm.

Eckington
Hereford & Worcs. PO, stores. A dormitory village of little interest except for Holy Trinity Church, which dates from the 12thC, and three pubs. Walk from Strensham Lock or Eckington Bridge.

MOORING
Overnight mooring by prior arrangement with the lock keeper at Strensham (0386 750355).

PUBS AND RESTAURANTS
◗ **Royal Oak** Bredon.
◗✕ **Fox & Hounds** Bredon. (0684 72377). Thatched 15thC inn with garden and restaurant.
◗ **Crown Inn** Eckington.
◗ **Bell Inn** Eckington.
◗ **Anchor Inn** Cotheridge Lane, Eckington. Wadworth real ale.

Pershore

Above Eckington Bridge, the river meanders beside the ever-present Bredon Hill, turning a full 180 degrees at the Swan's Neck. Nafford Lock adjoins the wilderness of Nafford Island, a nature reserve, and a path leads from here to Birlingham, 1 mile to the north west. The swing bridge across the lock must be left closed on leaving. The path over the sluice leads to Eckington, Woollas Hall and Great Comberton but, alas, there are no moorings by the lock, the next being those at Comberton Quay.

Navigational notes

1 The two bridges at Pershore are extremely difficult to navigate when there is 'fresh' water in the river. The navigable arches align awkwardly and the current rushes around the piers of the old bridge, causing turbulence.
2 When *filling* the chamber of Pershore Lock to lock up, open the ground paddle first, then open the gate paddle when it is submerged. When *emptying* the chamber to lock down, ensure the ground paddle is closed.

Woollas Hall A mile south of Nafford Lock. Elizabethan manor house with a three-storey porch, now divided into flats. Beyond the hall a track climbs to the summit of Bredon Hill.
Great Comberton
Hereford & Worcs. Stores. One of the timeless small villages which surround Bredon Hill – Little Comberton, Bricklehampton and especially Elmley Castle, with its half-timbered cottages and Church of St Mary, are worth visiting.
Pershore
Hereford & Worcs. All services, and swimming baths by the river. A busy market town with many well-kept Georgian buildings, set among fruit farms and market gardens. The fine six-arched 14thC bridge over the Avon no longer carries traffic – a three-arched structure built in 1928 now takes the load. The Abbey, now the Parish Church of Holy Cross, was built on the site of a wooden building erected in AD689 by King Oswald. This was replaced in AD983 by a new building commissioned by Ethelwold, and again by a later Norman building, finally consecrated in 1239. In 1288 a fire destroyed part of the Abbey (and much of the town) resulting in much rebuilding before the dissolution in 1539. Restoration was by Scott 1862-65. Of the original Norman building, the nave, crossing and transepts survive. The Church of St Andrew, very close by, is now a community centre. Perrott House in Bridge Street was built in 1760 by George Perrott, when he purchased the Lower Avon Navigation.

BOATYARDS
Ⓑ **Millside Boatyard** 37a Bridge Street, Pershore (0386 552849). Ⓦ Ⓟ Ⓓ Slipway, gas, boat and engine repairs, long-term mooring, chandlery, toilets, winter storage.

MOORING
See also Pubs and Restaurants. There are good overnight moorings above Eckington Bridge, and less attractive ones at Birlingham Wharf (Swan's Neck), Comberton Quay and Defford Road Wharf. The Recreation Ground moorings above Pershore Lock are convenient for the town, and thus very popular. There is also limited mooring below the lock.

PUBS AND RESTAURANTS
🍺 **Old Mill** Elmley Castle. Food, garden.
🍺 **Plough Inn** Elmley Castle. Own brew cider.
🍺 **Queen Elizabeth** Elmley Castle. Food, garden.
🍺 **Cider House** Woodmancote, Defford.
🍺 **Defford Arms** Garden.
🍺✗ **Angel Inn** Pershore (0386 552046). Riverside garden. Mooring by arrangement.
🍺 **Brandy Cask** Pershore. Mooring by arrangement.
🍺✗ **Star Hotel** Bridge Street, Pershore (0386 552704). Mooring by arrangement.

Wyre Piddle

The reach between the locks at Pershore and
Wyre Piddle is the shortest on the navigation,
being just 1 mile. Wyre Mill, called by the
traveller Charles Showell 'the ugliest, of which
the Avon is ashamed', is now used by the
Lower Avon Navigation Trust as a sailing and
social club. The lock is diamond-shaped, the
last of its kind on the river. Approaching from
downstream the weir creates a strong cross
current, especially after prolonged rain. Wyre
Piddle (the Piddle Brook runs behind the
village) spreads around the outside of a wide
bend, with gardens down to the river, and the
Anchor Inn providing a useful mooring for
patrons. The villages then skirt the flood plain
of the Avon, and there is little to see except for
the wild-life – those interested in herons will
be particularly pleased. Beyond the Coventry
Water Main Bridge the village of Cropthorne
sits on higher ground to the south east. Below
Jubilee Bridge are the remains of the last flash
lock on the river, dismantled in 1961.

Wyre Piddle
Hereford & Worcs. PO, stores. A main road
village with no public mooring. The church
has a Norman chancel arch and font, and an
early English bellcote.
Cropthorne
Hereford & Worcs. Store. An attractive village
of thatch and timbers on the 'Spring blossom
route'. Much local fruit and vegetable produce
is sold from small roadside stalls in this area.

MOORING

See also Pubs and Restaurants. There are
overnight moorings in the weir stream at Wyre
Lock.

PUBS AND RESTAURANTS

🍺✗ **Anchor Inn** Wyre Piddle (0386
552799). Bar meals and restaurant, large
riverside garden and the only mooring for the
village, by arrangement only.
🍺 **New Inn** Cropthorne.

Fladbury

The approach channel below Fladbury Lock is extremely narrow and steep sided, with restricted vision. The lock walls narrow towards the base and this should be borne in mind when two craft lock down together. The beautiful Fladbury Mill overlooks the weir – it was in use as recently as 1930, and ferry wires, difficult to see from upstream, stretch across the weir stream. On the north side, beyond the railway bridge carrying the main London to Worcester line, is Evesham golf course. Above Craycombe Turn are extensive woodlands, while to the south lie the inevitable water-meadows, with few buildings or roads near the river. There is another handsome mill at Chadbury Lock, which was restored in 1952-53, the first major project carried out by the Lower Avon Navigation Trust, who were helped by the Royal Engineers. Beyond the lock, the river passes the Abbey Manor House and a boatyard, before passing through Evesham in a wide loop.

Fladbury
Hereford & Worcs. PO, stores. A picturesque village of half-timbered houses and cottages around a square, once the home of William Sandys, who began making the Avon navigable in 1636. The Church of St John Baptist has a fine 14thC rib-vaulted porch and contains some fine brasses to John Throckmorton and his wife. About 1 mile to the north east is Craycombe House, built c1791 by George Byfield for George Perrott (*see Pershore, page 19*) and later restored by the author Francis Brett Young, who lived here from 1932 until he went to South Africa after the Second World War.
Wood Norton
Above the north bank below Chadbury Lock. Once the seat of the Duc d'Aumale and later the Duc d'Orléans, pretender to the throne of France, it now houses an engineering school run by the BBC, who have built some incongruous modern buildings to accompany the mansion.
Abbey Manor House
1 mile above Chadbury Lock, on the north bank, c1840. An obelisk in the grounds overlooks the site of the Battle of Evesham, 4 August 1265, when Simon de Montfort and his rebel barons were defeated by the Royalists under Prince Edward, resulting in some 4000 deaths. Another memorial, the Leicester Tower, built c1840, is visible in the woodland.

BOATYARDS
Ⓑ **Sankey Marine** Worcester Road, below the Abbey Manor House, Evesham (0386 442338). Ⓦ Ⓟ Ⓓ Gas, overnight mooring, long-term mooring, winter storage, slipway, chandlery, books and maps, boat sales, engine sales and repairs, toilets, showers. Restaurant and bar at *weekends.*

MOORING
See also Boatyards. Overnight mooring available at Craycombe Turn.

PUBS
🍺 **Anchor** Fladbury.
🍺 **Chequers** Fladbury.
🍺 **Gardener's Arms** The Green, Charlton.

Evesham

Care should be taken approaching Hampton Ferry, where a wire stretches across the river – this will be lowered when the ferry man hears three long blasts of your hooter. Above the ferry to the west is Clarke's Hill, where the monks of Evesham once grew vines. Beyond the A435 road bridge the Abbey Public Park opens out to the north, with riverside gardens giving way to the borough moorings and Workman Gardens to the east, below the handsome Workman Bridge, built in 1856. After passing through the centre arch of the bridge, you will see the lock to the left past the old mill stream. This marks the boundary between the Lower and Upper Navigation. There is a resident lock keeper here (0386 6511), who lives in an unusual triangular house built in 1972 to span the chamber of an earlier lock. He has a small shop and sells Lower Avon Navigation Trust licences. Lock open *09.00-18.00 Easter-May, 09.00-20.00 May-Sep, 09.00-1800 Oct-Nov, 10.00-16.00 Nov-Easter.* Craft should keep well away from the weir above the lock, passing close to the boatyard on the opposite bank. The river is then once again in open country, entering the Vale of Evesham, a major fruit and vegetable growing area. The wooden bridge at Offenham no longer exists but a cable ferry operates by the Bridge Inn, and a lookout should be kept for this obstruction.

Evesham
Hereford & Worcs. EC Wed. All services. A town which owes the major part of its prosperity to the fruit and vegetable growing in the Vale of Evesham – in the spring a mass of blossom, and in the autumn rich in local produce. All that remains of the once-important Benedictine abbey, founded in AD714 by Bishop Egwin and dissolved by Henry VIII in 1539, is the fine timbered gatehouse, a detached bell tower (1533) and a few ruins. Close by there are elegant Georgian buildings and half-timbered houses, Booth Hall (late 15thC) being a fine example. Close to the bell tower are two notable churches – St Lawrence (16thC) and All Saints (12thC). There is an annual regatta on *Spring Bank Holiday*, rowing boats can be hired and an ex-Thames steamer, the *Gaiety*, does trips.
Tourist Information Centre The Almonry Museum, Abbey Gate, Evesham (0386 446944).
Offenham
Hereford & Worcs. EC Sat. PO, tel, stores. Twelve centuries ago this was the headquarters of Offa, King of Mercia; today it is one of the few English villages to possess a maypole.

BOATYARDS
Ⓑ **Evesham Marina** Kings Road, Evesham (0386 47813). Ⓡ Ⓦ Ⓓ Pump-out, gas, narrowboat hire, overnight mooring, long-term mooring, winter storage, slipway, crane, books and maps, boat building, boat sales, engine repairs.

MOORING
See also Boatyards and Pubs and Restaurants. There is a single overnight mooring, for a fee, below the A435 bridge on the south side, and extensive borough moorings by Workman Gardens, for a fee. Weir Meadow Caravan Park, between Workman Bridge and the lock, has overnight moorings with full facilities for craft up to 24ft long. By arrangement, ring 0386 442417. Above Evesham Lock (fee).

PUBS AND RESTAURANTS
◗ **Cider Mill** Hampton.
◗✕ **Northwich Arms Hotel** Waterside, Evesham (0386 40322). Grill and Buttery. Moorings opposite, by arrangement.
◗✕ **Evesham Hotel** Coopers Lane, Evesham (0386 765566). Garden, moorings opposite.
◗ **Swan** Port Street, Evesham. Snacks.
◗✕ **Bridge Inn** by the ferry, Offenham (0386 446565). Mooring by arrangement.

Bidford-on-Avon

George Billington Lock is the first of the new
Upper Avon locks, built in the winter of 1969.
The unusual flood-proof lock keeper's hut, the
'Offenham light', is a more recent addition.
The new lock cut joins the river at right angles,
and care should be exercised when rejoining
the main course. Robert Aickman New Lock
soon follows, overlooked by Harvington Mill,
disused since the turn of the century. The
original Robert Aickman Lock was the first to
be built on the restored Upper Avon, but was
re-sited in 1982 due to erosion and silting of
the original course. The steep ridge of Cleeve
Hill closes from the south to a virtual cliff at
the water's edge below Cleeve Prior.

Navigational note
The navigation arch of Bidford Bridge is to the
far right when heading upstream.

Middle Littleton
Hereford & Worcs. Walk east from the Fish &
Anchor Inn to see the tithe barn thought to
have been built by John de Ombersley, Abbot
of Evesham from 1367 to 1377. Nearby is the
17thC manor house and St Nicholas's
Church.
Cleeve Prior
Hereford & Worcs. PO, stores. The manor
house (private) is a handsome 16thC building,
standing in well-kept grounds with a fine
display of yews. The Church of St Andrew still
retains some Norman and Early English work.
Bidford-on-Avon
Warwicks. PO, stores, bank. The irregularly-
arched bridge was built in 1482 by the monks
of Alcester, near the site of a Roman ford
which was finally removed in 1970. A new
bypass has brought peace to this pleasant
village of old timbered buildings, amongst
which is the solidly built former Falcon Inn –
Shakespeare is said to have taken part in a
drinking contest here. The Church of St
Lawrence, by the river, dates from 1276, but
was restored in 1835.

BOATYARDS

Ⓑ **Bidford Boats** Riverside House, 4 The
Pleck, Bidford-on-Avon (0789 773205).
Ⓢ Ⓦ Narrowboat hire, overnight mooring,
long-term mooring, winter storage, slipway,
boat sales, minor engine repairs.

MOORING

See also Pubs and Restaurants. There are free
overnight moorings at George Billington Lock
and Robert Aickman New Lock. Overnight
moorings are available, for a fee, at Abbots
Salford Caravan Site (unfortunately on the
opposite bank to Cleeve Prior), and at IWA
Lock (free). The public moorings at Bidford
are very good, but limited in number. There is
a single mooring available at Bell Court on the
town side, and more at Bidford Boats, both for
a fee. Upstream, at Barton, there are free
overnight moorings in the lock cut.

PUBS AND RESTAURANTS

🍺 **Fish & Anchor Inn** George Billington
Lock. Food, gardens. A private ferry crosses
the weir stream from the moorings. Mooring
at the pub for patrons.
🍺✕ **Golden Cross** Harvington (0789
772420). Smart, comfortable modernised pub
offering good value bar food *lunchtime and
evenings*, and Whitbread and Flowers real ales.
Restaurant open *D and Sun L*. Garden, B & B.
🍺✕ **White Lion Hotel** Bidford-on-Avon
(0789 773309). Comfortable hotel next to the
bridge, serving Everards real ale and *lunchtime*
bar meals. Restaurant meals *L & D*. Garden.
🍺 **Anglo-Saxon** High Street, Bidford-on-
Avon. Flowers real ale in a basic village local
near the bridge.
🍺 **Pleasure Boat** High Street, Bidford-on-
Avon. Riverside pub offering Ansells real ale
and food *lunchtime and evenings*.
🍺✕ **Cottage of Content** Barton (0789
772279). A picturesque 15thC pub with a
riverside garden. Flowers real ale, bar snacks
and restaurant meals (*L & D*).

Welford-on-Avon

Proceeding upstream, craft should follow the narrower right-hand channel below Bidford Grange – there were once two mills and a lock here, but now nothing remains. Beyond is the new Pilgrim Lock, built in the winter of 1970. The river flows through attractive meadowland, and pleasant orchards announce the village of Welford-on-Avon and W. A. Cadbury Lock, completed in July 1971. The river meanders round the village, passing a once-fine Victorian house inappropriately adorned with a modern chimney, before the multi-arched Binton Bridges, the former mill and the Four Alls pub are reached. Weston-on-Avon lies to the south on a very attractive stretch of deep water with many trees lining the banks. Luddington Lock was built in spring 1971 – there are overnight moorings here, but a sign informs 'sorry, no shop, no pub'.

Hillborough Manor Private. It is thought that Charles II fled here in September 1651 after being defeated by Cromwell at Worcester.

Welford-on-Avon
Warwicks. PO, tel, stores. The Church of St Peter is of Norman and early English origin, situated in the older and more attractive part of what is now a desirable commuter village. There is a maypole and several pubs. Weston-on-Avon lies a short distance to the east and can be reached by what is, in part, a riverside walk; visit the Church of All Saints, itself by the river.

Luddington
Warwicks. It is thought that Shakespeare may have been married here, in a church now replaced by a more recent building.

MOORING

See also Pubs and Restaurants. There are free overnight moorings at Pilgrim Lock, W. A. Cadbury Lock, Welford (no access to village), and below Binton Bridges (access to Welford) for a fee. There are also free overnight moorings above Luddington Lock.

PUBS AND RESTAURANTS

◗✕ **Four Alls** Binton Bridges (0789 756228). A smart riverside pub and restaurant with a garden, serving Flowers real ale. Its name, in the stained glass of the public bar, is explained thus:

> A King I rule over all
> A parson I pray for all
> A soldier I fight for all
> A farmer I pay for all

Overnight mooring by arrangement. (A similarly named pub, the 'Five-Alls', is situated in Chepstow.) W

◗ **Bell** Welford-on-Avon. A comfortable beamed pub in the village centre. Flowers real ale, bar snacks and children's room.

◗ **Shakespeare Inn** Chapel Street, Welford-on-Avon. A popular local housing the village library. Flowers real ale, bar snacks, and a large garden with a children's play area and barbecue facilities.

Stratford-upon-Avon

The River Stour joins the Avon from the south. The disused railway bridge here once carried the line from Stratford to Gloucester. Weir Brake Lock, which takes its name from the wooded bank to the south east of the river, was completed early in 1973; the weir was completed a few months later. Immediately beyond the disused Stratford to London railway bridge is the very deep Colin Witter Lock, reinforced by a series of rectangular steel girder frames to overcome the high ground pressures and overlooked by a monument to celebrate the reopening of the navigation. On sunny summer weekends the lockside and bridge is thick with gongoozlers enjoying the river, the boats and the extensive parkland. A block of flats now stands on the site of the old Lucy's Mill. Above the lock the river throngs with cruisers, trip boats and rowing boats, overlooked by the red-brick hulk of the Royal Shakespeare Theatre. The Stratford-on-Avon canal basin can be seen beyond the entrance lock below Tramway Bridge, which was built in 1823 to carry the Stratford and Moreton Horse Tramway from the Bancroft basin to Moreton-in-the-Marsh. It is now a footbridge. The 14-arched road bridge was built c1480 by Sir Hugh Clopton, once Lord Mayor of London, and was widened in 1814. The surroundings become quieter as the river gently winds to its effective head of navigation by The Red House, although shallow-draught craft may proceed to just below Alveston Weir.

Stratford-upon-Avon
Warwicks. EC Thur. MD Wed, Fri. All services.
Tourism has been established a very long time in Stratford. It was in 1789 that the first big celebrations in William Shakespeare's honour were organised by the actor David Garrick. They are now held annually on St George's Day, *23 April*, which is believed to be Shakespeare's birthday. An annual Mop Fair on the *12 October* reminds the visitor that Stratford was already well-established as a market town long before Shakespeare's time. (The first grant for a weekly market was given by King John in 1196.) Today, Stratford is well used to the constant flow of charabancs and tourists, ancient charm vying with the expected commercialism that usually mars popular places like this. There are wide streets of endless low, timbered buildings that house dignified hotels and antique shops: plenty of these are also private houses. On the river, hired punts and rowing boats jostle each other while people picnic on the open parkland on the banks. The Royal Shakespeare Theatre, opened in 1932, is a splendid institution on an enviable site beside the Avon, but the aesthetic appeal of its massive 'industrial' style is limited. It was designed by Elizabeth Scott to replace an earlier theatre, destroyed by fire in 1926.
Shakespeare Birthplace Trust Stratford-upon-Avon (0789 204016). This Trust was founded in 1847 to look after the five buildings most closely associated with Shakespeare; four of these are in Stratford (listed below) and the other is Mary Arden's cottage at Wilmcote (see page 178). *There is a standard opening time for these properties; any variation on this standard is shown in the individual entries. Open Apr–Oct 09.00-18.00 Mon–Sat, 10.00-18.00 Sun (to 17.00 Oct); Nov–March 09.00-16.30 Mon–Sat (closed Sun).* Admission charge.
Shakespeare's Birthplace Henley Street. An early 16thC half-timbered building containing books, manuscripts and exhibits associated with Shakespeare and rooms furnished in period style. Next door is the Shakespeare Centre. *Open Sun afternoons Nov–Mar.*
Hall's Croft Old Town. A Tudor house complete with period furniture – the home of Shakespeare's daughter Susanna and her husband Dr John Hall.
New Place Chapel Street. The foundations of Shakespeare's last home set in a replica of an Elizabethan garden.

Anne Hathaway's Cottage Shottery, 1 mile west of Stratford. Dating from the 15thC this fine thatched farmhouse was once the home of Anne Hathaway before she married William Shakespeare. It has a mature, typically English garden, and long queues of visitors in the summer'. The cottage was badly damaged by fire in 1969, but has since been completely restored. *Also open Sun afternoons Nov-Mar.*

Holy Trinity Church Attractively situated among trees overlooking the recently restored lock on the River Avon. It is mainly of the 15thC but the spire was rebuilt in 1763. Interesting misericords depict amusing scenes, and fine monuments include one of William Shakespeare who is buried in the chancel. His tomb bears a curse against anyone who dares to disturb it.

Shakespeare Royal Theatre (Box office 0789 292271). The home of the Royal Shakespeare Company, who produce Shakespeare plays to a very high standard *from Apr to Dec every year.*

Clopton Bridge A very fine stone bridge over the Avon, originally built by Sir Hugh Clopton c1480-90 – he later became Lord Mayor of London. The bridge nearby was built in 1823 to carry a horse-drawn tramway connecting Stratford with Shipston-on-Stour. It is now a footbridge.

Information Centre Judith Shakespeare House, 1 High Street, Stratford-on-Avon (0789 293127). Judith Shakespeare was William's younger daughter. In 1616 she married and moved into this former tavern, once called The Cage. It is a characteristic Elizabethan building of three storeys. Judith Shakespeare is buried in the graveyard of Holy Trinity church in Stratford.

BOATYARDS

There are trip boats and many rowing and motor boats for hire in Stratford-upon-Avon. Ⓑ **Stratford-upon-Avon Marina** by Clopton Bridge, Stratford-upon-Avon (0789 69669). ⓇⓈⓌⒹⒺ Pump-out, gas, narrowboat hire, day boats, overnight

mooring, long-term mooring, winter storage, slipway, groceries, chandlery, books and maps, boat building, boat sales, engine sales and repairs, toilets.

MOORING

See also Boatyards. There are free overnight moorings at Weir Brake Lock, below Stratford New Lock, by the Recreation Ground opposite the theatre, in the Stratford Canal Basin, and at the Old Bathing Place ¼ mile above Clopton Bridge.

BOAT TRIPS

Lady of Camelot Restaurant and conference boat for charter. Up to 60 people. Ring 0789 297459 for details.

PUBS AND RESTAURANTS

There are numerous restaurants, snack bars, fast-food places and pubs in Stratford-upon-Avon, many named for the benefit of visitors, such as 'The Pen & Parchment'. Also:

🍺 ✕ **Black Swan** (known as the Dirty Duck) Waterside. (0789 297312). Theatrical pub with a small terrace. Flowers real ale, bar snacks and restaurant meals (*L & D*).

🍺 ✕ **Arden Hotel** Waterside, opposite the theatre. (0789 294949). Courage and Ind Coope (Burton) real ale, restaurant meals (*L & D*), garden.

🍺 **Old Tramway Inn** Shipston Road. Davenports real ale in a one-roomed pub with a large garden. Meals at *lunchtime*.

🍺 ✕ **Shakespeare Hotel** Chapel Street (0789 294771). Fine old beamed hotel in the town centre. Visit the Froth & Elbow bar for Hook Norton, Davenports, Courage and Bass real ale. Meals (*L & D*), children's room, garden.

🍺 **Slug & Lettuce** Guild Street (0789 299700). Good choice of expensive real ale, and French cuisine (*L & D*). Garden.

🍺 **Ferry Inne** Alveston. Food, garden.

🍺 **Alveston Manor Hotel** Banbury Road.

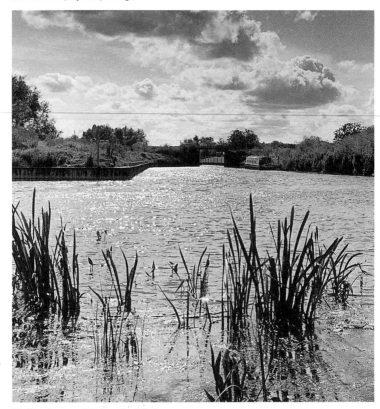

The River Avon near Offenham. *Derek Pratt.*

GRAND UNION

Maximum dimensions

Regent's Canal
Length: 72'
Beam: 14' 6"
Headroom: 8' 6"
Brentford and Paddington to Camp Hill top lock (Birmingham)
Length: 72'
Beam: 12' 6"
Headroom: 7' 6"
Camp Hill top lock to Aston and Salford Junctions
Length: 72'
Beam: 7'
Headroom: 7'
Aylesbury and Northampton Arms
Length: 70'
Beam: 7'
Headroom: 7' 6"

Manager

London Area: 071-286 6101
Cowley to Cosgrove: (044 282) 5938
Cosgrove to Foxton, Norton Junction to Braunston: (0788) 890666
Napton to Camp Hill: (0926) 492192
Camp Hill to Salford Junction: (0902) 409010

Mileage

Thames, BRENTFORD to:
Bull's Bridge: 6
Black Jack's Lock: 16
Watford: 22
Berkhamsted: 33
Bulbourne: 38
Leighton Buzzard: 47½
Fenny Stratford: 55
Cosgrove: 67
Stoke Bruerne: 73
Gayton Junction: 77
Buckby Locks: 89
Braunston: 93½
Napton Junction: 98½
Leamington Spa: 109
Shrewley: 115½
Salford Junction: 137

Locks: 166

Paddington Arm: 13½
No locks

The Grand Union Canal is unique among English canals in being composed of at least eight separate canals. This system links London with Birmingham, Leicester and Nottingham. Up to the 1920s all these canals were owned and operated by quite separate companies: there were five between London and Birmingham alone.

The original – and still the most important – part of the system was the Grand Junction Canal. This was constructed at the turn of the 18thC to provide a short cut between Braunston on the Oxford canal and Brentford, west of London on the Thames. Previously, all London-bound traffic from the Midlands had to follow the winding, narrow Fazeley, Coventry and Oxford canals down to Oxford, there to tranship into lighters to make the 100-mile trip down river to Brentford and London. The new Grand Junction Canal cut this distance by fully 60 miles, and with its 14ft wide locks and numerous branches to important towns rapidly became busy and profitable. The building of wide locks to take 70-ton barges was a brave attempt to persuade neighbouring canal companies – the Oxford, Coventry and the distant Trent and Mersey – to widen their navigations and establish a 70-ton barge standard throughout the waterways of the Midlands. Unfortunately, the other companies were deterred by the cost of widening, and to this day those same canals – and many others – can only pass boats 7ft wide. The history of the English canals might have turned out very differently had the Grand Junction's attempt succeeded.

The mere proposal of the building of the Grand Junction Canal was enough to generate and justify plans for other canals linked to it. Before the Grand Junction itself was completed, independent canals were built linking it in a direct line to Warwick and Birmingham, and a little later a connection was established from the Grand Junction to Market Harborough and Leicester, and thence via the canalised River Soar to the Trent. Unfortunately, part of this line was eventually built with narrow locks, thereby sealing the fate of the Grand Junction's wide canals scheme.

Meanwhile in London in 1812 the Regent's Canal Company was formed to cut a new canal from the Grand Junction's very busy Paddington Arm, round London to Limehouse, where a big dock was planned at the junction with the Thames. This was duly opened in 1820, narrowly escaping conversion at an early stage into a railway, and proved extremely successful. Ten years later a 1½-mile-long canal – the Hertford Union – was built: this remains a useful short cut from Regent's Canal to the River Lee.

These were the canals that made up the spine of southern England's transport system until the advent of the railways. When in this century the Regent's Canal Company acquired the Grand Junction and others, the whole system was integrated as the Grand Union Canal company in 1929. The new company, aided by the Government, in 1932 launched a massive programme of modernisation: widening the 52 locks from Braunston to Birmingham, piling and dredging, etc. But when the grant was all spent, the task was unfinished and broad beam boats never became common on the Grand Union Canal. The great attempt to break loose from narrowboat carrying had failed.

Limehouse

In the Greater London area little specific information is given that does not relate directly to the canal; but canalside pubs and restaurants are included together with some nearby places to eat and drink. Places and features of interest can be found in Nicholson's *London Guide.* The Regent's Canal begins at Limehouse Basin (previously known as Regent's Canal Dock) in London's dockland and climbs up round central London towards Paddington. It is mostly flanked by the backs of houses and factories which usually enclose the canal in a remarkably private and peaceful world of its own. The towpath can now be followed from Salmon Lane Lock along the whole length of the Regent's Canal to West London, and there are frequent access points. New visitor moorings have been provided at Camden, Islington (above City Road), Cowley Lock and Brentford, near the High Street. The IWA organise guided towpath walks *Feb-Nov,* details available on 071-586 2510/2556 (modest charge). The entrance to the Regent's Canal and to the River Lee Navigation from the Thames is through the rebuilt ship lock and across Limehouse Basin. The Hertford Union Canal (often known as Duckett's), is a useful short cut between the Regent's Canal and the Lee Navigation, running along the attractive Victoria Park (see page 108).

Navigational notes
1 The rebuilt Limehouse Basin Ship Lock can accommodate craft 98' x 25' 4" x 9' draught. It is *open daily 08.00-17.00 (but no access 1 hour either side of LW).* Ring 071-895 9930 for information.
2 As with most inner city canals, there is a risk of vandalism. Lock gates between Mile End and Limehouse are padlocked *between 15.30 – 08.30.*

Victoria Park Hackney. Beside the canal. Almost 300 acres of parkland which comes as a relief after so much townscape. Designed by James Pennthorne, a protégé of Nash, and laid out between 1842 and 1845.
Limehouse Basin Limehouse. The terminus of the Regent's Canal and of the Lee Navigation where they meet the Thames, the basin used to be crowded with ships, barges and narrow-boats. Once known as the Regent's Canal Dock, this basin is now a marina. R S W pump-out, mooring, launderette, toilets.

PUBS AND RESTAURANTS

🍺 **Rosemary Branch** 2 Shepperton Road N1. Free house with a good selection of real ale.
🍺 **Rose & Crown** 13 Mare Street E8. Handy pub serving Young's real ale and food *lunchtime and evenings.*
🍺 **Royal Cricketers** 211 Old Ford Road E2. Canalside pub with Whitbread and guest real ales. Meals *lunchtime and evenings (not Sun).* Garden.
🍺 **Fish & Ring** 141a White Horse Road, off Ben Jonson Road. Warm and friendly East End pub dispensing Davenports and Fuller's real ales.
🍺 **Queens Head** 8 Flamborough Street E14. Young's real ale and *lunchtime* food.
🍺✕**Grapes** 76 Narrow Street, Limehouse (071-987 4396). Fine riverside pub serving Taylor Walker and Ind Coope (Burton) real ale. Snacks and seafood restaurant.
🍺 **Barley Mow** 44 Narrow Street (071-265 4983). In the original Dockmaster's office, at the entrance to Limehouse Dock. Taylor Walker, Tetley's and Young's real ale in a splendid new waterside pub. Bar food.
🍺 **The House They Left Behind** Narrow Street. ¼ mile east of Limehouse Dock. The only building left standing in a demolished terrace, this shored-up pub offers a warm welcome and an appetising range of home-cooked food *lunchtime and evenings (not Fri and Sun evenings).* Vegetarians catered for. Webster's and Ruddles real ale. Outside seating.

Regent's Park

The canal continues to climb, passing two large basins before plunging under Islington through a ½ mile tunnel (forbidden to unpowered craft), then round the back of St Pancras and Camden Town passing Battlebridge Basin, site of the London Canal Museum. Here, at Camden High Road, the top locks are reached and the long level begins (27 miles of canal without a lock). Near the top lock is a castellated youth club; boatmen should beware of the many young persons rowing and canoeing nearby, and at Hampstead Road Locks BW have a Canal Information Centre in the lock cottage. Soon the industrial surroundings melt away and, rounding a right-angled bend, the canal suddenly enters London Zoo and Regent's Park – which look splendid from the water. (Do *not* attempt to tie up and walk into the Zoo without paying.) The canal continues through a long wooded cutting, then leaves Regent's Park and skirts the former Marylebone goods yard – now a housing estate – beyond which is the short Maida Hill Tunnel. One emerges into one of the finest stretches of urban canal in the country. Tree-lined and flanked by fine Regency houses, the Regent's Canal ends gloriously at Little Venice. To the left, under the new Westway bridge, is the vast Paddington Basin. To the right is the Paddington Arm of the former Grand Junction Canal. The two stop places seen at Little Venice were used for 'gauging' boats for tolls. There are good moorings and a BW operated pump-out by the Canal Office.

Navigational note
Commencing in 1993 and going on for several years, extensive redevelopmentwill be taking place in the area around St Pancras Basin. Boating facilities will be temporarily relocated at City Road Locks.

Islington Tunnel 960yds long, the tunnel was opened in 1816. In 1826 a towing boat was introduced, which pulled itself to and fro along a chain laid on the canal bed. This system remained until the 1930s.
Camden Lock A fascinating craft and canal centre, with a busy weekend market, around what was once a timber wharf. The castellated lock cottage now houses BW Regent's Canal Information Centre (071-482 0523).
Regent's Park Originally part of Henry VIII's great hunting forest in the 16thC. In 1811 the Prince Regent planned to connect the park and a new palace via the newly built Regent Street to Carlton House. Although never completed, the design by John Nash is very impressive: the park is surrounded by handsome Regency terraces and gateways. The sanctuary and the north east corner of the park are excellent points for watching migrant birds, including willow warblers, chiffchaff, white throats, redstarts and redpolls.
London Zoo Regent's Park (071-722 3333). The canal passes along the edge of the Zoo, one of the largest in the world. Lord Snowdon's aviary can be seen from the canal. The Zoo was originally laid out by Decimus Burton in 1827, but since then many famous architects have designed special animal houses. *Closed Christmas.*
Cumberland Basin A small canal basin by the Zoo which used to form the junction of the Regent's Canal Main Line with an arm that led off round the park to Cumberland Market near Euston Station. Much of the arm was filled in during the last war and the Zoo car park now sits on top of it. Cumberland Basin is now full of moored boats; there is also a floating restaurant.
Lord's Cricket Ground St John's Wood Road NW8 (071-289 1611). The ground of the MCC, which is also the governing body for British cricket.
Canalside walk From Lisson Grove (at the east end of Maida Hill Tunnel) to Regent's Park Zoo, 2 miles of the canal towpath make one of London's most attractive waterside walks. The bridges are nicely painted and wooden seats installed at intervals. With the

ducks, the overhanging trees, the passing
boats and London Zoo on either side, this is a
remarkable stretch of urban canal.
Little Venice A very canal-conscious area
centred on the junction of the Regent's and
Grand Junction canals, famous for its elegant
houses, colourful boats and excellent
canalside views. The island and pool were
named after Robert Browning. The area is
sometimes referred to as Paddington Stop.

BOATYARDS

BW St Pancras Basin Camley Street, NW1.
Apply to St Pancras Yacht Club (071-278
2805). R S W Toilet. Clubhouse open to the
public. *Sat afternoons & evenings. Sun
lunchtime & Wed evenings.*
Ⓑ **Turner Marinas** 57 Fitzroy Road, NW1
(071-722 9806). In Cumberland Basin.
R W Overnight mooring by arrangement,
chandlery, books and maps. Moorings in
Cumberland Basin, at Lisson Grove and
Blomfield Road, Little Venice, where there is
pump-out and gas.
London Narrow Boat Assn New Wharf
Road, N1 (071-837 9256). W S Temporary
moorings by prior arrangement only.
Laundry, baths.

BOAT TRIPS

London Waterbus Co. Camden Lock (071-
482 2550). A *30 minute* trip from Little Venice
through Regent's Park to the Zoo and then
continuing on to Camden Lock *Hourly service
both ways in summer, reduced service on winter
weekends.*
Jason's Trip Opposite Blomfield Road
moorings (071-286 3428). *1½ hour* trip in a
narrowboat through Regent's Park and the
Zoo to Hampstead Road Locks. Commentary
on return trip, advisable to book. Also *Lace
Plate* restaurant boat available for private hire.
Seats 12.
Canal Cruises 250 Camden High Street,
NW1 (071-485 6210/4433). Nb *Jenny Wren*
makes a *1½ hour* trip through Regent's Park,
the Zoo and Maida Hill Tunnel to Little
Venice and back. Advisable to book. Also *My
Fair Lady* cruising restaurant makes an *evening
dinner cruise Tue to Sat, and lunchtime cruise on
Sun.* Must book.
Lady Rose of Regents Little Venice, east of

BW canal office. (081-788 2669). Cruising
restaurant.

PUBS AND RESTAURANTS

🍺 **Bridge House** Little Venice, next to the
BW Canal Office. Charrington and Bass real
ale, and bar *lunches.*
🍺 **Warwick Castle** Warwick Place W9. At
Little Venice, decorated with old canal prints.
Charrington and Bass real ale, and bar *lunches.*
🍺 **Crockers** 24 Aberdeen Place NW8. Close
to Maida Hill Tunnel. A monument to
Victorian extravagance, this pub was built as
part of a hotel, when it was thought the
Marylebone railway terminus would be
situated here. Sampson and Wards Sheffield
real ale.
🍺 **Engineer** 65 Gloucester Avenue NW11.
Commemorates Brunel. Charrington and
Bass real ale.
🍺 **Lock Tavern** 35 Chalk Farm Road NW1.
By Hampstead Road Lock, this is a popular
pub. Charrington and Bass real ale.
🍺 **Waterside Inn** 82 York Way N1. Hoskins
and other guest real ales in a reconstructed
17thC building on Battlebridge Basin. Hot
food and *Sunday lunches.*
🍺 **Island Queen** 87 Noel Road N1. Near
City Road Locks, this is a busy pub noted for
its selection of topical 'puppets' hanging above
the bar. *Lunchtime* food, Bass and Charrington
real ale.
🍺 **Constitution** St Pancras Way NW1. Busy
canalside pub serving Courage real ale and bar
food *lunchtime.* Garden and self-cook
barbecue. Live music *at weekends.*
🍺 **Narrowboat** 119 St Peters Street N1.
Canalside pub with a strong canals theme, and
a canalside balcony. Bar meals *lunchtime,*
Fuller's, Bass and Charrington real ale.
✖ ❗ **Gallery Boat** Prince Albert Road NW1
(071-485 8137). Converted floating barge at
Cumberland Basin. Chinese (Peking-style)
restaurant. *Open L&D Mon-Sun.*
✖ ❗ **The Gourmet Pizza Company**
Camden Lock, Chalk Farm Road NW1 (071-
485 0360). Well-appointed overlooking the
canal, various craft workshops and brightly
painted barges. Seating outside in summer. 12
varieties of pizza including Chinese Duck and
English breakfast. *Open L&D Mon-Sun.*

Kensal Green

The Paddington Arm continues west. Starting at a big housing estate, one passes the backs of houses in Harrow Road and then goes along the side of the well-known Kensal Green Cemetery. There is a useful Sainsbury's with moorings, W and easy access immediately west of Kensal Green Bridge. The huge concrete structure sweeping out over the canal is the elevated Westway Road. The main Western region tracks run just below the canal to the south, and beyond them can be seen the towers of Wormwood Scrubs. Acton Lane Power Station straddles the canal; not far away are the twin townships of Harlesden and Willesden. The canal crosses the North Circular Road on a large aqueduct: a strange contrast between the tranquillity of the canal and the roaring traffic below.

Kensal Green Cemetery North bank of canal. Opened in 1833, the huge cemetery flanks the canal. The monuments are now all romantically overgrown, and scattered among trees. Water gates set in the wall indicate that at one time coffins for burial could be brought up by barge. Leigh Hunt, Thackeray, Macready, Trollope, Wilkie Collins and Blondin are among the famous buried here.
Porta Bella Dock Ladbroke Grove W10. A marina/market/office complex.
St Mary Magdalene Alongside the canal west of Little Venice. Built by Street, 1868-78, the church with its tall Gothic spire is now curiously isolated among modern flats. The richly decorated crypt is very striking.
Wormwood Scrubs South of canal. Expanse of open space with the famous prison on the southern boundary.

PUBS
- **Richardson's** Abbey Road. Recently modernised pub serving Whitbread real ale.
- **Grand Junction Arms** Acton Lane NW10. A large pub with good moorings and a children's playground. *Open all day* serving Young's real ale and bar food *evenings and all day Sat*. Vegetarians catered for, terraced garden.
- **Fisherman's Arms** 50 Old Oak Lane NW10. Friendly local serving Young's and Tetley's real ale. Bar food *lunchtime Mon-Fri*. Traditional disco *Fri evenings*.
- **Narrowboat** 346 Ladbroke Grove W10. Completely rebuilt following a road widening scheme. Fuller's real ale and moorings.
- **Flora** Lager only. Canalside garden and mooring.
- **Carlton Bridge Tavern** 45 Woodfield Road W9. A welcoming canalside pub serving Webster's and Ruddles real ale and food *weekday lunchtime*. Vegetarians catered for, children welcome until *20.00*. Moorings, garden, Irish music *Wed evenings*.
- **Paddington Stop** Formosa Street W9. Modern canalside pub *open all day*. *Lunchtime* bar snacks.

Greenford

The Paddington Arm continues west through
Alperton and Greenford. Between bridges 11
and 12 there is a useful Sainsbury's right by
the canal, with $\boxed{W}$ and moorings. The
surroundings are mostly flat, but Horsenden
Hill and Perivale Wood provide a long stretch
of beautiful hilly parkland and Sudbury Park
Golf Course adjoins the canal. Soon
afterwards the canal turns south into suburban
Middlesex.

BOATYARDS
ⓑ **Highline Yachting** Rowdell Road,
Northolt (081-845 9924). $\boxed{R}$ $\boxed{S}$ $\boxed{W}$ $\boxed{D}$ Gas,
overnight mooring, long-term mooring, winter
storage, toilet. *Closed Mon, Wed, Fri & Sun.*

PUBS
🍺 **Civil Engineer** by bridge 18.
🍺 **Black Horse** Black Horse Bridge,
Greenford. Bustling traditional pub, *open all
day,* serving Fuller's real ale. Food available
lunchtime Mon-Fri. Vegetarians catered for.
Children's play area, garden and overnight
mooring for patrons.
🍺 **Pleasure Boat** Ealing Road, Alperton. A
wooden skiff over the entrance porch echoes
this pub's name. Tetley's and Young's real ale
and *lunchtime food Mon-Fri.* Vegetarians
catered for. Children welcome *until 20.00.*
Garden with play area. *Friday night* is music
night.
🍺 **Ballot Box Inn** Horsenden Lane North.
North of bridge 13.

Bull's Bridge

Continuing south through the industrial
estate, the Paddington Arm soon reaches the
junction with the main line of the Grand
Union at Bull's Bridge. Here is a large BW
yard – formerly the Grand Union Canal
Carrying Fleet depot – where maintenance
boats are built and repaired. Turning left leads
east towards Brentford and the Thames past a
colourful collection of houseboats: turning
right goes to Birmingham and the north.
Along here the canal now enters the indivisible
conurbation of Hayes, Harlington, West
Drayton and Yiewsley: a good area for shops
and pubs.

Hayes & Harlington
Middx. EC Wed. All services. Much-
industrialised area, home of such famous
brand names as Nestlés, Heinz and EMI.
Southall
Middx. EC Wed. All services. Extensive modern
shopping centre.
Martinware Pottery Collection Southall
Public Library, Osterley Park Road. (081-574
3412). Representative collection of
Martinware, including birds, face mugs and
grotesqueries. Of exceptional interest to
admirers of 'art nouveau'. *Closed Sun & Mon.*

BOATYARDS

ⓑ **Willowtree Marina** West Quay Drive,
Yeading, Middx (081-841 6585). Ⓡ Ⓢ Ⓓ
Pump-out, gas, visitor moorings, slipway,
workshop facilities, DIY, chandlery,
launderette, showers, toilets, restaurant, wine
bar.
T & D Murrell Bull's Bridge Junction. (081-
848 4485). Ⓡ Ⓢ Ⓦ Ⓔ Overnight mooring,
long-term mooring, boat sales.

PUBS AND RESTAURANTS

🍺 **Woolpack** North of bridge 198. Courage
real ale and a selection of strip tease artistes
Mon-Sat. Servery food *lunchtime Mon-Fri.*
Garden, discos *Tue, Thu, Fri.* Unsuitable for
children.
🍺✕ **Blue Anchor** Hayes. Canalside, at
bridge 199. Smart one-bar pub serving
Ruddles, Webster's and Fuller's real ale.
Lunchtime food.
🍺 **Grand Junction Arms** Southall.
Canalside, by bridge 201. A cosy family pub
serving a varied selection of food *lunchtime and
evenings every day.* Webster's and Ruddles real
ale. Children welcome, garden. Disco *Fri
evening.*
🍺 **Hambrough Tavern** Southall. Canalside,
at A4020 bridge. Fairly plush new pub serving
Young's and Wadworth real ale together with
food *lunchtime Mon-Fri.* Puddings a speciality.
Outside seating, no children in the bars.

Brentford

This section follows the main line of the
Grand Union east from Norwood down to the
junction with the Thames at Brentford. At
Norwood is a BW maintenance yard; here
begins the 11-lock drop to the river, including
the Hanwell flight of six locks. It is in parts an
interesting and attractive stretch: Osterley and
Syon parks are nearby. The River Brent joins
the canal at the bottom of Hanwell Locks;
there is a rare intersection of canal, road and
railway at the top of these locks and several of
the bridges are of the brick arched type more
commonly seen on the rural canals. Near the
big M4 embankment is a very attractive cast
iron 'roving' bridge, dated 1820. Immediately
below this bridge, is a very poorly signed and
unprotected weir, *hazardous* when there is
fresh water in the river. Towards Brentford,
the towing path disappears under the roof of a
large BW warehouse – an odd experience for a
walker. Kew Gardens is just across the
Thames. Access for walkers to the towpath is
easily gained at the top and bottom (from
Green Lane) of Hanwell Locks and at
Brentford Locks (from Brentford High
Street), but there is no towpath from
Brentford Locks to the Thames.

Navigational notes
1 Norwood top lock and Hanwell bottom lock
are locked at *20.00 (summer)* and *18.00
(winter)* and re-open at *08.00.* Last entry to
the flight by *18.30* and *16.30* respectively to ensure
sufficient time to clear the locks before
closure.
2 The Thames at Brentford is tidal;
Teddington Locks are 5 miles upstream.
Application to navigate the non-tidal Thames
should be made in advance to the National
Rivers Authority, 2nd Floor, King's Meadow
House, Reading, Berks, RG1 8DQ (0734
535000). Craft entering the canal from the
Thames without the necessary BW licence
may complete the formalities at Brentford
Depot office at Brentford Locks. No licence is
required on the tidal Thames. Brentford and
Thames Locks are controlled by lock keepers
and are of course subject to the tide. They
operate for two hours either side of high water
and the lock keeper can be informed of your
imminent arrival on 081-560 1120.

Osterley House Isleworth (081-560 3918).
Set in a large park – a superb remodelled
mansion with elegant interior decorations by
Robert Adam, 1760-80. Gobelins and
Beauvais tapestries and fine carpets.
Elizabethan stables in large park. *Open 11.00-
17.00. Closed Mon.* Access is unfortunately on
the south side of the M4, 1½ miles from the
canal. But Osterley Park tube station is close
to the entrance, which is just north of the A4.
Boston Manor House Boston Manor Road,
Brentford, ½ mile north of bridge 208 (081-
560 6597). Tudor and Jacobean house with
excellent examples of period ceilings. *Open
summer afternoons.* Nearest tube station:
Boston Manor (¼ mile north of the house).
The National Music Museum High Street,
Brentford (081-560 8108). In the church at
the foot of the tall gas holder east of the locks.
Exceptional collection of automatic, old and
odd musical instruments. Many of them are
demonstrated during the *90-minute* guided
tour. *Open Sat & Sun afternoons. Closed Nov-
Feb.*
Syon House Brentford (081-560 0881).
Entrance 300yds west of Brentford Locks on
A315. Seat of the Duke of Northumberland.
Noted for its fine Adam interior and period
furniture, also its paintings. Its historical
associations go back to the 15thC. *Open
summer afternoons. Closed Fri & Sat.*
Syon Park Gardening Centre Park Road,
Brentford (081-580 0134). Very wide
selection of plants and gardening equipment
for sale.
Syon Park Gardens Brentford (081-560
0881). 55 acres of Capability Brown gardens.
In the grounds are the Gardening Centre, Live
Butterfly House and Motor Museum.
Gardens *closed Xmas Day & Boxing Day.*

Kew Gardens Kew (081-940 1171). On the south bank of the Thames, opposite Brentford. (Access from the south side of the Gardens or from the Thames towpath.) One of the world's great botanic gardens, with thousands of rare outdoor and hothouse plants. Kew Palace, also worth a visit, was built in 1631 in the Dutch style. *Open daily 10.00-sunset.* The famous glasshouses *open 11.00, closing times vary.*

BOATYARDS

BW Norwood Yard at Norwood top lock. (081-574 1220). R S W

ⓑ **Adelaide Marine** Adelaide Dock, Endsleigh Road, Southall (081-571 5678/4428). R S W D E Pump-out, wide beam and narrowboat hire, gas, coal, chandlery, wet dock. slipway, crane, boatbuilding, repairs. DIY facilities, *24hr* emergency call out.

ⓑ **Anglo-Welsh** Adelaide Dock, Endsleigh Road, Southall (081-571 5678). Narrowboat hire.

ⓑ **Brent Marine** Brent Wharf, High Street, Brentford (081-847 1538). W E Gas, overnight mooring, long-term mooring, winter storage, crane, chandlery, boat building, boat storage, engine sales and repairs. Toilet and showers.

ⓑ **Brentford Dock Marina** (081-568 0287). Tidal access 2½ *hours* each side of high water. R S W Gas, overnight mooring, long-term mooring, chandlery, provisions, books and maps, minor boat and engine repairs, boat sales, outboard engine sales, toilet.

PUBS

🍺 **Old Oak Tree** Southall (at bridge 202). Canalside pub serving Courage real ale and food *weekday lunchtime. Open all day.*

🍺 **Lamb** Norwood (at bridge 203). Courage real ale and *lunchtime food Mon-Sat* in this canalside pub. Garden, moorings.

🍺 **Fox** Green Lane, Hanwell (at bottom of Hanwell Locks 50yds from canal). In virtually a village location this pub offers a selection of real ales and *lunchtime* food. Vegetarians catered for. Large garden. Children welcome.

🍺 **Mary O'Riordan's** Brentford High Street (north of Brentford Lock). Single roomed pub serving Fuller's and Bateman's real ale. Sandwiches *weekday lunchtime.* Live traditional Irish music *Tue-Fri evenings.*

🍺 **Six Bells** Brentford High Street (north of Brentford Lock). Basic town pub serving Fuller's real ale. Bar food and breakfasts *from 09.00.* B & B.

🍺 **The Magpie and Crown** Brentford High Street (between Brentford and Thames Locks). Welcoming family atmosphere and offers an interesting variety of good value food *lunchtime Mon-Fri.* Real ales include Courage, Webster's and Badger. Outside seating.

🍺 **Beehive** Brentford High Street (north of Thames Lock). Traditional town pub with a fine blue and green tiled exterior. Fuller's real ale, food available *all day Mon-Sat.*

Ice and snow at Denham. *Derek Pratt.*

Continued on page 38 (top map)

Cowley Peachey Junction

The canal begins to bend towards the north, passing at bridge 192 a new building erected on the site of Colham Wharf. An incised stone from the wharf has been preserved and built into the new building, and can be seen from the road. At Cowley Peachey Junction, the Slough Arm branches off to the west. Cowley Lock marks the end of the 27-mile pound and the start of the climb up the Colne valley and the Chiltern Hills. Uxbridge, just to the north, signals the limit of the outer-suburban belt that surrounds London. Uxbridge Lock has an attractive setting with its lock cottage, a turnover bridge and a tall modern flour mill standing nearby in grounds that are splendidly landscaped down to the water's edge. The *Paddington Packet Boat* used to run daily from Paddington to Cowley – one of the few passenger boats plying regularly along the Grand Junction Canal. It was pulled by four horses and had precedence over all other boats, so it covered the 15-mile lock-free run in a time that was remarkable at the beginning of the 19thC.

BOATYARDS

Ⓑ **Denham Yacht Station** By bridge 184. (0895 39811). Ⓦ Ⓓ Ⓔ Pump-out, gas, narrowboat hire, overnight mooring, long-term mooring, winter storage, chandlery, books and maps, boat building, boat sales, engine repairs, toilets, club house.

Ⓑ **Uxbridge Boat Centre** Uxbridge Wharf, Waterloo Road, Uxbridge (0895 52019). Ⓡ Ⓢ Ⓦ Ⓓ Ⓔ Gas, overnight mooring, long-term mooring, winter storage, slipway, dry dock, crane, DIY facilities, groceries, chandlery, books and maps, boat building, boat and engine repairs, engine sales, toilet. *Closed Mon (also Sun Dec & Jan)*.

Ⓑ **Highline Yachting** Packet Boat Lane, Cowley Peachey, Uxbridge (0895 442290). Ⓡ Ⓢ Ⓦ Ⓓ Pump-out, gas, overnight mooring, long-term mooring, covered wet dock, chandlery, provisions, books and maps, boat building, boat and engine sales and repairs, toilet. *Closed Sun & Mon*.

BOAT TRIPS

Colne Valley Passenger Boat Services (0895 812130). Trips from the Swan & Bottle. **Pisces, Gemini I & II** Owned and operated from Cowley Lock by the London Borough of Hillingdon. Education Department, 265 High Street, Uxbridge (0895 50111).

PUBS AND RESTAURANTS

🍺 **Crown & Treaty** Oxford Road, Uxbridge, near bridge 185. A very handsome pub dating from 1576, where unsuccessful negotiations were held between King and Parliament during the Civil War. Wethered real ale and *lunchtime food*. Traditional jazz *Sat evenings*.
🍺 **Dolphin** At bridge 186. Friendly local serving Courage real ale and food. Small canalside garden with roses.
🍺 **General Elliot** St John's Road, Uxbridge. At bridge 186. A quiet canalside pub of great character, serving Ind Coope (Burton) and Benskins real ale. Garden.
✕ ▮ **Shovel** Cowley Lock (0895 33121). Restaurant, steak bar and bar, with canal decor. *L & D*.
🍺 **Paddington Packet Boat** Down the road from bridge 190. Fuller's real ale and *lunchtime* food in a fine traditional pub.
🍺✕ **Turning Point** Packet Boat Lane, Cowley Peachey. Beside Highline Yachting. (0895 440550). A well kept family pub and restaurant serving Rayments and Greene King real ale. Bar food and à la carte restaurant menu available *lunchtime and evenings*. *Sunday roasts 12.00-19.00*.
🍺✕ **de Burgh Arms** Near bridge 192 (0895 442018). Smart and comfortable pub with a grill bar (*L & D*). Taylor Walker, Benskins and Ind Coope (Burton) real ale.

Continued at bottom of next page

N

Langley

Langley station

B470

SLOUGH ARM

Iver

Iver station

Frays River

5M 0L
Slough

MAIN LINE

190

B

Cowley Peachey Junction

91

192

Cowley

Iver

Striking off to the west from Cowley Peachey
Junction, this 5-mile lock-free arm leads in an
almost straight line to Slough. Built as late as
1883 (the last canal to be built in Britain
except for the Manchester Ship Canal), it
sweeps easily over several aqueducts and
through a long cutting. West of Iver the water
is amazingly clear, and there are often
attractive weeds and reeds to be seen growing
in the canal in summer.

Iver
Bucks. EC Wed. PO, tel, stores, garage, station.
The church has a Saxon nave with Roman
bricks visible in the walls. Norman arches,
medieval art and Tudor monuments. The
700-year-old tower owes its great height to the
15thC bell chamber.
Old Slade Nature Reserve 1 mile south of
Iver station. Gravel pit taken over by the
Berkshire, Buckinghamshire and Oxfordshire
Naturalists' Trust and now a wealth of bird
and animal life.
Iver Grove Shredding Green, Iver (north of
the boatyard). A fine mansion built by Sir
John Vanbrugh in 1724. Not open to the
public.

PUBS
- **Chestnuts** Langley.
- **North Star** by Langley Station.
- **Fox & Pheasant** Thorney Lane, Iver.
- **Swan** High Street, Iver. Food.
- **Red Lion** Shredding Green, Iver. Food.

Continued on page 39

27M 49L
Marsworth

Cowley Peachy
2¾M 4L

Denham
Denham deep lock 11' 1" **87**

182

(closed)

River Colne

MAIN LINE

183

A40(T)

Frays River

R
88 Uxbridge lock 4' 7"

continued page 36

Denham

The main line of the canal continues northwards up to the Colne valley past the village of Denham and across Harefield Moor, a stretch of common land of considerable interest to naturalists. Denham Lock, with a rise of 11ft 1in, is the deepest on the Grand Union. The large mooring site of the Harefield Cruising Club and marina is in one of the flooded gravel pits that are linked to the canal here.

Langley
Bucks. EC Wed. PO, tel, stores, station. A new town development; but there are unspoiled woodlands at Langley Park.
Denham
Bucks. EC Wed. PO, tel, stores, station. West of the canal and of the River Colne, Denham is split into two parts: the new part is north of the railway. In the old village is the church set among the cottages. It contains a Doom painting of 1460 and some Renaissance effigies and monuments. Denham Court, which stands in the Colne meadows, and Denham Place, the 17thC home of the Vansittart family, are both fine examples of English architecture.

PUBS

All these are 1 mile north west of the lock, by footpath through the country park:
- **Falcon** Denham. Snacks.
- **Green Man** Denham.
- **Swan** Denham.

Grand Union Slough Arm

Slough

The Slough Arm continues westwards under the A412 to its terminus, passing dull housing and industrial estates on its way to the terminal basin.

Slough
Berks. EC Wed. MD Tue. PO, tel, stores, garage, station, cinema. This is the largest town in Berkshire; it is a new town, undistinguished architecturally and remembered more for its very wide range of light industries and its immortalisation in verse by John Betjeman who wrote (in 1981):
'Come, friendly bombs, and fall on Slough
It isn't fit for humans now
There isn't grass to graze a cow.'
St Mary's Church is, however, interesting for its stained glass by Kempe and Alfred J. Wolmark: the church was completed in 1876. Herschel Park, in the town centre, is also worth a visit.

PUBS

- **Nags Head** near Slough Basin.
- **Grapes** south of the basin.
- **Rising Sun** further south of the basin.

B416

Cowley Peachy
5M   0L

Slough
Slough station

A412

continued page 37

Harefield

Leaving Widewater Lock, the canal continues north up the Colne valley through a landscape of interesting contrasts which contains woods, mills, lakes and a large sewage works. Black Jack's Lock is beautifully framed by a small mill and a tiny timbered cottage used as a restaurant, while Copper Mill Lock is just upstream of an attractive group of canalside buildings. Old chalk quarries adjoin the canal as it turns north east towards Rickmansworth. Meanwhile flooded, worked-out gravel pits cover the floor of this wooded valley. Stocker's is yet another lock with an interesting group of old farm buildings close by: they date from the 16thC.

Navigational note
There is a strong cross current between bridge 177 and Copper Mill Lock.

Springwell and Stocker's Locks This stretch is of interest to naturalists: there is a great variety of plants along here, and disused watercress beds are nearby. Orchids have been found growing in the adjacent chalk pits.
Copper Mill An interesting canal settlement. The big mill was once a paper mill, but after the canal was built it turned to making copper sheets for the bottoms of boats. The old cast iron bridge by the pub has now been replaced by a concrete one. South of here is the unnavigable Troy Cut, which leads to the very ancient Troy Mill.
Harefield
Middx. PO, tel, stores. Harefield represents the first escape from the stranglehold of outer London suburbia. The church set at the foot of the hill is almost a small museum: Norman masonry, box pews, 16thC screen, 19thC Gothic gallery, Georgian pulpit, and a huge collection of monuments including brasses, and work by Grinling Gibbons, Rysbrack and Bacon.

BOATYARDS

Ⓑ **Harefield Marina** Beside bridge 180. (0895 822036). Ⓓ Moorings, crane, slipway, gas, repairs, chandlery.

PUBS AND RESTAURANTS

Fisheries Inn Canalside at bridge 177. A very fine old pub virtually surrounded by water. Ind Coope (Burton) and Benskins real ale, extensive range of bar meals *lunchtime and evenings*, and a nice garden.
✕ ❢ **Black Jack's Mill Restaurant** Harefield (089 582 3120/2205). In a startlingly pretty situation overlooking Black Jack's Lock. International cuisine *L & D* (no credit cards).
Horse & Barge By bridge 180. Recently refurbished in a tasteful and restrained manner, with a comfortable and spacious lounge and a Victorian conservatory bar. The large canalside garden has colourful flowerbeds and an adventure playground. Ruddles, Webster's and Coombe real ale, good food *lunchtime and evenings*.

Rickmansworth

Continuing north east, the canal reaches Batchworth Lock on the outskirts of Rickmansworth. (There are in fact two locks here, one of them leading up into the River Chess which is navigable for a short distance. Northbound navigators should take the right hand lock to stay on the Grand Union Canal.) Here the River Colne comes in from the east and the Chess from the north west, while the Gade continues to accompany the canal to the north east. Just before the lock is a useful Tescos, complete with moorings for patrons. Past Rickmansworth is Common Moor, north of this is Croxley and the outskirts of Watford. A commemorative plaque at Iron Bridge Lock, unveiled by the Duke of Marlborough, is inscribed 1787-1987, to mark 200 years of the Grand Union Canal's existence. The canal keeps well away from this town and climbs instead into the superb Cassiobury Park, a long and lovely stretch of wooded parkland. The A404 crosses at Rickmansworth and the A412 at Croxley.

Cassiobury Park The canal flows through the park, once part of the 17thC gardens of the Earls of Essex. The avenue of limes was planted by Moses Cook in 1672 and many of the trees are as old as 300 years. The park stretches for 190 acres and is adjoined by Whippendell Woods. Watford's carnival takes place here every *Whitsun*.

Croxley Green
Herts. PO, tel, stores, garage, station. Despite being swamped by new housing, part of the old village survives around the green, where there are several attractive houses. There is a large medieval barn south of the village.

Rickmansworth
Herts. EC Wed. PO, tel, stores, station, cinema. Very little of the medieval town remains today: the Vicarage in Church Street has late medieval timberwork, but 18thC and 19thC alterations are intermingled. Despite this, there are several other buildings well worth a look: the 17thC Bury and the timber-framed but much restored Priory, both lying near the 19thC Church of St Mary, which lends a wonderful feeling of unity because it is almost entirely the work of one man – Sir Arthur Blomfield. The town centre is north of bridge 173.

Batchworth Lock Canal Centre beside Batchworth Lock (081-992 8776). Static canal exhibits together with nb. *Albert* in Ovaltine livery. *Open 12.00-17.00 daily (closed Mon).*

Rickmansworth Aquadrome Bury & Batchworth Lakes. The canal flows along the south east edge of the lakes. Facilities for all types of water sport, especially sailing. Picnic areas for onlookers, and swimming in Bury lake. *Open daily.* An aqua show is held *every Whit Mon.*

BOATYARDS

Ⓑ **Bridgewater Basin** Cassio Bridge Wharf, Croxley Green, Watford (0442 863615). Ⓦ Ⓓ Ⓔ Gas, overnight mooring, long-term mooring, winter storage, slipway, chandlery, books and maps, boat sales, engine sales and repairs.

BOAT TRIPS

Arcturus Cruises Cassio Wharf, Watford. Part or whole day cruises by narrowboat, for parties of up to 54 passengers. Public trips *Sun afternoon* from lock 77. (Enquiries to 043 871 4528).

PUBS

◗ **New Halfway House** near Cassio Bridge (169).
◗ **White Bear** Near Batchworth Lock. Cottagey pub dispensing Courage real ale and *lunchtime food (Mon-Fri).*

Kings Langley

The canal climbs in a northerly direction through Cassiobury Park to Grove Mill, a water mill where the mill stream doubles as a private canal arm. Just north of the mill is the deservedly famous ornamental stone bridge ordered by the Earl of Essex before he would allow the Grand Junction Canal Company to cut a navigation through his park. The canal winds considerably along this valley as it follows the course of the River Gade. This results in several wide stretches; do not attempt to turn in these without ascertaining the depth. The M25 north orbital road and the A41 cross the canal as it approaches the lovely village of Hunton Bridge. A little further north is Kings Langley, where there is a useful store and off-licence just west of bridge 158. This is a good area for those who like pubs.

Kings Langley
Herts. EC Wed. PO, tel, stores, station. Once a country village but now ravaged by the heavy motor traffic that thunders through the town. Its name derives from its royal associations; there are still the remains of a palace in the town. The tomb of Edmund de Langley, brother of the Black Prince, lies in the Norman Church of All Saints. Sir John Evans, the famous archaeologist, is also buried here.

Abbots Langley
Herts. EC Wed. PO, tel, stores, station (shared with Kings Langley). The Church of St Lawrence has 12thC arcades to the nave and a 14thC south chapel, an octagonal Perpendicular font and a 14thC wall painting of Saints Thomas and Lawrence.

Hunton Bridge
Herts. PO, tel, stores. Peaceful canalside village, with a spired church and the pleasing Langleybury Park.

PUBS AND RESTAURANTS

▸ **Rose and Crown** High Street, Kings Langley. A quite exceptional, heavily beamed, traditional pub combining live jazz, good food, a range of well kept real ales and a striking interior. Reputed to be the best jazz venue outside London, musicians perform *Sun lunchtime and Tue, Thu and Sat evenings* in the intimate surroundings of a wood panelled bar lit by a stained glass lantern window. Tables stand in alcoves hung with old enamel advertising signs and photographs of jazz 'greats'. Tetley's, Young's, Ind Coope (Burton), Greene King, Wadworth and Marston's are all dispensed from two well appointed bars, and an imaginative range of food and snacks are available *lunchtime and evenings (not Sat or Sun evenings)*. Traditional Sunday roasts, vegetarians catered for. Outside seating.

▸ **Swan** High Street, Kings Langley. A friendly traditional one room pub serving Greene King and Adnams real ale. Rolls always available. Regular quiz nights.

✕ ▸ **La Casetta** 18 High Street, Kings Langley (0923 263823). Hospitable Italian restaurant in a delightfully random timber framed building, dating from 1509. *L Mon-Fri, D Mon-Sat. Booking essential at weekends.*

▸ **Saracens Head** High Street, Kings Langley. There are always four real ales to choose from in this traditional pub. Regular ales include Fuller's, Wadworth and Marston's. Bar food *lunchtime Mon-Sat*. Vegetarians catered for. Outside seating.

▸ **Dog and Partridge** Old Mill Lane, Hunton Bridge. Benskins real ale and food *lunchtime Mon-Fri*. A fine old village pub.

▸ **Kings Head** Hunton Bridge. A village pub of great character, with an extensive canalside garden. Benskins, Ind Coope (Burton) and Tetley's real ale, and food *lunchtime and evenings (not Sun evenings)*. Imaginative adventure playground.

Map labels (top to bottom, left side):

N

144

57

58

Bourne End

145

146

Pix farm

59

60 Winkwell locks 13' 7"

Winkwell

147 Winkwell swing bridge

61 B

62 Boxmoor top lock 6' 8"

Boxmoor

11M   24L
Marsworth

Cowley Peachy
18¾M   28L

A4177

148

The Fishery

B4505

Fishery lock 7' 1" 63

149

station

River Bulbourne

150

A414

Hemel Hempstead

Boxmoor lock 7' 1" 64

River Gade

151

152

153

BW Apsley yard

SW

Apsley

Apsley mills

Apsley station

67-65 Apsley locks 16' 0"

154

Nash mills

68 Nash Mills locks 12' 2"

SW

Hemel Hempstead

The canal begins to climb more steeply to the north west, passing several large paper mills in Apsley and the quaint double arch of bridge 154. The River Gade leaves the canal for Hemel Hempstead, a handsome modern town standing back from the canal beyond spacious urban parkland known as Boxmoor. The canal turns further west, accompanied now by the little River Bulbourne. The busy railway line is never far away, interrupting the peace of this very attractive valley. Watercress beds are to be found along here; they owe their existence to the mineral waters from the many chalk springs of the Chilterns which are the source of the River Bulbourne. The nearby A41 is fortunately shielded by trees; its many petrol stations, pubs and shops may be useful .

Navigational notes
1 A BW key is required to operate Winkwell Swing Bridge.
2 Beware of mooring between locks 57 and 58, as the water level can drop overnight.

Hemel Hempstead
Herts. EC Wed. MD Thur, Fri, Sat. PO, tel, stores, garage, station, cinema. A developing, well-planned new town with excellent shops.
Piccotts End Medieval Murals 138 Piccotts End. Remarkable 14thC wall paintings in a hall believed to have been a pilgrims' hospice. Also an Elizabethan painted room.

BOATYARDS
Ⓑ **Middlesex and Herts Boat Services** Winkwell Dock, Winkwell, Bourne End (0442 872985). R S W D E Pump-out, gas, long- and short-term mooring, dry dock, crane, boat and engine repairs, boat building and fitting out, *24 hour* emergency breakdown call out, DIY facilities, specialist welding.
BW Apsley Yard Ebbems Road, Apsley (0442 56910). R S W

BOAT TRIPS
Reach Out Projects Base Nash Mills, south of bridge 155. (0707 332321). Specialists in boat hire for youth work and the disabled..

PUBS AND RESTAURANTS
◗✗ **Three Horseshoes** By bridge 147, Winkwell (0442 862585). A popular inn with a real fire, an over 30s bar and Benskins and Ind Coope (Burton) real ale (the John Bull Bitter is *not* real ale). Meals at *lunchtime (not Sun),* garden.
◗ **Fishery Inn** Fishery Road, Boxmoor. A large, friendly canalside pub serving Ind Coope (Burton) real ale and meals *lunchtime and evenings (not Sun).* Family room, large garden with swings and slides.
◗ **Old Kings Arms** High Street, Hemel Hempstead, in the old town. Historic pub serving Charles Wells real ale. *Lunchtime* food.
◗ **Three Blackbirds** 194 St John's Road, Boxmoor. Ind Coope (Burton) and Benskins real ale in a friendly pub with an emphasis on games. Meals *lunchtime and evenings (not Sun),* family room, garden.
◗ **Steam Coach** St John's Road, Boxmoor. Small friendly pub offering Ind Coope (Burton) and Benskins real ale and food *lunchtime and evenings (not Sun).* Children's room, garden, folk club *on Monday.*
◗ **Heath Park** St John's Road, Boxmoor. Large pub, convenient for the shops. Younger real ale, food *lunchtime and evenings (not Sun).*
◗ **Albion** Durrants Hill Road, Apsley. Benskins real ale in a friendly canalside pub. Meals *lunchtime and evenings (Mon-Fri),* snacks *lunchtime Sat.* Large, pretty garden and family room.
◗ **Fountain** London Road, Apsley. There is live music *Wed and Sun* in this pub, which offers Benskins and Friary Meux real ale. *Lunchtime* food (*Mon-Sat*), garden.
◗ **White Lion** London Road, Apsley. Quiet, friendly pub with an open fire where you can enjoy Coombe and Webster's real ales, and food *lunchtime and evenings (not Sun).* Children welcome.

Berkhamsted

The canal now enters Berkhamsted by its back door and steals inconspicuously through the middle of the town, the northern limit of the Grand Union as a barge canal. Leaving Berkhamsted and still climbing up the Chilterns, one passes Northchurch, where a pump draws canal water supplies from a deep borehole in the chalk beds. The summit level is reached at Cowroast Lock which, in the days before the pump was installed at Northchurch, used to be the scene of long lines of boats tied up in the dry summers as the canal engineers struggled to maintain the water supply in the three-mile summit level – which was constantly being drained by the use of locks at either end. (It is perhaps worth noting that every time a boat crosses this summit level it draws off nearly 200,000 gallons of water.) At Cowroast Lock the old toll office still stands.

Navigational note
BW request that no wide beam craft moor on line between here and Braunston.

Ashridge House *Herts.* 3½ miles north of Berkhamsted. (0442 843491). Built in 1808 as a large romantic mansion in the Gothic taste by James Wyatt, the house gives an impression of what his famous Fonthill must have been like; the chapel is particularly splendid. The grounds were laid out by Capability Brown, and altered later by Repton. *Gardens only open, on weekend afternoons.*
Northchurch
Herts. EC Wed. PO, tel, stores. Built round the flint church which contains some Saxon work, and fine 19thC stained glass. In the High Street are several timber-framed houses.
Berkhamsted
Herts. EC Wed. MD Sat. All services. Good-looking large town with buildings of all periods, the A41 running through the middle. The High Street is dominated by the Church of St Peter, which contains work from practically every period, including a restoration by Butterfield of 1871. There are several brasses. Only the ruins of the Norman castle remain where William I received the offer of the English crown in 1066. The 17thC Sayer almshouses are completely intact. The Common is known as a haven for wild birds including nightjars, woodcocks, grasshopper warblers, redpolls and bramblings.

BOATYARDS
Ⓑ **Cowroast Marina** By Cowroast Lock, Tring (0442 823222). Ⓡ Ⓢ Ⓦ Ⓓ Pump-out, gas, narrowboat hire, overnight mooring, long-term mooring, slipway, wet dock, chandlery, books and maps, boat sales, boat and engine repairs.
Ⓑ **Bridgewater Boats** Castle Wharf, Berkhamsted (0442 863615). Ⓦ Ⓓ Pump-out, gas, narrowboat hire, overnight mooring. Their base has won an environmental award.

PUBS
🍺 **Cow Roast** Cowroast Lock. Large, smart 17thC inn near the marina. Benskins, Taylor Walker and Ind Coope (Burton) real ale and meals *lunchtime and evenings (not Sun).* Garden.
🍺 **Crystal Palace** Station Road, Berkhamsted. Panelled pub near the castle remains. Benskins real ale, food *lunchtime and evenings (not Sun).*
🍺 **Boat** Gravel path, by bridge 142. Fuller's real ale.
🍺 **Brownlow Arms** Ravens Lane, Berkhamsted. Quiet backstreet pub serving Aylesbury real ale. Garden.
🍺 **Rising Sun** George Street, Berkhamsted. Excellent canalside local close to Bridgewater Boats. Benskins real ale, meals *lunchtime and evenings (not Sun),* garden.
🍺 **Bull** High Street, Berkhamsted. Pleasant pub with canalside garden. Benskins and Friary Meux real ale and *lunchtime food (not Sun).*

AYLESBURY ARM
See page 46

2 Dixon's gap
bridge

Marsworth narrow locks 1-8

6¼M 16L
Aylesbury

Marsworth
Marsworth Junction
BW Marsworth yard

continued
page 47 130

131

Tringford pumping
station

Startop's end
R W

Tring reservoirs

132 Lower Icknield way
bridge

B489

reservoirs

45-39 Marsworth locks
42' 3"

50 ft

WENDOVER ARM

New Mills

Bulbourne Junction
W

Bulbourne

N

N

BW Bulbourne
workshops

B488

133 Upper Icknield
way bridge

134

TRING SUMMIT LEVEL

2¼M 7L
Marsworth

Cowley Peachy
27¼M 45L

135

Tring station

Aldbury

A41(T)

136

Bulbourne

The canal continues north west through the long wooded cutting that contains the Tring summit level. At the hamlet of Bulbourne are the BW workshops where to this day traditional wooden lockgate-making is carried out by a small team of craftsmen. Just to the west the old Wendover Arm joins the canal, constantly feeding water into the summit level. This arm no longer goes to Wendover, but it is still navigable for small boats as far as Little Tring and the Tringford pumping station. There is also a landscaped picnic and barbecue area. Back at Bulbourne Junction, the first of the Marsworth locks begin to wind down the hill past the reservoirs; at the bottom of the flight there is an interesting double-arched bridge, a sight often repeated between here and Stoke Bruerne 33 miles to the north. This type of bridge was built by the Grand Junction Canal Company in the expectation that the locks would later be paired – a programme that was never completed. 100yds north of the double bridge is Marsworth Junction, dominated by the BW workshops. At the northern the main line bears round to the north east, while the Aylesbury Arm (7ft wide only) starts its fall west through the first eight narrow locks towards Aylesbury.

Marsworth
Bucks. PO, tel, stores, garage. A quiet scattered village centred around the Grand Union Canal and the Aylesbury Arm. The Icknield Way, a Roman road, passes the village. Dunstable Downs rise to the south east, gliders are a common sight and occasionally a hot air balloon may be seen floating along in the sky.
Tringford Pumping Station At the present terminus of Wendover Arm. Built by the Grand Junction Canal Company to pump water up from the three reservoirs just down the hill, and from the 100-acre Wilstone reservoir over to the west. This water, plus the supply from springs in Wendover was – and still is – fed down the arm into the Tring summit level. Originally the pumping station housed big beam engines, but these were · replaced in the 20thC by heavy diesels. Now quiet, smooth, electric motors perform this vital task, lifting some four million gallons of water each day. The system was recently overhauled, having been in constant use since 1929.
Tring Reservoirs South of Startops End (bridge 132) and beside Marsworth locks. Four reservoirs with many wildfowl and waterside birds, notably the Black Tern and the Great Crested Grebe. Also abundant marsh and water plants. National nature reserve, managed by the Nature Conservancy, 20 Belgrave Square, London SW1. Public access is permitted along waymarked pathways.
Bulbourne
Herts. Tel. Canalside settlement around the BW workshops which are a well-preserved example of early 19thC canal architecture, with characteristic fanlights. To the north east is the long railway cutting built by Robert Stephenson in 1834-38, an engineering feat of the age.
Aldbury
Herts. PO, tel, stores. A charming village pond and stocks are sheltered below the hillside which rises to the east towards Ashridge. Note the quaint cottages along Stocks Road and to the north east and west of the Church of St John the Baptist, which dates from the 13thC. The monument to the third Duke of Bridgewater (an urn and a Greek Doric column) was erected on the brow of the hill beyond Stocks Road in 1832 to commemorate his pioneering work for the English canals.
Aldbury Common 1½ miles east of bridge 135 past Tring station. Acres of open land which adjoin Berkhamsted Common, Ashridge Park and Ivinghoe Common.

BOATYARDS
BW Bulbourne Workshops Bulbourne (0442 822261). Home of the maintenance

yard and the lock-gate making team. No services.

BW Tring Yard Marsworth (044 282 5938).

PUBS

🍺 **Red Lion** Vicarage Road, Marsworth. A splendid village pub with an open fire and bars on two levels, dispensing Banks and Taylor, Bass, Hook Norton and Wadworth real ale. Local information is displayed on a noticeboard in the public bar. Food *Mon-Sat,* with home-made curry a speciality.

🍺 **White Lion** Startops End, Marsworth. Canalside at bridge 132. A large pub serving Marston's and Younger real ale. Meals *lunchtime and evenings (not Sun),* children's room, garden.

🍺 **Grand Junction Arms** Bulbourne. Canalside at bridge 133. Quiet, attractive pub with a large garden, serving Benskins and Ind Coope (Burton) real ale in a bar with an open fire. Meals *lunchtime and evenings (not Mon).*

🍺 **Queens Head** Marsworth, near bridge 132.

🍺 **Royal Hotel** Station Road, Tring. Hotel with two bars, where Chiltern and Greene King real ale can be enjoyed. Food *lunchtime and evenings (not Sun),* children's room, garden, accommodation.

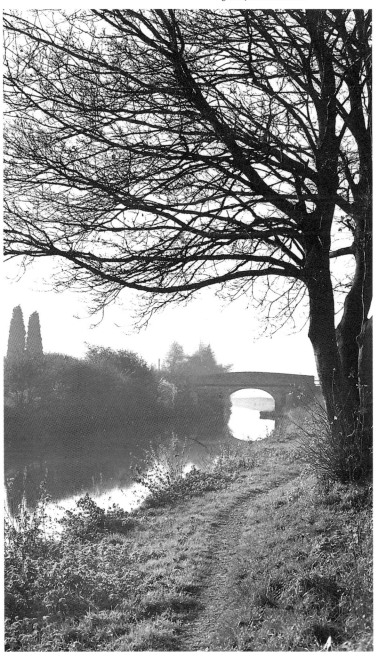

The Tring Summit of the Grand Union. *Derek Pratt.*

Continued on page 47
(bottom)
→ N

Broughton

16

15

14

14

13

12

11

10

To Aston Clinton 9
Redhouse lock 13

Buckland lock 12

8

Puttenham

4¼M 5L
Aylesbury

Marsworth
2M 11L

7

10 & 11
Puttenham locks

6

Wilstone

5

9 Wilstone lock

4

3 Wilstone bridge

Puttenham

The Aylesbury Arm continues to fall to the west. Totally isolated and remote, it is one of the most peaceful stretches of canal in the country, passing through modest farmland with good views of the Chiltern Hills over to the east and, in the distance to the west, of tall new buildings in Aylesbury. The locks are 7ft wide, and the bridges too are narrow. This canal was once semi-derelict, but an energetic programme of dredging and lock repairing restored it to a good navigable condition.

Navigational note

Locks 14 and 15 are padlocked. BW key required.

Wilstone
Herts. PO, tel, stores. Quiet village running away from the canal to Wilstone reservoir, a national nature reserve.

PUBS AND RESTAURANTS

🍺 **Prince of Wales** North of bridge 15. White walled pub with bars on two levels. Aylesbury real ale.

🍺✕ **Bell** 1 mile south of bridge 9. (0296 436055). Large rambling old inn with internationally famous cuisine (*L & D*). Marston's real ale.

🍺 **Rising Sun** South of bridge 9. A lively and cheerful roadside pub serving Courage real ale and *lunchtime* meals.

🍺 **Buckingham Arms** Wilstone.

🍺 **Half Moon** Wilstone. Nicely refurbished old inn. Aylesbury and Everards real ale, *lunchtime* food (*not Sun*). Open fire, garden.

Marsworth

The main line heads north east and continues its descent through Marsworth locks before entering the remote countryside beyond Ivinghoe. There is a useful licensed canal shop, The Ship, by bridge 130.

PUBS
⬤ **White Lion** Startops End, Marsworth. Canalside at bridge 132. A large pub serving Marston's and Younger real ale. Meals *lunchtime and evenings (not Sun)*, children's room, garden.
⬤ **Red Lion** Vicarage Road, Marsworth. A splendid village pub with an open fire and bars on two levels, dispensing Banks and Taylor, Bass, Hook Norton and Wadworth real ale. Local information is displayed on a noticeboard in the public bar. Food *Mon–Sat*, with home-made curry a speciality.
⬤ **Grand Junction Arms** Bulbourne. Canalside at bridge 133. Quiet, attractive pub with a large garden, serving Benskins and Ind Coope (Burton) real ale in a bar with an open fire. Meals *lunchtime and evenings (not Mon)*.

Aylesbury

The canal now runs under the Aylesbury ring road and drops down through the last two locks into the town; boaters should be aware of the iron girder bridge 18 which is extremely narrow. Aylesbury basin itself is spacious and full of boats, although there is no longer a boatyard as such. However, there are moorings for visitors, and pubs nearby, and all the amenities of the town centre are a mere three-minute walk away.

Aylesbury
Bucks. EC Thur. MD Wed, Sat. PO, tel, stores, garage, station, cinema. A busy market town where the 20thC has not taken over completely; the centre of Aylesbury is made up of a number of attractive squares, and the 13thC church lies hidden in its secluded churchyard a short distance away. There are some interesting Georgian buildings too. 'The King's Head', dating from the 15thC, has outstanding windows, gateway and courtyard, and Oliver Cromwell's chair in the bar.
Buckinghamshire County Museum Church Street, Aylesbury (0296 88849). Illustrates county archaeology, geology and history, local crafts, costume, natural history. Also small collection of prints and paintings. *Closed Sun.*

PUBS
⬤ **Bell Hotel** Market Square, Aylesbury. A traditional country town pub, serving Wethered real ale and food *lunchtime and evenings*.
⬤ **Kings Head** Market Square, Aylesbury. 15thC inn owned by the National Trust, with original timber front and stained-glass windows. Bass and Brakspear real ale, meals *(L & D)*.
⬤ **Old Millwrights Arms** Walton Road, Aylesbury. ¼ mile west of bridge 17. Aylesbury, Chiltern and Morrells real ale in a friendly 30s style pub. *Lunchtime* food.
⬤ **Ship** Walton Street, Aylesbury, beside the canal basin. Ind Coope real ale and snacks.
⬤ **White Swan** Walton Street, Aylesbury. Lively 16thC pub serving a good choice of real ale and meals *lunchtime and evenings* (booking advised).

Ivinghoe

Northwards from Marsworth the canal falls steadily away from Dunstable Downs and the Chilterns, leaving the hills as a backdrop to the west. As the hills give way to open grasslands, the canal becomes more remote, a quiet, empty section that terminates in the peace of Grove Church Lock. Villages are set back from the canal, only Slapton, with its superb pub, being under 1 mile away. The main feature of the section is the locks, carrying the canal down from the Chilterns toward Leighton Buzzard and the Ouzel valley; these occur frequently, often in remote and attractive settings. The railway and the B488 run parallel to the canal to the west; there is a station at Cheddington.

Grove
Bucks. An attractive group formed by the bridge, lock, lock cottage and the tiny church, a 14thC chapel with a later bell turret.
Slapton
Bucks. EC Thur. PO, tel, stores. Compact residential village; the Perpendicular church contains several brasses of the 15th and 16thC.
Cheddington
Bucks. EC Thur. PO, tel, stores, garage, station. 1 mile north of bridge 126. A residential area spread around the station, clearly a commuter development. The church contains a richly carved Jacobean pulpit. On the hills south of the village are the remains of a medieval field cultivation.
Mentmore House
1½ miles west of Horton Lock. A Tudor-style stone mansion built in the 1850s by Sir Joseph Paxton for the Rothschild family. Large plate glass windows, central heating and fresh air ventilation made the house advanced for its time, reflecting the ingenuity of the architect.
Whipsnade White Lion
On Dunstable Downs, visible from the canal from around Slapton and Cheddington. The lion was cut in 1935 and is over 480ft long.
Ivinghoe
Bucks. EC Wed. PO, tel, stores, garage. 1 mile east of bridge 123 or 126. An attractive although greatly expanded village, which centres round the large 13th and 14thC church, notable for its crossing tower and Jacobean pulpit. The main street, leading west from the church, contains the old town hall, partly 16thC. ¼ mile south of the village is Pitstone Green Mill, a post mill scheduled as an ancient monument.
Iron Age Hill Fort
1 mile north east of Ivinghoe, on top of Beacon Hill. The triangular hill fort encloses six acres: within this area stands a bowl barrow thought to date from the Bronze Age. There is a tumulus to the south and another to the east of Beacon Hill.

BOATYARDS

Ⓑ **Grebe Canal Cruises** Pitstone Wharf, Cheddington (0296 661920). Ⓡ Ⓢ Ⓦ Ⓓ Pump-out, gas, narrowboat hire, day boat hire, long-term mooring, winter storage, slipway, books and maps, boat sales, boat and engine repairs, gift shop, toilet. *Closed winter weekends.*

BOAT TRIPS

Grebe Canal Cruises Pitstone Wharf, Cheddington (0296 661920). Trips *every weekend May-Sep, daily in school holidays.* Also private charter for up to 60 persons.

PUBS

⬤ **Carpenters Arms** Slapton, north east of bridge 120. Superb thatched pub dispensing Benskins and Ind Coope (Burton) real ale straight from the barrel. Open fire, unspoilt public bar decorated with old carpentry tools. Excellent food *lunchtime and evenings*, garden. Well worth finding.
⬤ **Duke of Wellington** Cook's Wharf, Cheddington Road, Pitstone. Large, quiet and friendly pub. Adnams and Marston's real ale, meals *lunchtime and evenings.*

Leighton Buzzard

The canal now runs parallel to the River Ouzel
to the east and, leaving the open fields behind,
passes through the joined towns of Linslade
and Leighton Buzzard, effectively acting as a
boundary between them. Leighton Buzzard
station is actually in Linslade. The A418
crosses the canal in the town centre. Leaving
these towns, the canal enters the valley of the
Ouzel and meanders sharply, following the
river. Steep hills rise to the east and west,
thickly wooded to the east. A low towpath
hedge allows fine views of this beautiful valley.
This section contains a good mixture of canal
townscape and landscape, Grove and
Leighton Locks both having attractive and
well-kept lock houses.

Leighton Buzzard
*Beds. EC Thur. PO, tel, stores, station, garage,
cinema, take-away food (near the bridge).* A
picturesque market town with a superlative
church. 17th and 18thC houses and half-
timbered cottages are to be found in the
streets leading to the Market Cross, which has
stood for some 600 years in the centre of the
town. There are also some fine 19thC
buildings; note particularly Barclay's Bank. In
North Street stand the almshouses founded by
Edward Wilkes in 1633 on condition that the
bounds of the parish be beaten every Rogation
Monday. The custom is still maintained, and
on *23 May* a choir boy stands upon his head in
front of the almshouses while the appropriate
extracts from the donor's will are read.
All Saint's Parish Church Dates from 1288
and is notable for its 191ft tower and spire and
the 15thC wooden roof. It retains its ancient
sanctus bell, 13thC font, misericords, brasses
and a medieval lectern. The medieval graffiti
are interesting and include a depiction of
Simon and Nellie arguing about whether the
Mothering Sunday Simnel cake should be
boiled or baked.
Linslade
Bucks. PO, tel, stores, garage, station. Linslade
is virtually a residential extension of Leighton
Buzzard. Traces of the old village can just be
found to the north, especially the church, near
the canal, easily recognised by its battlements;
the front and parts of the structure date from
the 12thC. West of the church is a railway
tunnel with delightfully incongruous neo-
Gothic portal in grey brick.
Ascott House 2 miles to the west, along the
A418 from Linslade (0296 688242).
Attractive, irregular timber-framed house
built in 1606, with extensive additions made
in 1874 and 1938. Collection of paintings,
French and Chippendale furniture, oriental
porcelain. Twelve acres of grounds and
gardens containing rare trees. *Opening times
are liable to vary – ring for details.*

BOATYARDS

Ⓑ **The Wyvern Shipping Company**
Rothschild Road, Linslade (0525 372355).
Ⓡ Ⓢ Ⓦ Ⓓ Ⓔ Pump-out, gas, narrowboat
hire, long-term mooring, dry dock, books and
maps, boat building, engine repairs, toilets.

BOAT TRIPS

Leighton Lady Canal Cruises Ring 0525
384563 for details.

PUBS

🍺 **Globe Inn** Globe Lane, Linslade.
Canalside, near bridge 111. Over £2½ million
disappeared in 20 minutes during the Great
Train Robbery, which happened close to the
site of this old, low beamed pub. Marston's,
Greene King and Ruddles real ale are
available, together with a wide range of
inexpensive food *lunchtime and evenings.* Warm
family atmosphere, children's play area. Music
nights *in winter.* Canalside terrace.
🍺 **Bedford Arms** By bridge 114. Webster's
real ale and food *lunchtime and evenings* in a
busy town pub that stays open *all day.* B & B.
🍺 **White Horse** Between bridge 114 and the
railway station, Linslade. Friendly one bar
local serving Aylesbury and Bass real ale.

Soulbury

The canal meanders along the Ouzel valley to the north west through beautiful scenery. The hills rising steeply to the west and the natural woods to the east make the canal seem like a river, which is rare on the Grand Union. As the valley widens, the canal continues its steady fall towards Bletchley, following the Ouzel closely. Flat meadows reaching to the west precede the approach to Bletchley. All the locks, the Soulbury flight of three, and one at Stoke Hammond, form an attractive canalscape, the double-arched bridges showing where the locks were once doubled. Remains of the supplementary locks can still be seen at Soulbury alongside the small pumping station that returns water back up the flight whenever necessary. Next to the flight is Tom Allen's metalworks, for wrought iron and canal souvenirs. The railway and the B488 run closely to the west of the canal.

Stoke Hammond
Bucks. EC Sat. PO, tel, stores, garage. Set above the canal to the west, the village overlooks the valley as it spreads untidily along the B488. The church, weighted down by its squat central tower, contains a decorative 14thC font.

Soulbury
Bucks. 1 mile west of the Three Locks. PO, tel, stores. The church contains a monument in white marble by Grinling Gibbons, 1690. To the south is Liscombe House, a rambling 17thC brick mansion with a fine Gothic façade of 1774, set in a large landscaped park.

BOATYARDS
Ⓑ **Willowbridge Marina** Stoke Road, Bletchley (0908 643242). Ⓡ Ⓢ Ⓦ Ⓟ Ⓓ Pump-out, gas, overnight mooring, long-term mooring, winter storage, slipway with gantry crane, chandlery, provisions (hot pies, stamps), books and maps, boat and engine sales and repairs, toilet, showers, laundry, off-licence, telephone.

PUBS AND RESTAURANTS
🕮 **Dolphin** Stoke Hammond. Pleasant pub with an open fire and piano. Aylesbury real ale and *lunchtime* food.
🕮✕ **Three Locks** Stoke Hammond (0525 27393). Ⓦ Ⓡ Lunches, afternoon teas, Aylesbury and Everards real ale in a very attractively sited canalside pub. Terrace.

Bletchley

The canal runs through open country, but to
the south lie the suburbs of the rapidly
expanding town of Bletchley. There is a canal
shop at Fenny Stratford Lock. Once north of
the town the canal again meanders gently
through villages, still following the course of
the River Ouzel as far as Woolstone. There is
only one lock on this section, but the old
arched accommodation bridges abound. The
main railway leaves the canal south of
Bletchley, but another line, to Bedford,
crosses at Fenny Stratford. There is a station
close to the canal here. Through the whole of
the Milton Keynes area to Wolverton the tow
path is excellent – either gravel or tarmac.

Little Woolstone
Bucks. A tiny hamlet with a pub and a garage.
Great Woolstone is even smaller. Willen Lake
is best approached from bridge 83.

Woughton on the Green
Bucks. PO, tel, stores. The village is attractively
scattered round a huge green flanked by the
canal to the west. There are houses of all
periods, mixed in a random but harmonious
manner and presided over by the church built
on a mound to the east.

Simpson
Bucks. PO, tel, stores. A main-road village,
much redeveloped as a suburb of Bletchley,
but still retaining elements of independence.
The church is mainly 14thC; note the wooden
roof and a monument by John Bacon, 1789.
Beyond Woughton Park to the north is
Walton Hall, the Open University.

Bletchley
*Bucks. EC Wed. MD Thur, Sat. PO, tel, stores,
garage, station, cinema.* This formerly
agricultural and lace-making town is now a
large, modern place that has swallowed up its
neighbour, Fenny Stratford. A small part of
the 12thC St Mary's Church remains; much
restoration and alteration has been done.

Fenny Stratford
Bucks. PO, tel, stores, garage, station. The town
is now merged into Bletchley. The building of
the red-brick church, 1724-30, was inspired
by Browne Willis, the antiquarian; as a result
it is an early example of Gothic revival. The old
pump house is now a gift shop and cafeteria,
run by handicapped youth.

BOATYARD

Ⓑ **Milton Keynes Marina** A new facility.

PUBS AND RESTAURANTS

🍺 **Wayfarer Hotel** East of bridge 82a.
Aylesbury real ale in a new hotel on the shore
of Willen Lake. Meals *lunchtime and evenings*.
🍺✕ **Barge** Newport Road, Little Woolstone
(0908 679596). Smart old pub with a carvery.
Charrington and M & B real ale, garden.
🍺 **Cross Keys** Newport Road, Great
Woolstone. Thatched village pub with a prize-
winning garden, serving Charles Wells real
ale, meals *lunchtime and evenings (not Mon &
Tue evenings)*.
🍺 **Woughton House Hotel** Woughton on
the Green. Aylesbury real ale in a country
hotel. Meals *lunchtime and evenings*, garden.
🍺✕ **Moorings** beside Milton Keynes
Marina. A Toby Grill.
🍺 **Ye Old Swan** Opposite the church,
Woughton on the Green. 17thC tavern with
Dick Turpin associations. Ushers and
Wilson's real ale, *lunchtime* food, garden.
🍺✕ **Plough** Simpson, by the aqueduct.
Charles Wells real ale, and a lovely garden.
Bar meals and a full à la carte restaurant
lunchtime and evenings.
🍺 **Beacon** Mount Farm Lake, Bond Avenue,
Bletchley. Aylesbury, Everards and Ind Coope
(Burton) real ale, meals *lunchtime and evenings*,
garden. A circular upper gallery gives views
over the lake. Nine-hole pitch and putt,
football pitches and facilities for other games.
🍺 **Red Lion** Fenny Stratford Lock. Garden
for children, camping, groceries. Ⓡ Ⓦ
🍺 **Plough** West of bridge 98. Modern pub
serving Benskins and Ind Coope (Burton) real
ale and snacks. Garden.

Milton Keynes

Continuing north west, and then at Great
Linford turning sharply to the west, the canal
runs through attractive, lightly wooded
scenery that gradually gives way to hills and
follows the Ouse valley, clinging to the south
side. Either side, where once were open fields,
the new town of Milton Keynes has been built.
Willen and Great Linford are well worth
visiting. There are no locks, but a variety of
bridges. At Great Linford Wharf there is a
winding hole that marks the junction with the
Newport Pagnell branch, closed many years
ago. At New Bradwell the canal crosses a dual-
carriageway on a splendid new aqueduct,
completed in 1991.

New Bradwell
Bucks. PO, tel, stores, Chinese take-away. A
Victorian railway town, built on a grid of
extreme monotony and regularity. The
church, by Street, 1858, is of interest,
especially for its Victorian stained glass. The
19thC Bradwell Windmill is now restored.
Access from bridge 72 where there are good
moorings.

Great Linford
Bucks. PO, tel, stores. Great Linford is
magnificent: a traditional village street
running away from the canal, with a
marvellous group formed by church, manor,
farm and almshouses, all in rich golden stone.
The 14thC church right alongside the canal
contains Georgian box pews and pulpit, and
fine 19thC stained glass. The almshouses are
17thC with strong Dutch gables. The manor,
symmetrical, dignified and elegant in a totally
18thC way, completes the picture.

Milton Keynes
*Bucks. All services and a major shopping centre
accessible by bus from bridge 82a.* An exciting
new town development encompassing
Bletchley and the scattered villages to the
north. Work on the 22,000-acre area began in
the early 1970s and the original population of
40,000 has grown to around 100,000.
Strategically placed between Birmingham and
the capital, close to the M1 and the main
railway line, the Development Corporation
has been successful in attracting many
companies to the area. The housing schemes
are imaginative, and well endowed with green
space and trees. Great emphasis is placed on
the social and recreational needs of the
population and in this respect the new town
makes good use of the canal.

Willen
Bucks. ½ mile east of bridge 81. PO box, tel. A
hamlet wholly dominated by the Wren church,
which is well worth a visit. All the interior
fittings are original, and the plaster work,
pews, organ case and font should be seen. The
170-acre lake is a watersports centre, with
sailing, canoeing, etc.

PUBS
- **New Inn** Canalside near bridge 72.
Friendly, stone built pub offering Charles
Wells real ale and good value food *lunchtime
and evenings.* Garden
- **Black Horse** Canalside at Black Horse
Bridge. A popular pub with a choice of bars
and open fires in the winter. Aylesbury,
Tetley's and Ind Coope (Burton) real ales are
served, and there is a wide variety of
reasonably priced food from a servery *at
lunchtime* and in the dining room *in the
evenings.* Vegetarians catered for. *Open all day
in the summer.* Canalside seating, large play
area, mooring. Live music *Fri.*
- **Giffard Park** Canalside at bridge 78. A
large modern pub serving Castle Eden,
Flowers and a guest real ale together with a
wide range of food. *Open all day, including
Sun,* food is available 11.00-22.00. Family
room, children's play area and canalside
seating. Mooring.
- **Eager Poet** Nr Pennylands Marina, bridge
79a, Milton Keynes. Modern pub with
facilities for the disabled. Wethered and
Brakspear real ale, bar food. The name was
chosen as the result of a competition (a keen
Milton). Clever, isn't it?

Bowlers Bridge, Simpson, on the Grand Union. *Derek Pratt.*

9¾M 7L Gayton Jnc
Marsworth 28¼M 18L

Cosgrove

The canal continues westwards past industrial Wolverton, and then turns north west prior to crossing the Ouse valley by means of an embankment and aqueduct. Hills now begin to dominate the landscape to the west as the canal follows the course of the River Tove, an indication of the climb ahead up to Stoke Bruerne. After Wolverton the canal becomes more remote, with only Cosgrove exploiting it. The railway 1 mile to the east provides the only intrusion. There is plenty of canalscape; Wolverton Aqueduct, Cosgrove Lock ending the 11-mile Fenny Stratford Pound, Cosgrove Bridge and the disused and long abandoned Buckingham Arm branching away to the west. (Part is now a nature reserve, and a nature trail follows the disused canal.) After Cosgrove and the old junction, the A508 runs to the west.

Castlethorpe
Bucks. PO, tel, stores. A quiet village, thatched houses around a green, 1 mile north east of Castlethorpe Wharf. The main railway running in a cutting below the village is the only disturbance. Parts of the church date back to 1200, although the tower was built in 1729. To the north is the site of a castle.

Cosgrove
Northants. EC Wed. PO, tel, stores. The village climbs west away from the canal, its spread visually terminated by the wooded church. The best parts are by the canal: a range of warehouses, a curious pedestrian tunnel under the canal, and a splendid stone bridge charmingly decorated in the Gothic taste, built in 1800. Its style is unique among canal bridges, and there is no obvious reason for its solitary splendour. The Georgian house that dominates the west bank by the lock is Cosgrove Hall; in 1958 a Roman bathhouse was discovered in front of the hall.

Wolverton
Bucks. EC Wed. MD Fri. PO, tel, stores, garage, station. Ignore the regularity of New Wolverton, and continue further west where the remains of the old village still survive among the trees. The Norman-style church was built in 1815, its large size perhaps anticipating the coming of the railway! By the church is the rectory with a handsome portal, built in 1729.

Great Ouse Aqueduct
North of Old Wolverton the canal crosses the Ouse via an iron trunk aqueduct, a square cast-iron trough carried on stone pillars. Built in 1811, it replaced a brick structure that collapsed in 1808. This in turn had replaced nine locks that enabled the Ouse to be crossed on the level, a system abandoned because of the danger of floods.

BOATYARDS

Ⓑ **Cosgrove Marina** The Lock House, Cosgrove (0908 562467). Ⓡ Ⓢ Ⓦ Ⓓ Pump-out, gas, overnight mooring, long-term mooring, winter storage, chandlery, boat building, boat sales, engine sales and repairs, toilets, *24 hour* mobile breakdown service, boat painting.

BOAT TRIPS

Linda Cruises Cosgrove Lock (0604 862107). Regular *Sun afternoon cruises during the summer* in nb. *Linda*. Party bookings *all year round.*

PUBS

🍺 **Navigation** Castlethorpe Wharf, Cosgrove. Spacious and friendly pub with a large open fire. Offers Morland and a fine range of guest real ales. Families welcome. Bar food *lunchtime and evenings.* Canalside garden.
🍺 **Barley Mow** Cosgrove, by bridge 65. Snacks, large garden with swings and a slide, mooring.
🍺 **Galleon Inn** Old Wolverton. Attractive and comfortable inn with a balcony overlooking the garden and canal; many curios decorate the walls. Ind Coope (Burton) and Wadworth real ale, meals, garden and children's room.

Yardley Gobion

The canal leaves the low hills to the west and passes through open fields to Grafton Regis, where the hills reappear. A quiet, rural stretch, with only the noise of the railway. The villages lie set back to the west, but are easily approached. Accommodation bridges occur with even regularity, mostly old brick arches. After Grafton Regis the River Tove joins the canal and then branches away to the west after ¼ mile; there is a winding hole by this junction. At once the canal starts the seven-lock climb to Stoke Bruerne, via single wide locks. The A508 crosses after the second lock; there is a handy slipway nearby.

Stoke Park Approached via Stoke Bruerne, or along a footpath that leaves the canal at lock 20. The park is then ½ mile west of the canal. Built 1629-35 by Inigo Jones for Sir Francis Crane, head of the Mortlake Tapestry Works, the symmetrical façade with its flanking pavilions and colonnade made Stoke Park House (now demolished) one of the earliest Palladian or classical buildings in England. The exterior only and the gardens may be visited. *Open Jul-Aug, Sat & Sun only.*

Grafton Regis
Northants. EC Sat. PO, tel, stores. A quiet stone village that runs gently westwards from the canal, it still preserves a strong manorial feeling. The large church, near the canal, is mostly 13th and 14thC, but contains a Norman font. There is also a fine Neo-classical monument by Flaxman, 1808.

Yardley Gobion
Northants. PO, tel, stores, off-licence. A small thatch and stone village, set on a slope to the west of the canal. The village is by-passed by the busy A508, which has prompted much new development. The church, built in 1864, is now out of reach of the traffic, and is serene once more.

BOATYARDS

Ⓑ **Baxter Boatfitting Services** Yardley Gobion (0908 542454). Ⓡ Ⓢ Ⓦ Ⓓ Ⓔ Pump-out, gas, overnight mooring, long-term mooring, winter storage, slipway, day hire boat, crane, dry dock, chandlery, provisions and farm produce, books and maps, boat building, boat and engine sales and repairs, toilet, laundry, baths, B & B.

PUBS

🍺 **White Hart** Grafton Regis. On the busy A508, west of the canal from bridge 57. John Smith's, Ruddles and Courage real ale. Food *lunchtime and evenings.* Garden.
🍺 **Coffee Pot** Yardley Gobion. South of bridge 60. Food.

Stoke Bruerne

Now the hills become more dominant,
especially to the west and north west,
anticipating Blisworth Tunnel. After the
tunnel and the thickly wooded approach
cutting, the hills recede to the west, and the
canal, becoming wider but shallow at the
edges, reaches Gayton Junction through open
fields. The villages are very much on top of the
canal, partly because of the landscape, and
partly because of their importance to the
canal; Stoke Bruerne is an ideal canal village.
After Stoke Bruerne Top Lock the level
remains unchanged for several miles. A deep
cutting leads to Blisworth Tunnel, the longest
in Britain still open to navigation. The
Waterways Museum at Stoke Bruerne makes
this altogether an exciting stretch. The A43
crosses in the middle of Blisworth, but
Blisworth station is closed.

Blisworth
Northants. PO, tel, stores, garage. A large brown
stone village built around the A43, it climbs
up steeply from the canal, which passes
through in a cutting shortly after leaving the
tunnel. The church, mostly 14thC, is just to
the east of the canal, but appears to sit astride
it. There are houses of all periods, the most
striking built of local stone in the 18thC.
Blisworth stone was quarried extensively. On
the road that runs above the tunnel, marked
by the regular grey caps of the air vents, are
several elegant stone houses: one, now a farm,
is handsomely titled in carved lettering,
'Blisworth Stone Works'.

Blisworth Tunnel
At 3057yds long, Blisworth is the longest
canal tunnel open to navigation in Britain. No
towpath, but the channel is wide enough to
allow the passing of two 7ft boats, so keep to
the right. *Boats over 7ft beam must give advance
notice to the section inspector on 0788 890666 so
that boats can be prevented from entering the
tunnel at the opposite end.*
The Grand Junction Canal was completed
and opened in 1800 with the exception of this
tunnel. The first attempt at excavation failed,
and so a tramway was built over Blisworth
Hill, linking the two termini. Boats arriving at
either end had to be unloaded onto horse-
drawn waggons, which were then pulled over
the hill, and reloaded onto boats. A second
attempt at the tunnel was more successful,
and it opened on 25 March 1805. Originally
boats were legged through. (Note the leggers'
hut at the south end.) 1984 saw the
completion of the British Waterways Board's
£4.3 million restoration project.

Stoke Bruerne
Northants. EC Sat. PO, tel, stores. Perhaps the
best example of a canal village in this country.
Built mostly of local Blisworth stone, the
houses flank the canal, clearly viewing it as a
blessing. To the west the hilly landscape warns
of the approaching tunnel under Blisworth
Hill. The Perpendicular church with its
Norman tower overlooks the village, while the
warehouses and cottages along the wharf have
become a canal centre, greatly encouraged by
the presence of the Waterways Museum. As a
canalscape Stoke Bruerne has everything: a
pub, locks, boat scales, a double-arched
bridge, museum and canal shops and a nearby
tunnel.

Waterways Museum Stoke Bruerne (0604
862229). Housed in a fine old stone
warehouse, a unique collection brings to life
the rich history of over 200 years of canals.
Exhibits include a traditional narrowboat,
boat weighing scales, a reconstructed butty
boat cabin, steam and diesel engines, and
extensive displays of clothing, cabinware,
brasses, signs, models, paintings,
photographs, and documents. Museum shop
selling canal literature, maps, postcards,
souvenirs and other ephemera. *Open daily
(except Christmas, Boxing Day and winter
Mon).* Charge. Pleasure trips to Blisworth
Tunnel mouth *during summer* from the
museum.

BOATYARDS

Ⓑ **Grand Junction Boat Company** Canal Maintenance Yard, Blisworth Arm, Northampton (0604 858043). Ⓡ Ⓢ Ⓦ Ⓓ Pump-out, gas, coal, chandlery, books and maps, boat building and repairs, engine sales and repairs, *24 hour* emergency breakdown call out.

D Blagrove Wharf Cottage, Stoke Bruerne (0604 862174). Ⓓ Ⓔ Canal carriers, coal sales, B & B.

Ⓑ **Blisworth Tunnel Boats** Gayton Road, Blisworth (0604 858868). Ⓡ Ⓢ Ⓦ Ⓓ Ⓔ Pump-out (*not Sat, ring in advance*), gas, narrowboat hire, day hire boats, overnight mooring, long-term mooring, wet dock, chandlery, souvenirs, books and maps, boat and engine repairs, boat sales, toilet.

BOAT TRIPS

Linda Cruises Stoke Bruerne (0604 862107). *Daily trips* on nb. *Charlie Easter-Oct, and weekends all year.* Party bookings.

Boat Inn Stoke Bruerne (0604 862428). *Weekend trips May-Oct* on nb. *Indian Chief.* Otherwise a wide range of party bookings on this 40 seater narrowboat with bar, snacks and disabled lift.

PUBS AND RESTAURANTS

☞ **Royal Oak** Blisworth. Food, garden for children.

☞ **Boat Inn** Stoke Bruerne. Bustling canalside pub serving Marston's, Theakston and Banks's real ale, together with food *lunchtime and evenings.* Vegetarians catered for. Families are welcomed in the bar and adjacent tea room. Informal music sessions are encouraged. *Christmas* boaters caberet nights. Groceries, canalside garden.

✕ **Old Chapel Tearooms** Chapel Lane, Stoke Bruerne (0604 863284). Coffee, teas and cakes. Exhibition of waterways art. *Open daily 10.00-18.00.*

✕❢ **Bruerne's Lock Restaurant** Stoke Bruerne. Classic English fare (*L & D*). Reservation is advised (0604 863654).

Wootton Lock, Northampton Arm of the Grand Union Canal. *Derek Pratt.*

Milton Malsor

At Gayton Junction the Northampton Arm of the Grand Union branches away to the north east. It falls steeply through 5 miles of open country to Northampton where it connects with the navigable River Nene and thus with Peterborough, the Fens and ultimately the Wash. There are no villages on the canal, and the main feature of interest is the flight of 17 locks down to Northampton. Most of the long flight is visible from the top, as is Northampton in the distance. Several traditional drawbridges cross the canal, which look very pretty but are hard work to operate. Only the M1 bridge, a long concrete tunnel, interferes with the unchanged feeling of the arm. A guide sheet is obtainable from the box at Gayton Junction.

Rothersthorpe
Northants. EC Sat. PO, tel, stores. A comfortable mixture of brick and stone built round a large square. The church contains a Tudor pulpit. To the west of the village is a large circular dovecot with 900 nesting places.

Milton Malsor
Northants. PO, tel, stores. Attractive, meandering brick stone village, spreading east towards the 14thC church. Around the church are several elegant stone houses of the 17th and 18thC, making an exploration on foot worth while. New houses have been well incorporated with the old.

BOATYARDS
Ⓑ **Alvechurch Boat Centre** Gayton Marina, Blisworth (0604 858685). On the Northampton Arm, 400yds from Gayton Junction. Ⓡ Ⓢ Ⓦ Ⓓ Pump-out, gas, narrowboat hire, overnight mooring, long-term mooring, winter storage, boat sales and repairs, toilets, gift shop. BW and River Nene licences. Telephone.

PUBS
▰ **Chequers** North Street, Rothersthorpe. There is an open fire on chilly days in this village pub which serves Manns real ale and snacks.
▰ **Greyhound** Towcester Road, Milton Malsor. A fine village pub in 17thC cottages, once occupied by workers from the brewery next door (now closed). There is an open fire in the bar, where Manns real ale and *lunchtime* food can be enjoyed. Garden.
▰ **Compass** Green Street, Milton Malsor. Small 18thC village local dispensing Manns real ale. Snacks (*not Sun*) and garden.

14

16

13

75 Hardingstone lock

N

N

River Nene

A45(T)

9

14 Wootton lock

13 8 drawbridge

M1

12
11
10 6 drawbridge

1-13 Rothersthorpe locks
Rothersthorpe
8
7
6
5 5 drawbridge
4
3
2
1 W

NORTHAMPTON
ARM

3

Ⓑ

MAIN LINE
continued page 60

47

5M 17L
Northampton

A43

**Milton
Malsor**

2

48 RS
W BW Gayton yard
Gayton Junction

MAIN LINE

Northampton

Continuing north east and then swinging east after Hunsbury Hill, the canal leaves the open country behind as it approaches Northampton. Housing estates fringing the canal soon appear. The entry into the town passes factories, disused wharves and railway junctions before reaching Cotton End Wharf. Anyone considering stopping in Northampton is advised to pass through the bottom lock and into the Nene Navigation, where surroundings are more inviting.

Navigational note
The River Nene is a fully navigable river from Northampton down to the Wash. At Peterborough, which is 60 miles and 37 locks away, the river becomes tidal. It connects with the Middle Level Navigations and the Great Ouse and adjoining rivers.

Northampton
Northants. EC Thur. MD Wed, Sat. PO, tel, stores, garage, station, cinema, theatre. The centre of the town was destroyed by fire in 1675, and so little remains of Northampton's industry. Only an archway of the 12thC castle remains, one of the best-known Norman castles. Thomas à Becket was tried here in 1164. There are several churches of interest, including a rare round Norman one of c1110. The richly decorated Town Hall was built during the 19thC in the Gothic style.
Abington Museum Abington Park. Period rooms, toys, bygones. Northampton lace, ceramics, natural history exhibited in a manor castle. *Closed Sun in winter.*
Central Museum and Art Gallery Guildhall Road. Archaeology, antiquities, paintings, furniture and the finest collection of historical footwear in Europe, including Queen Victoria's wedding shoes and ballet shoes of Nijinsky.
Delapre Abbey London Road (A50). ½ mile south of canal. A former Cluniac nunnery, founded in 1145, the Abbey underwent major alterations in the 16th and 17thC. *Open Thur & Sat afternoons.* South of the Abbey park is Eleanor Cross, one of three surviving crosses set up by Edward I in 1290 to mark the last resting places of Queen Eleanor on her way to burial in Westminster Abbey from Harby in Leicestershire where she had died.
Battle of Northampton 10 July 1460 ½ mile south of Northampton Lock, between Delapre Abbey and Hunsbury Hill. A significant battle in the Wars of the Roses in which the Lancastrian King Henry was defeated by Edward of York. Beaumont, Shrewsbury, Egremont and Buckingham were slain and many bodies floated in the River Nene.

PUBS AND RESTAURANTS

🍺✕ **Plough** Bridge Street, Northampton (0604 230554). A plush Victorian hotel offering real ale in the comfortable lounge. *Lunchtime bar meals, restaurant (closed Fri-Sun)* and carvery (*D and Sun L*).
🍺 **Bull & Butcher** Bridge Street, Northampton. Sturdy local pub dispensing real ale and *lunchtime* bar snacks (*not Sun*). Accommodation.
🍺 **King William IV** Commercial Street, off Bridge Street, Northampton. A wide range of real ales in this pub. *Lunchtime* bar meals.
🍺 **Saddlers Arms** Bridge Street, Northampton. 18thC listed building with a wood panelled bar, a cosy snug and a large lounge. Davenports real ale is there to enjoy, along with *lunchtime* bar meals *(not Sun)*.
🍷 **W & R Shipman** The Drapery (northerly continuation of Bridge Street), Northampton. Old and long established wine bar just off the Market Square, with many unique and interesting features. Wines, spirits and Sam Smith real ale (in half pints only). *Lunchtime snacks. Closed Sun.*

Gayton Junction

Continuing north west after Gayton Junction, the canal enters a relatively empty stretch of agricultural land, open fields falling away to the north and steep hills to the south through which the railway cuts its way parallel to the canal. At Banbury Lane Bridge there is an attractive group of buildings – once the Anchor pub and wharf. As it approaches Bugbrooke, the only village on this stretch, it begins to meander as the hills become more dominant. There are no locks, but a large number of old brick arched bridges provide some interest. The canal is accompanied by the A5 and M1, both in the distance, while the B4525 crosses at Bugbrooke.

Bugbrooke
Northants. PO, tel, stores, garage. Although much rebuilding has taken place in the north, there are still fine 18thC houses to the south and a pretty Baptist church of 1808. The parish church is set by itself in parkland and is mainly 14thC incorporating a 12thC chapel. A well proportioned building of golden stone, it was sensitively restored in 1921. Look for the plaque in the belltower, which warns, in rhyme, against improperly dressed bellringers. One of the great pleasures of this manorial village is the well marked footpaths and bridleways.

Gayton
Northants. PO, tel, stores. Set on a hill to the west of the canal junction, the village seems to be composed of large, handsome stone houses, ranging in style from the 16thC to the 19thC; trees among the houses increase the rural grandeur. The large church with its ornamented tower maintains the unity of the village.

PUBS AND RESTAURANTS
🍴✕ **Old Wharf Inn** Cornhill Lane, Bugbrooke (0604 832585). By bridge 36. A new pub serving Ind Coope (Burton) and Tetley's real ale, and bar meals *lunchtime & evenings.* À la carte restaurant (booking advisable), large garden and ample moorings.
🍴 **Bakers Arms** High Street, Bugbrooke. Garden.
🍴 **Five Bells** 14 Church Lane, Bugbrooke. Very fine old pub opposite the church serving *lunchtime* food (*not Sun*) and real ale. The garden is shaded by willows and the tables are well spaced. Swings, a climbing frame and pet rabbits will amuse the children.
🍴 **Eykyn Arms** Gayton. Two roomed pub serving Adnams and Charles Wells real ale. *Lunchtime* food. Noteworthy key ring collection.
🍴✕ **Queen Victoria Inn** Gayton (0604 858438).

Bugbrooke

Bugbrooke Downs

Lower farm

43 Banbury Lane bridge

Gayton

Gayton Junction

continued page 58

12½M 7L
Norton Jnc

Marsworth
37½M 25L

Northampton arm

BW Gayton yard

Weedon

The canal begins to meander sharply because of the hills encroaching to the west; at the same time the landscape becomes more dramatic as the valley steepens on both sides of the canal. Weedon is passed on a long embankment that dominates the village, and then a quiet open stretch follows which gives way to the landscaped woods of Brockhall Park. The canal avoids most villages, passing directly only through Weedon, where there is much of interest: aqueducts over a road and the River Nene, an embankment, the old wharf (private) and the elegant barracks. There are good moorings above the church. Several transport routes merge now to produce a strange picture of three totally different means of transport running parallel: the old Roman road, Watling Street (A5), keeping as straight a course as possible through the hills; the canal, its junior by 1800 years, now looking more outdated than the Roman road; the London–Midland railway line and the 20thC motorway complete the set of contrasts. Of all the thousands of travellers passing through this area every hour, it must surely be those who travel on the canal who enjoy it the most as they compare the canal's dignity and quiet progress to the noise and rush of the roads and the railway.

Weedon
Northants. EC Thur. PO, tel, stores, garage. The canal passes much of Weedon via an embankment, and so the village seems to be set in a valley. Sandwiched curiously between railway and canal embankments is the Victorian church with a Norman tower. Upper Weedon runs west from the canal, a long L-shaped street flanked by fine houses of all periods. To the north are the remains of Weedon barracks, begun in 1803; at one time very extensive, including a Royal Pavilion to be used by George III in case of invasion, the barracks were built here because it was the furthest point from any coast! Many buildings survive, although the canal arm cut to serve the barracks was closed when the railway was electrified.

Nether Heyford
Northants. PO, tel, stores. A small residential village dwarfed by pylons on all sides. The canal skirts the village. A large Roman building was discovered to the east of the village in 1699.

BOATYARD
Ⓑ **Concoform Marine** The Boatyard, High Street, Weedon (0327 40739). Ⓦ Ⓟ Ⓓ Pump-out, gas, narrowboat hire, overnight mooring, long-term mooring, slipway. *Closed Sun & Mon in summer, and winter weekends.*
Ⓑ **Waterways Services** High Horse Wharf, Heyford Lane, Weedon (0327 42300). Ⓡ Ⓢ Ⓦ Ⓓ Pump-out, gas, long-term mooring, boat building, boat sales, engine sales and repairs, toilets.
Ⓑ **Stowe Hill Marine** Stowe Hill Wharf, Weedon (0327 41365). Ⓡ Ⓢ Ⓦ Ⓓ Gas, overnight mooring, long-term mooring, winter storage, slipway, groceries, chandlery, books and maps, boat building, boat sales, engine sales and repairs, toilets, gifts.

BOAT TRIPS
Saucy Sue 47-seat boat available for party hire. Details from Waterways Services, Weedon (0327 42300).

PUBS AND RESTAURANTS
🍺 **New Inn** Weedon, near bridge 24.
🍺✗ **Crossroads Hotel** Weedon (0327 40354). A selection of real ale, bar food *lunchtime and evenings.* Children welcome.
🍺 **Narrowboat** Weedon. Beside bridge 26, this is a busy pub serving Charles Wells real ale. A good selection of bar food *is always available.* Canalside seating, mooring.
🍺 **Globe** Weedon. Near bridge 24. Small friendly hotel serving Marston's and Ruddles real ale. Bar food *lunchtime and evenings.* Children welcome, accommodation.

Norton Junction

Continuing north west the canal follows a valley whose course is closely shared with the M1, A5 and the main railway. Despite all these, there is a quiet, wooded stretch past Brockhall Park. Now the landscape opens out and the M1 and the railway take over. Whilton and Buckby Locks climb up to Norton Junction, accompanied by attractive terraces of red-brick cottages – in one of these, by lock 8, there is a canal craft shop. By lock 9 are the remains of Long Buckby Wharf, while opposite there is a useful farm shop selling fresh produce, groceries and home-made pies. All the locks have side ponds, now disused, and ivy leafed toadflax grows in the lockwalls. The system for pumping water back up the flight has been restored, using an electric pump. Above Buckby Locks is Norton Junction, where the Leicester section branches off to the north (this is covered in the *Nicholson/Ordnance Survey Guide to the Waterways 2: Central*). The main line continues west towards Braunston.

Buckby Wharf
Northants. PO box, tel, stores.
Whilton
Northants. PO, tel, stores. 1 mile east of the canal at the end of a road that goes nowhere. Whilton is quiet and unchanged, especially at the east end. There are several fine stone houses, including a pretty Georgian rectory.
Brockhall
Northants. PO box. A large, lightly wooded landscaped park climbs gently east away from the canal. In the centre a manorial brown stone village and church are still intact and remote despite the M1 roaring through the west end of the park. The Hall is Tudor in part, with fine 18thC interiors; large trees screen it from the motorway.

BOATYARDS

ⓑ **Whilton Marina** Whilton Locks (0327 842577). Ⓢ Ⓦ Ⓟ Ⓓ Ⓔ Gas, overnight mooring, winter storage, slipway, dry dock, groceries, chandlery, books and maps, boat sales, engine sales and repairs, toilets, showers.
ⓑ **Weltonfield Narrowboats** Weltonfield Farm, by bridge 2 on the Leicester section (0327 842282). Ⓡ Ⓢ Ⓦ *not Sat* Ⓓ Ⓔ Pump-out, gas, narrowboat hire, overnight mooring, long-term mooring, dry dock, boat lift, chandlery, books and maps, boat building, boat sales, engine sales and repairs, toilets.

PUBS AND RESTAURANTS

🍺✕ **Stag's Head** Watford Gap (0327 703621). A canalside pub and restaurant (*L & D*), serving Adnams real ale.
🍺 **New Inn** Canalside, at Buckby Top Lock. Cosy alcoved free house, serving Marston's and Wilson's real ale and *lunchtime* food. .
🍺 **The Locks** By bridge 15. Large modern pub serving Charles Wells real ale and meals *lunchtime and evenings*. Family room.

Welton

From Norton Junction to Braunston the canal
turns westward through hills and wooded
country. At first there are good views to the
north and north east, with the embankment
carrying the Leicester line branching away to
the north. The canal then runs into a wooded
cutting which leads to Braunston Tunnel.
Before Welton Wharf, the feeder from the
Daventry reservoir, built 1804, is reached; the
Welton feeder enters by bridge 6 and the
Drayton feeder enters the canal at the east end
of Braunston Tunnel. A similar cutting
follows the tunnel, and then the landscape
opens out although the hills stay present on
either side. The flight of six wide locks takes
the canal down towards Braunston, a big canal
centre. A canal shop by Braunston Bottom
Lock stocks fresh fruit and veg, milk, bread,
crafts, chandlery and coal. It is open *daily
08.00-20.00 Jun-Sep, 08.00-18.00 for the rest of
the year.*

Towpath note
Sections of the towpath are totally impassable
between Norton Junction and Braunston Top
Lock. It is a similar picture between
Braunston Turn and Napton Junction.

Braunston Tunnel Opened in 1796, to bore
through the Northamptonshire heights, the
tunnel is 2042yds long. Its construction was
hindered by quicksands, and a mistake in
direction has given it a slight 'S' bend.
*Two boats of 7ft beam can pass in this tunnel, but
wide beam boats must get permission from BW on
0788 890666 to arrange a passage.*
Welton
Northants. Tel. The village climbs up the side
of a steep, winding hill, which makes it
compact and attractive, especially round the
church.

BOATYARDS
Ⓑ **Weltonfield Narrowboats** Weltonfield
Farm, by bridge 2 on the Leicester Section
(0327 842282). Ⓡ Ⓢ Ⓦ (*not Sat*) Ⓓ Ⓔ
Pump-out, gas, narrowboat hire, overnight
mooring, dry dock, boat lift, chandlery, books
and maps, boat building, boat sales and
repairs, toilet.

PUBS
⬤ **Admiral Nelson** By lock 3, Little
Braunston. Dating from 1730 and originally a
farmhouse, this building still retains much of
its traditional charm. Warmed by a log fire in
winter, there is home cooked food *lunchtime
and evenings every day.* Breakfast, morning
coffee and afternoon teas are also available
during the summer. Webster's, Batemans and
Ruddles real ale, and Northamptonshire
skittles for amusement. Canalside garden.
⬤ **White Horse** High Street, Welton. ¾ mile
from the canal. Attractive pub serving
Webster's real ale and food *lunchtime and
evenings.* Garden.
⬤ **New Inn** Canalside, at Buckby Top Lock.
Cosy alcoved pub, serving Marston's and
Wilson's real ale, and *lunchtime* food. Next
door is Ginger's Canal stores, for provisions
and souvenirs.

Braunston

Long rows of moored craft, including many narrowboats, flank the canal at Braunston and there is a fine selection of old buildings. A large marina with many beautifully restored buildings situated on an arm to the south meets most boating needs; note also the iron side-bridge and the 18thC dry dock. The arm in fact was part of the old route of the Oxford Canal before it was shortened by building a large embankment (Braunston Puddle Banks) across the Leam valley to Braunston Turn. The entrance to this arm was thus the original Braunston Junction. Leaving Braunston, the canal runs south west towards Napton Junction. This stretch of the Oxford Canal was used jointly by the Grand Junction Company, and as a result the Oxford charged excessive toll rates in an attempt to get even with their rival, whose more direct route to London had attracted most of the traffic. Flowing through open country with a background of hills to the south, the canal is curiously quiet and empty after the activity around Braunston. The land is agricultural, with few houses in sight. There are no locks, no villages and few bridges, making this a very pleasant rural stretch of canal, although the state of the towpath, nonexistent in many places, will be a great disappointment to walkers. The A425 crosses through Lower Shuckburgh.

Navigational note
BW request that no wide beam craft moor on line between here and Berkhamsted.

Lower Shuckburgh
Warwicks. PO box. A tiny village along the main road. The church, built in 1864, is attractive in a Victorian way, with great use of contrasting brickwork inside. The farm, west of bridge 104, sells eggs.

Braunston
Northants. PO, tel, stores, butcher. Set up on a hill to the north of the canal, so that the spire of Braunston church dominates the valley for miles around. The village is really a long main street, with houses of all periods that give the feeling of a spacious market town. The village is a very well known canal centre, and as such is no less significant today than when the Oxford and Grand Junction Canals were first connected here.

BOATYARDS

Ⓑ **Braunston Boats** Bottom Lock, Braunston (0788 891079). Ⓦ Ⓓ Pump-out, gas, narrowboat hire, long-term mooring.
Ⓑ **Braunston Marina** The Wharf, Braunston (0788 891373). Under the fine bridge dated 1834. Ⓡ Ⓢ Ⓦ Ⓓ Gas, pump-out, overnight mooring, long-term mooring, winter storage, dry dock, wet dock, chandlery, boat building, engineering – all services. Toilets.
Ⓑ **Boatserve** The Wharf, Braunston (0788 891971).
Ⓑ **Midland Chandlers** Canalside, Braunston (0788 891401).
Ⓑ **Union Canal Carriers** Canalside, Braunston (0788 890784). Ⓢ Ⓓ Pump-out, gas, narrowboat hire, overnight mooring by arrangement, long-term mooring, books and maps, boat building, boat sales, engine sales and repairs. *24 hour* breakdown service (0788 812156 *evenings*).

PUBS AND RESTAURANTS

Ⓟ✕ **Boatman** Braunston (0788 891313). Once the Rose & Castle, now a comfortable and friendly modern hotel/restaurant/pub. Ruddles and Wilson's real ale. Interesting bar menu at reasonable prices. Children's room, canalside garden with swings and overnight moorings for patrons.
Ⓟ **Old Plough** High Street, Braunston. Imposing 17thC pub of great character, serving Ind Coope (Burton) and Ansells real ale, and food *lunchtime and evenings*. Garden.
Ⓟ **Wheatsheaf** The Green, Braunston. A locals' pub with a striking red bar, dispensing Courage, Webster's and Ruddles real ale. Snacks.

Napton Junction

Continuing west from Lower Shuckburgh, the canal flows through wide open fields to Napton Junction, where the Oxford Canal continues to the south and the Grand Union branches north towards Birmingham. The empty landscape rolls on, broken by Calcutt Locks, towards Stockton where there is a sudden change. Hills come close to the canal, broken by the quarries and thick woods along the south bank. The quarries produce Blue Lias, a local stone, and cement which was used in the construction of the Thames Embankment. Huge fossils have been found in the blue lias clay, which is the lowest layer from the Jurassic period. This industrial belt contrasts with the open landscape that precedes and follows it. Stockton Locks continue the fall towards Warwick. The B4100 crosses before Stockton locks.

Stockton
Warwicks. EC Sat. PO, tel, stores, fish & chips, Indian take-away. Stockton is a largely Victorian village in an area dominated by the smoking chimneys of the cement works to the west. The church is built of Blue Lias, quarried near Stockton Locks.

BOATYARDS
Ⓑ **Calcutt Boats** Calcutt Top Lock, Stockton, Rugby (092 681 3757). Ⓢ Ⓦ Ⓓ Pump-out, gas, narrowboat hire, overnight mooring, long-term mooring, slipway, crane, dry dock, groceries, chandlery, books and maps, boat building, boat sales, engine sales and repairs, breakdown service.

PUBS AND RESTAURANTS
🍺 **Blue Lias** Canalside, at bridge 23. Well kept and attractive pub with a canalside garden and farmyard with animals. Be prepared for the uneven interior brickwork, which may look staighter when you have enjoyed some Flowers, Bass, Marston's or Theakston real ale. Bar meals *lunchtime and evenings (not Sun). Open all day.*
🍺 **Boat** Canalside at bridge 21. A pleasant old pub serving Bass real ale. Grills and bar meals *lunchtime and evenings*. Play area, children welcome.
🍺✗ **Barley Mow** School Street, Stockton. M & B real ale in a modernised pub. Chargrill steaks and bar meals *lunchtime and evenings*. Outside seating on the green, opposite the church.
🍺 **Crown** High Street, Stockton. A refurbished village pub, with settles in the lounge. Ansells real ale and bar meals *lunchtime and evenings*.

Long Itchington

Continuing west, the canal leaves the industry around Stockton and runs through open arable land flanked on both sides by hills. The pleasant emptiness is broken by the locks that occur steadily through this section, continuing the fall to Warwick. Of interest are the top two locks at Bascote, which form a staircase. The A423 crosses at Long Itchington, a village with a large number of pubs, including two on the canal.

Long Itchington
Warwicks. PO, tel, stores, garage. A large housing estate flanks the busy A423; the village proper lies to the north west, and is very attractive. Apart from several pubs there are houses of the 17th and 18thC, and a largely 13thC church whose spire was blown down in a gale in 1762. There are impressive poplars around the village pond. St Wulfstan, who later became Bishop of Worcester, was born here in 1012.

BOATYARDS
Ⓑ **Warwickshire Fly Boat Company** Stop Lock Cottage, Stockton (092 681 2093). By the Kayes Arm. Ⓢ Ⓦ Ⓓ Pump-out, gas, skippered 12-berth narrowboats, overnight mooring, long-term mooring, winter storage, slipway, crane, dry dock, groceries, chandlery, books and maps, boat sales, boat building, engine sales and repairs, toilets, showers, laundry.

PUBS AND RESTAURANTS
🍺 **Two Boats Inn** Canalside at bridge 25. An unusual pub, where the lounge resembles a log cabin. A good selection of real ale includes Flowers, Bass, Theakston and Hook Norton. Bar meals *lunchtime and evenings*. Garden.
🍺 **Green Man** Long Itchington, past the church. A fine traditional country pub with a very low ceiling in the lounge. Davenports real ale, family room.
🍺 **Buck and Bell** Long Itchington, overlooking the village green. You would be forgiven for thinking this pub had closed. A unique experience.
🍺✗ **Harvesters** Church Road, Long Itchington, opposite the village store. Small, popular local serving Hook Norton plus a guest real ale. Meals *lunchtime and evenings*. Outside tables.
🍺 **Jolly Fisherman** Long Itchington. Large pub overlooking the village green and pond. Ansells and Banks's real ale, and a wide range of food *lunchtime and evenings (not Sun evenings)*, garden. Interesting period records on the juke box. Children welcome. Music *Fri & Sat*. Queen Elizabeth I stayed in the black-and-white-timbered building opposite.

Royal Leamington Spa

After Fosse Locks the canal continues west through attractive and isolated country to Radford Semele, where there is a fine wooded cutting. Emerging, the canal joins the A425 and then carves its private course straight through Leamington. Midway through the town the canal enters a deep cutting that hides it from the adjacent main road and railway. The A425 accompanies the canal through Leamington. There are good moorings and shops by bridge 40.

Royal Leamington Spa
Warwicks. EC Mon, Thur. PO, tel, stores, by bridge 40, garage, station, cinema. During the 19thC the population of Leamington increased rapidly, due to the late 18th and 19thC fashion for spas generally. As a result the town is largely mid-Victorian, and a number of Victorian churches and hotels dominate the town, several designed by J. Cundall, a local architect of some note who also built the brick and stone town hall. The long rows of villas, elegant houses in their own grounds spreading out from the centre, all express the Victorian love of exotic styles – Gothic, Classical, Jacobean, Renaissance, French and Greek are all mixed here with bold abandon. Since the Victorian era, however, much industrialisation has taken place.
Art Gallery & Museum Avenue Road. British, Dutch and Flemish paintings of the 16th and 17thC. Also a collection of modern art, pottery and porcelain through the ages and a specialist series of 18thC English drinking glasses. Victorian costume and objects. *Open Mon–Sat and Sun afternoons.*
All Saints' Church Bath Street. Begun in 1843 to the design of J. C. Jackson, the church is of Gothic style, not always correct in detail. The north transept has a rose window patterned on Rouen Cathedral; the west window is by Kempe.
Jephson Gardens Alongside Newbold Terrace, north of bridge 40. Beautiful ornamental gardens named after Dr Jephson (1798–1878), the local practitioner who was largely responsible for the spa's high medical reputation.
Radford Semele
Warwicks. EC Thur. PO, tel, stores, garage. A main road suburb of Leamington, Radford Semele takes no notice of the canal that runs below the village, alongside the River Leam and the closed railway line to Rugby. Among the bungalows are some fine large houses, including Radford Hall, a reconstructed Jacobean building. The Victorian church is set curiously by itself, seemingly in the middle of a field.
Offchurch
Warwicks. Tel. A scattered residential village reflecting the proximity of Leamington. It takes its name from Offa, the Saxon King of Mercia, reputedly buried near here. The church, with its tall grey stone tower, contains some Norman work. To the west lies Offchurch Bury, whose park runs almost to the canal. Originally this was a 17thC house, but is has since been entirely rebuilt. The façade is now early 19thC Gothic.

PUBS AND RESTAURANTS

🍺 **Royal Exchange** Tachbrook Road, Leamington Spa. 100yds north of bridge 41. Charles Wells real ale.
🍺 **Bridge** Canalside at bridge 40. Ansells real ale and food. Canalside terrace and mooring for patrons.
✕ ❢ **Grand Union Restaurant** At bridge 40 (0926 21323). Good menu with an interesting and varied selection of dishes. *L & D.* Booking essential.
🍺 **Stags Head** Offchurch. Ansells real ale and food in a popular thatched pub. Garden with swings.
🍺 **White Lion** Southam Road, Radford Semele. Smart village pub, once a coaching inn, built in 1622. Davenports real ale and food *lunchtime and evenings.* Garden.

Within the map:

N →
River Avon
48
47
45
44
43
A425
Victoria park
42
A445
station
A452
41
40
A452
39
A4099
38
Royal Leamington Spa
urban development
37
River Leam
36
12M 23L
Kingswood
Napton
9¾M 23L
35 Radford Road bridge
Radford Semele
Offchurch Bury park
34 Bull bridge
23 Radford bottom lock 7' 3"
R
33
22
Offchurch

Warwick

After leaving Leamington the canal swings
north west under the A425 and then crosses the
railway and the River Avon on aqueducts.
Warwick is best approached from bridge 49, as
the canal skirts round the town to the north.
After climbing the two Cape Locks, it swings
south to Budbrooke Junction, where the old
Warwick and Napton Canal joined the
Warwick and Birmingham. Turn to the west,
pass under two large road bridges, and then the
first of the 21 locks of the Hatton flight appears,
with the distinctive paddle gear and gates
stretching up the hill ahead, a daunting sight
for even the toughest boatman. Consolation is
offered by the fine view of the spires of
Warwick as you climb the flight. There is a
small shop selling maps and canalia between
locks 45 and 46. On reaching the top, the canal
turns to the west, passing the wooded hills that
conceal Hatton village and Hatton Park.

Hatton
Warwicks. This heavily wooded village is
scattered around the top of the Hatton Locks.
The church, set by itself, is partly
Perpendicular, partly Victorian. North of
Hatton, and seemingly inseparable from it, is
Haseley, also surrounded by woods; its small
church is pretty and relatively unrestored, still
retaining its box pews. Parts of it date from the
13thC. There is a craft centre here.

Warwick
Warwicks. EC Thur. MD Wed, Sat. All services.
A historic town with medieval buildings.
Church of St Mary's Of Norman origin, it
contains a large 12thC crypt. Unfortunately,
much of the building was burnt down in 1694
and only the 14thC chancel and the
Beauchamp chapel were left. The most
striking feature of the rebuilt church is its
pseudo-Gothic tower.
Warwick County Museum Market Place.
Mainly local natural history, geology,
archaeology and the history of Warwickshire.
Includes the Sheldon tapestry map of
Warwickshire which dates from 1588. *Closed
Sun morning.* Free.
Court House Jury Street. The present
building, which dates from 1725, was built on
the site of a 16thC civic building.
Warwick Castle Castle Hill. The exterior is a
famous example of a 14thC fortification.
Inside are pictures by Rubens, Van Dyck and
Velazquez. *Open daily.*

BOATYARDS
ⓑ **Stephen Goldsbrough Boats** Hatton
(0564 778210). Boat painting and repairs,
DIY facilities, dry dock.
ⓑ **Kate Boats Warwick** The Boatyard,
Nelson Lane, Warwick (0926 492968).
Ⓢ Ⓦ Ⓓ Pump-out, gas, narrowboat hire,
overnight mooring, long-term mooring,
winter storage, groceries, chandlery, books
and maps, boat building, boat sales, engine
repairs, toilets.
ⓑ **Saltisford Canal Trust** Saltisford Arm,
Warwick (0926 490006). Ⓡ Ⓢ Ⓦ Pump-out
(please telephone), boat repairs, laundry,
information centre and museum, visitor
moorings, small boat hire, shop and good
access to town.
ⓑ **Delta Marine Services** Nelson Wharf,
Warwick (0926 499337). Ⓡ Ⓦ Ⓓ Pump-out,
gas, boatbuilding and repairs, engine sales and
repairs, moorings, DIY facilities, wet dock. *24
hour* emergency breakdown call out.

PUBS
🍺 **Waterman** Hatton. Comfortable pub
offering an extensive bar menu *lunchtime and
evenings every day. Open all day.* Garden.
🍺 **Dun Cow** Saltisford. ¼ mile east of bridge
51. Town pub serving M & B real ale. Food
lunchtime and evenings (not Sun evenings).
🍺 **Cape of Good Hope** Cape Locks,
Warwick. Welcoming canalside family pub
serving good food *lunchtime and evenings every
day.* Boddingtons and a guest real ale.

Looking down Hatton Locks towards Warwick. Note the distinctive caps on the ground paddle mechanism. *Derek Pratt.*

Kingswood

The canal now enters the wooded cutting that
precedes Shrewley Tunnel. After the tunnel
the hills surround the canal on all sides as it
travels through steep wooded folds. A tall
embankment carries it to Rowington, and
then this gives way to wooded meadows that
continue to Kingswood and the junction with
the Stratford-on-Avon Canal. There are no
locks, a relief after the exhausting Hatton
flight; instead the curious tunnel and the
junction provide canal interest. The villages
on this stretch tend to be scattered and
shapeless, but there are plenty of facilities near
at hand, and Packwood House is worth a visit.
The railway continues to flank the canal to the
west, occasionally interrupting the peaceful
landscape: there is a station at Lapworth
(Kingswood). The Stratford-on-Avon Canal is
covered on pages 171 to 180.

Kingswood
Warwicks. Tel, garage, station. The village is
scattered over a wide area from the Grand
Union Canal to the Stratford-on-Avon Canal.
The centre is 1 mile to the west, around the
ambitious 15thC church, and the area
immediately around the canal is residential, its
character determined by the railway station.
The main feature of interest is the canal
junction with the Stratford-on-Avon Canal
and resulting basin. Note particularly the iron
turnover bridge by the lock at the junction,
which is split to allow the towing rope to pass
through without being unhitched from the
horse. Such bridges are a feature of the
Stratford-on-Avon Canal.
Wroxall
Warwicks. 1½ miles north east of Rowington.
Little remains of the Benedictine abbey
founded in c1135; the 14thC nave and 17thC
tower of its church, and fragments of the
buildings around the cloisters survive. The
mansion, a gloomy Victorian pile set in
wooded parkland, replaced a Tudor house
bought by Sir Christopher Wren for his son in
1713.
Rowington
Warwicks. Tel. A residential village of Tudor-
style houses, handsome but suburban. Hidden
among them are occasional 17thC and 18thC
buildings, while near the canal the 13thC
church retains some furnishings and a fine
peal of bells.
Shrewley
Warwicks. PO, tel, stores. Runs in an untidy
line along a minor road crossing the north end
of the tunnel. Most of the village is recent
ribbon development. Useful as a source of
supplies.
Shrewley Tunnel 433yds long, the tunnel
was opened in 1799 with the completion of the
Warwick and Birmingham Canal. It is
remarkable for the very clearly defined path
over the top of the hill that a towing horse
would use while its boat was 'legged' through
the tunnel. This horsepath in fact goes
through its own miniature tunnel for 40yds
and emerges at the north west end above and
beside the canal tunnel.
*This tunnel allows two 7ft boats to pass: keep to
the right.*

PUBS

🍺 **Navigation** Canalside at Kingswood. A comfortable pub with a real fire and an attractive garden, busy in summer. M & B and Bass real ale. Food *lunchtime and evenings (not Sun evenings), and summer* barbecues.

🍺 **Tom o'the Wood** Finwood Road, Rowington. Fine 16thC beamed canalside pub serving Flowers and Marston's real ale, and meals *lunchtime and evenings*. Vegetarians catered for. Garden, children welcome. It is named after one of the three windmills which used to exist in the village, and contains many items of memorabilia.

🍺 **The Case is Altered** Just off Five Ways, Haseley. A 45-minute walk from bridge 62, but worth it. Pass Rowington Hall, then north east past South Lawn, to find set amidst beautiful countryside this completely unspoilt pub, with an open fire in the bar. The real ale, Ansells and Flowers, is drawn straight from the barrel using barrel handpumps.

🍺 **Cock Horse** Old Warwick Road, Rowington. A pretty country pub with a menagerie of rabbits, guinea pigs and waterfowl to keep the children amused. Flowers real ale and meals *lunchtime and evenings*.

🍺 **Durham Ox** Shrewley. Built circa 1764, this beautifully kept traditional country pub prospered with the advent of the canal, then later the railway. It was named after a famous beast, reared locally, and which at the age of 5 years weighed 3,024 lbs. M & B real ale and bar snacks, Garden.

Shrewley Tunnel, with the pedestrian tunnel next to the boat tunnel. *Derek Pratt.*

Map labels (left column):

74 Castle bridge
N
73 Waterfield bridge
Grimshaw hall
73A Kixley Foot bridge
Kixley wharf
72 Kixley bridge
Knowle
B
71
RS
W
47-51
Knowle locks
41' 10"
A4023
Knowle Hall
W
A41
70 Heronfield bridge
69 Black Boy bridge
A41(T)
68 Bakers Lane bridge
12¼M 11L
Bordesley
Kingswood
2M 0L
67
66 Rising bridge

Knowle

After Kingswood the canal moves north,
passing though a long straight stretch where
the flat landscape is temporarily
overshadwoed by electricity pylons; Knowle
Locks introduce more hilly countryside again,
and this green and pleasant land continues
right through to Solihull, concealing the
nearness of Birmingham. The flight of five
wide locks at Knowle used to be six narrow
ones, until the 1930s: the remains of the old
ones can still be seen alongside the new,
together with the side ponds (originally built
to save water). The locks are comparatively
deep, and very hard work, but they are well
maintained and beautifully painted up. They
are also the northernmost wide locks for many
miles now, since all the Birmingham canals
have narrow locks. Both Baddesley Clinton
and Knowle are set back from the canal
(Knowle station is fully 2 miles away), but
both warrant a visit.

Packwood House *NT property.* Hockley
Heath, 2 miles west of bridge 66 (056 43
2024). Timber-framed Tudor house, enlarged
in the 17thC. Collection of tapestry,
needlework and furniture. Park with formal
grounds and 17thC yew garden laid out to
represent the Sermon on the Mount, the trees
taking the place of Jesus and his followers.
*Open afternoons only Easter-Sep, Wed-Sun & B.
Hols.* Charge.

Knowle
W. Midlands. EC Wed. PO, all services. Despite
its proximity to Birmingham, Knowle still
survives as a village, albeit rather self-
consciously. It is blighted by the A41, which
roars through the middle, threatening to
destroy the number of old buildings that
remain. These date from the Middle Ages and
include such gems as Chester House, which
illustrates the advances in timber frame
construction from the 13th to the 15thC. The
church, consecrated in 1402, is large, formal
and elegant, and battlemented all round. Just
to the west is the timber-framed Guildhouse.
½ mile north of the village is Grimshaw Hall,
a gabled 16thC house noted for its decorative
brickwork. There are good views of it from the
canal.

Baddesley Clinton
Warwicks. PO, tel, stores. The village is a mile
from the canal at bridge 66, but nearer are the
church and the hall, set amid parkland. The
church is mostly 16th and 17thC, but the hall
is earlier – a typical late medieval manor built
in a mixture of brick and stone. Much of the
brickwork dates from the Queen Anne period,
the stables and parkland completing the
feeling of unity. NT. *Open Wed-Sat 14.00-
18.00 during the summer.*

BOATYARD

Ⓑ **Stephen Goldsbrough Boats** Knowle
Hall Wharf, Kenilworth Road, Knowle (0564
778210). Gas, boat fitting and repairs, engine
sales and repairs, surveys. *24 hour* emergency
breakdown call out.

PUBS AND RESTAURANTS

▰✕ **Wilsons Arms** Warwick Road, Knowle.
A Toby Grill pub which dates from the 16thC.
The older part still retains its character. M & B
and Bass real ale, meals *lunchtime and evenings.*
Outside seating.
▰✕ **Bridgewater** (0564 771177). Canalside
at bridge 75. A smart new residential hotel
serving Tetley's and Ansells real ale. Bar meals
lunchtime and evenings. Restaurant meals
evenings and Sun lunch. Booking advisable.
▰ **Black Boy** At bridge 69. A traditional pub
with a canalside garden. Bass real ale, bar
meals *lunchtime and evenings.* Children
welcome.
✕ ❢ **Lion Rock** 1 mile east of bridge 66 at
Baddesley Clinton (0564 782731). Well
worth the walk for an *evening* out at this
exceptional Cantonese restaurant.

Solihull

Continuing north west through wooded
country, the canal crosses the River Blyth on a
small aqueduct and enters the long wooded
cutting that carries it all the way to Olton
Bridge. This attractive screen conceals the
expanding suburban areas. The presence of
suburbia means that supplies are available in
plenty, but the embankment makes access
rather difficult. There is, however, a canalside
farm shop just south of bridge 78, (*open Mon-
Sat*). Catherine de Barnes is the last village
easily approached. There are no locks, and the
bridges tend to be high above the water.
Traffic noise and the presence of Birmingham
city airport, 2 miles to the north, tend to
disturb the illusion of peace created by the
cutting. The B4102 and the B425 cross the
canal, while the A41 bisects Solihull.

Solihull
*W. Midlands. EC Wed. PO, tel, stores, garage,
cinema, station.* A modern commuter
development, with fine public buildings. What
used to be the town centre, dominated by the
tall spire of the parish church, is now a
shopping area. The church, built of red
sandstone, is almost all 14thC. The interior
contains work of all periods: 17thC pulpit and
communion rail, 19thC stained glass.
Elmdon Heath
W. Midlands. EC Thur. PO, tel, stores, garage.
Suburb of Solihull. The athletic navigator in
need of supplies can climb up the
embankment by bridge 79 and find all he
needs – but the return journey can be difficult
if laden.
Catherine de Barnes
W. Midlands. Tel, stores, garage. A higgledy-
piggledy village in an area of isolation
hospitals, far from the romanticism implied by
the name. However, a convenient supply
centre with easy access from the canal before
the bulk of Birmingham.

BOATYARD
Ⓑ **Stephen Goldsbrough Boats** Hen Wood
Wharf, Solihull (0564 778210). Ⓡ Ⓢ Ⓦ Ⓓ
Pump-out, gas, long-term mooring.

PUBS
🍺 **Greville Arms** Damson Lane, Elmdon
Heath. Basic town pub. Snacks.
🍺 **Red House** Hermitage Road, Solihull. M
& B real ale and *lunchtime* food (*Mon-Fri*).
🍺 **Boat Inn** Catherine de Barnes. A well kept
Miller's Kitchen pub, offering Greenhall
Whitley, Tetley's and Davenports real ale.
Meals available *lunchtime and evenings*.

Tyseley

Continuing north west into Birmingham, the wooded cutting ends abruptly and, from this point on, housing estates and disused wharves accompany the canal. Olton Stores, by bridge 84, is a friendly and helpful place where you can stock up with groceries and fruit and vegetables. Boaters should be wary of rubbish in the canal as the city is approached. Factories flank the waterway, and presently these give way to a short stretch of open wasteland to which Tyseley Goods Yard forms a suitable backdrop. Then the factories take over again, and access to and from the canal becomes increasingly difficult. Camp Hill Locks and all the succeeding locks are narrow: only boats of 7ft beam or less can pass. After passing through subterranean vaults formed by the criss-crossing of railway viaducts, Camp Hill Bottom Lock and Bordesley Junction are reached.

Birmingham Railway Museum 670 Warwick Road, Tyseley (021-707 4696). ¼ mile south west of bridge 88. Both static and working exhibits, with at least one locomotive in steam each weekend. Things to see include a Royal Mail van and a 1908 royal saloon car. The museum also rebuilds locomotives for themselves and for other preserved steam railways, and these are on view. Courses are run on 'how to drive a steam engine', but booking is essential. Restaurant and shop. *Open 10.00-17.00 every day except Christmas period.* Charge.

Birmingham

The Birmingham and Warwick Junction
Canal runs north from Bordesley Junction to
join the Birmingham & Fazeley and Tame
Valley canals at Salford Junction. It was
opened in 1844 to by-pass the heavily-locked
stretches of the B & F at Ashted and Aston.
The 2¼-mile cut runs through industrial
surrounds. The five very tidy Garrison Locks
carry the canal down to the Erdington level,
where there is a stop lock (left open). The area
of the junction itself is completely covered by
elevated motorways, which join here in a huge
multi-level interchange; this provides an awe-
inspiring contrast between the old and the new
forms of transport. Beyond Bordesley
Junction the canal continues towards the
Birmingham Canal Main Line, passing
Digbeth Basin, and a very fine collection of
old wharf buildings climbing the six Ashted
Locks and 13 Farmer's Bridge Locks to join
the Birmingham & Fazeley Canal at Farmer's
Bridge Junction.

Navigational notes
1 There is a risk of vandalism here, so moor
only at recognised and secure sites in the city,
such as Gas Street, Cambrian Wharf or
boatyards (by arrangement).
2 Garrison and Camp Hill Top Locks are both
kept locked. You will need your BW key to
open them.

Grand Union canal
continued from
previous page

Birmingham

W. Midlands. EC Wed. MD Thur. All services.
It is strange to think that the medieval town
that centred round the parish church and the
moated manor originally stood on the site of
the present Smithfield market. The Bull Ring,
a modern shopping centre, used to be the
village green. Industrial and commercial
development continued with such speed
during the 19thC that Birmingham began to
be considered as the trade centre of the
Midlands. The town is famous for such men
as John Baskerville, William Murdoch, Joseph
Priestley, Matthew Boulton and James Watt.
Farmer's Bridge A canalside development
at Cambrian Wharf in which four skyscrapers,
a new canal pub and a restored 18thC street
complete with gaslights are grouped beside a
canal basin.
Saltley Reservoir Joins the Saltley Canal
below Garrison Locks. A rare wildlife haven in
the city.
Tourist Information Centre 2 City Arcade,
Birmingham (021-643 2514).

BOATYARDS

Ⓑ **Alvechurch Boat Centres** (Brummagem
Boats) Sherborne Street Wharf, Oozell's
Street Loop west of Farmer's Bridge Junction
(021-455 6163/0691). ⓇⓈⓌⒹⒺ
Pump-out, gas, narrowboat hire, day boat
hire, overnight mooring, wet dock, books and
maps, boat building, boat sales, toilet.

BOAT TRIPS

Sherborne Wharf Trips for parties of up to
48 people. Details from 021-455 6163.

PUBS

🍺 **Australian Bar** Bromsgrove Street, ½ mile
south east of Gas Street Basin. *Lunchtime*
snacks.
🍺 **White Lion** Horse Fair, ½ mile south east
of Gas Street Basin.
🍺 **St Paul's Tavern** Ludgate Hill, in the
jewellery quarter. Near Farmer's Bridge
Locks.
🍺 **Long Boat** Farmer's Bridge Top Lock,
Kingston Row, Birmingham 1. Canalside.
Food.
🍺 **Prince of Wales** Cambridge Street. Past
the Long Boat, turn left and the pub is on the
right.
🍺 **Crown** Broad Street, 200yds west of Gas
Street Basin. Out back is the old Butler's
Brewery, used before it became part of
Mitchells and Butler in 1898.

Ashted Locks, Aston Science Park, Birmingham. *Derek Pratt.*

KENNET & AVON

Maximum dimensions

Reading to Bath, junction with River Avon
Length: 72'
Beam: 7'
(or 70' x 13'9")
Headroom: 6' 6"
Bath to Hanham Lock
Length: 75'
Beam: 16'
Headroom: 8' 9"

Manager

(0380) 722859

Navigational note

Although the Kennet & Avon Canal is now open throughout its entire length, limited water supply to sections of the navigation is resulting in restricted use of some lock flights. Those particularly affected are Crofton and the Caen Hill flight at Devizes where it is likely that a booking system will be in operation. On some occasions restricted use of locks on the Widcombe flight at Bath and at Wootton Rivers may be enforced. For details contact The Manager.

Mileage

READING to
Aldermaston Wharf: 10
Tile Mill Lock: 8
Newbury Lock: 18½
Kintbury: 24½
Hungerford: 27½
Crofton Top Lock: 35
Pewsey Wharf: 41½
Devizes Top Lock: 53½
Bradford-on-Avon: 65½
Dundas Aqueduct: 70
Bath, junction with River Avon: 75¼
HANHAM Lock (start of tidal section): 86½
Bristol Docks: 93
AVONMOUTH entrance to Severn
Estuary: 100¾

Locks: 105

The Kennet & Avon Canal is one of the most splendid lengths of artificial waterway in Britain, a fitting memorial to the canal age as a whole. It is a broad canal, cutting across southern England from Reading to Bristol. Its generous dimensions and handsome architecture blend well with the rolling downs and open plains that it passes through, and are a good reminder of the instinctive feeling for scale that characterised most 18th and early 19thC civil engineering.

The canal was built in three sections. The first two were river navigations, the Kennet from Reading to Newbury, and the Avon from Bath to Bristol, both being canalised. Among early 18thC river navigations the Kennet was one of the most ambitious, owing to the steep fall of the river. Between Reading and Newbury 18 locks were necessary in as many miles, as the difference in level is 138ft. John Hore was the engineer for the Kennet Navigation, which was built between 1718 and 1723 and included 11 miles of new cut. Subsequently Hore was in charge of the Bristol Avon Navigation, carried out between 1725 and 1727. These river navigations were interesting in many ways, often because of the varied nature of the country they passed through. The steep-sided Avon Gorge meant that a fast-flowing river had to be brought under control. Elsewhere the engineering was unusual: for example the turf-sided locks on the Kennet, now being replaced with brick structures.

For the third stage, a canal from Newbury to Bath was authorised in 1794. Rennie was appointed engineer, and after a long struggle the canal was opened in 1810, completing a through route from London to Bristol. The canal is 57 miles long, and included 79 broad locks, a summit level at Savernake 474ft above sea level and one short tunnel, also at Savernake. Rennie was both engineer and architect, anticipating the role played by Brunel in the creation of the Great Western Railway; in some ways his architecture is the more noteworthy aspect of his work. The architectural quality of the whole canal is exceptional, from the straightforward stone bridges to the magnificent Neo-classical aqueducts at Avoncliffe and Limpley Stoke. Rennie's engineering, however, left something to be desired; the summit level was too short, and so pumping stations had to be installed at Crofton and Claverton to maintain the water level and feed the locks; in other places the canal bed was built over porous rock, and so leaked constantly, necessitating further regular pumping.

Nevertheless, the canal as a whole was a striking achievement. West of Devizes the canal descends Caen Hill in a straight flight of 16 locks. In total 29 locks are navigated within two miles of Devizes. The many swing bridges were designed to run on ball bearings, one of the first applications of the principle. The bold entry of the canal into Bath, a sweeping descent round the south of the city, is a firm expression of the belief that major engineering works should contribute to the landscape, whether urban or rural, instead of imposing themselves upon it as often happens nowadays.

Later the Kennet & Avon Canal Company took over the two river navigations, thus gaining control of the whole through route. However traffic was never as heavy as the promoters had expected, and so the canal declined steadily throughout the 19thC. It suffered from early railway competition as the Great Western Railway duplicated its route, and was eventually bought by that railway company. Maintenance standards slipped, and this, combined with a rapidly declining traffic, meant that navigation was difficult in places by the end of the 1914-18 war. The last regular traffic left the canal in the 1930s, but still it remained open, and the last through passage was made in 1951 by nb. *Queen*, with the West Country artist P. Ballance on board. Subsequently the canal was closed, and for a long time its future was in jeopardy. However, great interest in the canal had resulted in the formation of a Canal Association shortly after the 1939-45 war, to fight for restoration. In 1962 the Kennet & Avon Canal Trust was formed out of the Association, and practical steps towards restoration were under way. Using volunteers to raise funds from all sources, and with steadily increasing inputs from BW, the Trust has catalysed the reopening of the entire navigation as a through route from Reading to Bristol. This achievement was commemorated on 8th August 1990, with HM The Queen navigating through Lock 43, at the summit of the Caen Hill flight, which now bears her name. However, this must be seen as very much a beginning and not an end. Water supplies to the long pounds and the summit level have still to be secured by a combination of back pumping on several lock flights and the sealing of the remaining areas of porous canal bed. This will require substantial capital expenditure by BW and the Trust, while the waterway will always incur considerable ongoing running costs. Basic facilities such as water and pump-outs are still few and far between and will only appear in response to demand.

Natural history

This canal forms a unique series of freshwater habitats which vary along its length according to depth of water, aspect, height of the banks and the time of year.

The stonework of bridges, locks and aqueducts provides additional habitats for shallow-rooting plants. The three ferns, harts-tongue, wall-rue and black spleenwort, are of special interest. Where the lock walls are capped with limestone, lime-loving plants such as fairy flax and quaking-grass are found.

For much of its length the canal is bordered on one or both banks by trees, including several species of willow, and bushes, predominantly hawthorn. A detailed survey in 1972 showed that plants along the towpath vary little, growing in profusion along its length. There are many kinds of grasses; other frequent species are white deadnettle, hogweed, meadow cranesbill, ground ivy and fine specimens of the ratstail plantain. Apart from the marsh marigold, the yellow iris and the greater pond sedge, there are few flowers at the water's edge and on the canal bank until after mid-summer when purple loosestrife, the three-petalled arrowhead and flowering rush, together with the clusters of small creamy-white flowers of meadowsweet and pink-tinged angelica, contrast with the tall reed-grass and reedmace (often mistakenly called 'bulrush'). Rooting just in the water, the most common plant is the branched bur-reed. It has a profusion of leaves but the green, spherical, prickly-looking flowers are often sparse. Large tufts of tussock sedge, clumps of water dock and short stretches of common reed, having all the leaves on the tall stems turning to face away from the wind, can be found at the water's edge. Of all the marginal plants, perhaps the most handsome is the flowering rush, which is commonest near Bath. Deeper water supports such plants as yellow water-lily, water crowfoot and several pondweeds that root in the mud but hold their leaves and flowers above the water surface. A few plants are entirely submerged, the commonest being hornwort, which grows in long bushy, brittle tassels.

In the summer and autumn much of the water surface is covered with small floating plants that are moved by the wind. There are species of duckweed and a water fern, azolla, accidentally introduced from North America, which turns the canal red in autumn. The weed is only killed by a hard frost, when it sinks to the bottom and decays.

A botanist has recorded 190 different species of plants associated with the presence of the canal along a four-mile stretch near Melksham. The different plant zones make not only for numerical and visual diversity but also for the diversity of animals dependent on them. Mute swans, coots and moorhens nest and take refuge in the dense vegetation at the water's edge, water voles feed on it and use rushes and grass to line their nests. These are four of the canal's largest animals but they, like all wildlife, are part of the food chains that depend on the oxygen in the water and the light that filters into it. Amongst the tangle of submerged green plants and their roots lives a host of small animals, many visible only under a microscope. Some of the water snails, the large swan mussels (8in long), freshwater shrimps and flatworms feed on decaying plant matter, while others such as water beetles, water spiders, water boatmen, dragonfly nymphs and the strange water stick insects, represent the hunting predators, actively seeking out their quarry, which is often much larger than themselves. Many of these freshwater creatures are found only in the comparatively still water of canals and ponds, for they would be swept away in the streams and rivers. They provide food for water shrews, fish, frogs and, occasionally, grass snakes, which can be seen on sunny days curled up on the towpath or swimming across the canal in a few regular haunts.

The shy little grebe, with its trilling call, has spread from Wilton Water and now nests, on platforms made by willow branches dipping into the water, as far west as Devizes. Kingfishers have returned to the localities they frequented prior to the severe winters of the early 1960s and single herons are regular fishermen along the canal, though their diet also includes frogs etc. The abundance of newly-emerged insects attracts many small birds to the canal. In spring, the bushes are sometimes full of chiff-chaffs and willow warblers, eagerly feeding after their long flight from their winter quarters. Later, sedge and reed warblers arrive, take up their territories along the canal, sometimes singing all day and night, and build their nests in rushes and reeds. Swallows and house martins leave their nesting sites in the villages on summer evenings to feed over the canal, skimming low to pick up insects off the surface of the water. In late summer brambles growing on the banks are in flower, attracting butterflies to feed on them. The commonest are meadow brown, speckled wood, small tortoiseshell, peacock,

brimstone and the quaintly named gatekeeper. In autumn, pied wagtails converge on the canal pounds near Devizes at dusk to roost in the rushes. By December they number around 300.

The canal offers a wealth of interest and for students of all ages it can serve as an open-air natural history laboratory. If restoration work succeeds in producing the healthy ecological balance that has emerged near Bath, then naturalists, anglers and all other users will benefit.

The Kennet & Avon Canal Trust, The Wharf, Couch Lane, Devizes, Wilts. Tel: 0380 721279.

Seend Cleeve, Kennet & Avon Canal. *Derek Pratt.*

5' 3" Southcot lock *104*

Milkmaid's footbridge

105 Fobney lock 7' 8"

Reading

River Kennet

Berkeley avenue bridge

New ring road bridge
County lock *106*
Bridge street bridge

Bear Free wharf

Traffic light controls

High bridge

Watlington street bridge
Kings road bridge

B Reading General station

Blake's lock 3' 4"

18½M   21L
Newbury

Brentford
60M   21L

Kennet mouth

A329

A4

River Thames

Reading

The River Kennet leaves the Thames east of
Reading. The mouth of the river is marked by
gasometers and the main railway, which runs
parallel to the south bank of the Thames. The
Kennet leads south west towards the centre of
Reading, passing Blake's Lock, the only lock
maintained by the Thames Conservancy that
is not actually on the Thames. A variety of
sensitive new developments complement the
river's passage through this section of the
town. The Kennet through Reading is narrow,
shallow and fast-flowing, being a river
navigation; also there are several sharp blind
bends in the town, so great care in navigation
is needed. Keep a sharp lookout for other
boats and remember to allow for the flow of
the river. The river cuts across the middle of
the town, and so access to all facilities is easy.
Rows of riverside cottages and a surprising
variety of bridges decorate the Kennet in
Reading, High Bridge being the most central
access point. The Kennet passes over a weir
with County Lock adjoining. The weirs are a
feature of river navigation that should be
treated with respect, as the current they create
can often affect the course of a boat, especially
when making a slow approach to a lock. The
river gradually leaves the town, passing
through Fobney Meadow to Fobney Lock.

Navigational note
The Kennet & Avon Canal locks require
windlasses of an intermediate gauge – 1⅛in
instead of the normal 1in or 1¼in.

Reading
Berks. EC Mon, Wed. MD Mon. All services.
The town lies at the extremity of the Berkshire
Downs and the Chiltern Hills, where the
Thames becomes a major river. It is the
Victorian architecture that makes this town
interesting, as the university buildings are not
to everyone's taste. Canal walkers in Reading
will find there is no towing path in the centre
of town; however, west of Reading the whole
canal is a public right of way. (Because of the
risk of vandalism only recognised mooring
sites should be used.)
Blake's Lock Museum Gasworks Road,
Kenavon Drive, Reading (0734 590630).
Housed in a handsome pumping station built
in the 1870s, the museum depicts all aspects
of navigation in and around Reading. There
are also reconstructions of a printer's
workshop, a bakery and a barber's shop, and
displays of local industry. *Open 10.00–17.00,
14.00–17.00 Sat & Sun. Closed Mon.* Free.
Temporary mooring for visitors.
Abbey Ruins Fragmentary remains of this
12thC abbey built by Henry I lie on the edge
of Forbury Park. The 13thC gatehouse,
altered by Scott in 1869, still stands.
The Gaol Forbury Road. Designed by Scott
and Moffatt in 1842–44 in the Scottish
Baronial style. Oscar Wilde wrote his *Ballad of
Reading Gaol* while imprisoned here.
Museum of English Rural Life White
Knights Park. A fascinating collection of relics
of old English agriculture, and a small display
of painted canal ware with a set of tools used
for making narrowboats. *Closed Sun, Mon,
B.Hols.*
Museum & Art Gallery Friar Street. has an
exceptional natural history and local
archaeology collection. Also prehistoric
collection. *Open weekdays.*
Tourist Information Centre Central
Library, Belgrave Street, Reading (0734
55911).

BOATYARDS
Ⓑ **Reading Marine Co.** Gasworks Road,
Reading (0734 573917 or 509123). Ⓡ Ⓦ Ⓓ
Pump-out, gas, boat hire, slipway, boat and
engine repairs, mooring, chandlery, toilets.
BOAT TRIPS
Kennet Cruises 69ft trip boat *Lancing* for
charter and public trips. Also one narrowboat
for hire. For details ring 0734 871115.

PUBS AND RESTAURANTS

Horn St Mary's Butts, Reading. North of Bridge Street Bridge. Courage real ale, food.

Fisherman's Cottage Kennetside, Reading. A pretty 18thC canalside pub, west of Blake's Lock, serving Fuller's real ale. Food, garden. Children welcome.

Jolly Anglers Kennetside, Reading. East of Blake's Lock. There is a quaint façade to this pub which marks the last refreshment point before the Thames. Courage real ale,

pub food, garden, children welcome.

Lynhurst Arms Queen's Road, Reading. South of Watlington Street Bridge. Whitbread real ale, food.

Wharf Wine Press King's Bridge, Reading. A modern canalside wine bar and restaurant.

Kennet Arms East of Berkeley Avenue Bridge. Courage real ale pub serving bar snacks.

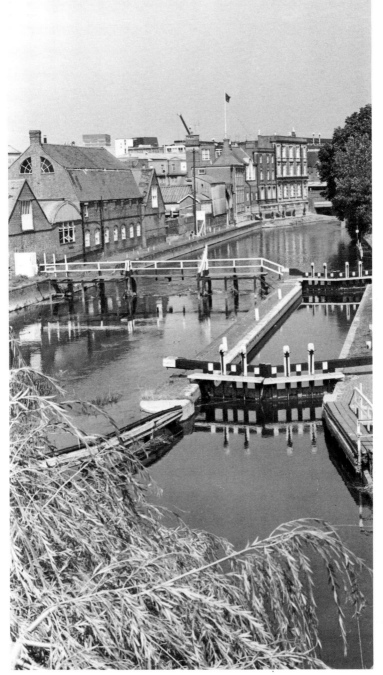

County Lock and Weir, Reading. There are several blind corners downstream. *Derek Pratt.*

Map labels (left page):

Sulhamstead
6' 4"
Tyle Mill Lock **99**
Tyle Mill swing bridge
SW
A4
River Kennet
Weir
Sulhamstead swing bridge
Sulhamstead lock **100**
4' 1"
Gravel Quarry Bridge
Theale
Shenfield mill
12M 14L
Newbury
Thames
6½M 7L
Theale swing bridge
Sheffield lock **101**
2' 2"
7' 7" Garston lock **102**
M4
Hissey's bridge
7' 0" Burghfield lock **103**
Swans bridge
Burghfield bridge
Weir

Theale

Continuing west, the canal passes Burghfield Bridge, a handsome stone arch. The Kennet winds through water-meadows, the straight stretches marking the canal sections. The M4 motorway and the railway inevitably affect the peace and quiet of this stretch, although the country to the south of the Kennet improves steadily as it progresses westwards. Berkshire is well-known as orchard country. At Theale there is the first of the swing bridges that occur along the Kennet & Avon. Fortunately, since the completion of the M4, this bridge has reverted to carrying relatively infrequent road vehicles, so the passage of a boat no longer causes a major traffic hold-up. Opening the bridge is hard work, but there are instructions to help you. Make sure that you close the traffic barriers first of all and open them behind you. Theale village is ½ mile north of the bridge. After Theale, the Kennet flows steadily through wooded fields towards Sulhamstead and reaches Tyle Mill after a pleasant tree-lined straight cut. The nature reserves of Cumber Lake to the north and Woolwich Green Lake to the south can be reached by a short walk from Sulhamstead Lock. Originally gravel pits excavated since 1960, the lakes offer an undisturbed habitat for all forms of wildlife. The moorings at Tyle Mill and at Burghfield are administered by BW. Ring 0380 722859.

Navigational note
Garston Lock has a slight bend in it. Two 'long' narrowboats can have difficulty fitting in side-by-side.

Sulhamstead
Berks. A scattered village ¼ mile south east of Tyle Mill, but with no real centre. There are several large houses standing in their own grounds; the most impressive is Folly Farm, built by Lutyens in 1906 in a William and Mary style. In 1912 Lutyens extended the house, this time using a Tudor style. The mixture of the two periods is most successful. The house is *private*.

Theale
Berks. EC Wed. PO, tel. Stores, garage, bank, chemist, station. ¼ mile north west of Sheffield Lock. Although largely a Reading suburb, Theale has been given a new lease of life by the opening of the bypass and the M4 motorway. The main street is now quiet and relatively traffic-free, and the Georgian terraces can be enjoyed. The large church with its tall tower is interesting. It was designed by E. W. Garbett and built 1820-32 in a style based entirely on Salisbury Cathedral. Theale station is half-way between the town and Theale swing bridge.

PUBS AND RESTAURANTS
Falcon High Street, Theale. An 18thC pub serving Courage real ale. Bar food and garden.
Railway Theale, next to the station. The pub nearest the canal in this village. Halls real ale, bar food and garden.
Lamb at Theale Courage real ale and bar food.
Red Lion Theale. Halls real ale and bar food.
Crown Inn Theale. Wethered real ale. Food (*not Sun*).
Cunning Man Burghfield Bridge. A family pub with large canalside garden. Courage real ale. Food, including burger bar and ice-cream parlour. Restaurant serving vegetarian food.
Mulligan's Fish and Chips Restaurant and Oyster Bar Bath Road, Sulhamstead. Half mile north of Tyle Mill.

Woolhampton

Leaving Tyle Mill the canal continues south west, constantly joining and leaving the River Kennet. Swing bridges are very common, often carrying busy roads. The A4 runs parallel for many miles, but always keeps its distance; the Great Western Railway also runs parallel but much closer.

Woolhampton
Berks. PO, tel, stores, garage, station. A village on the A4 that owes its existence to the days of mail coaches on the old Bath road. There is a good mixture of buildings in the main street, several pubs and hotels. Up on the hill to the north of the village are the Victorian church, the Georgian buildings of Woolhampton Park and Douai Abbey and School, the latter a fine group of 19thC buildings with more recent additions.

Aldermaston
Berks. PO, tel stores. Attractively placed at the foot of a wooded hill, 1½ miles to the south of Aldermaston Wharf (along a minor road), the village is particularly fine. Mellow brick houses of all periods face each other across the sloping main street, which has survived the inroads of traffic. At the top of the street is the pebble-dashed church, and Aldermaston Court, a private house containing magnificent 17thC woodwork.

Aldermaston Wharf
Berks. PO, tel, stores, station. A small canalside settlement bisected by the busy A340. The old swing bridge has been replaced with a hydraulic lift bridge, push-button operated with the aid of a BW key. It cost the local council £250,000 to build.

Ufton Green
Berks. A lush, peaceful hamlet built round a small triangular green. All that remains of the church is one flint wall, standing proudly in the middle of a field, and capped with a marvellous mantle of ivy.

BOATYARDS

BW Padworth Yard near Aldermaston Wharf (0734 712277). Information about the canal, and moorings on the navigable sections. Special K & A-sized windlasses for sale.

PUBS AND RESTAURANTS

■✕ **Row Barge** Station Road, Woolhampton. This canalside pub offers both restaurant and bar food, catering for vegetarians (*no food Tue evenings*). Real ales include John Smith's and Courage. Children welcomed, garden. Music *alternate Tuesdays.*
■ **Falmouth Arms** Woolhampton. Eldridge Pope real ale and bar food.
■✕ **Angel Inn** Woolhampton. An imposing ivy-clad building in the centre of the village. The pub serves a variety of guest beers along with Wethered real ale. There is a wide range of food, including vegetarian, served in both the bar and restaurant, including Sunday lunch. Garden, children welcome, B & B.
■✕ **Butt Inn** Aldermaston Wharf. Wethered and Flowers real ales. Food. Children welcome. Garden.
■✕ **Hind's Head** Aldermaston. An imposing building which faces up the main street. Formerly The Congreve Arms, until it changed hands following the devastation of a great fire. The Hind's Head once brewed its own beer, selling at 2d a pint; now Wethered real ale is served from the bar. The pub also offers good food in both bar and restaurant, catering for both vegetarians and curry fans. Garden, children welcome. B & B.

← N

88 Bull's lock
5' 9"

A4

89 Widmead lock 3' 7"

River Kennet

2M   4L
Newbury
Thames
16½M 17L

Thatcham

Long Cut swing
bridge

90 Old Monkey Marsh lock 6' 8"

Thatcham swing bridge

Thatcham station

91 Colthrop lock 7' 7"
Colthrop bridge

92 Midgham lock 7' 9"
Midgham bridge

A4

Cranwell's swing bridge

93 Old Heale's lock 8' 11"

Thatcham

The canal leaves Midgham Park to the north
and continues due west thorugh water-
meadows, the woods and hills receding to the
south. At Colthrop a large industrial estate
appears unexpectedly beside the canal; much
of it consists of paper mills. Thatcham station
is conveniently beside the canal; a hotel is
nearby. The village itself is a mile to the north
west. The canal now flows very straight
through isolated water-meadows under a
railway bridge to Bull's Lock. This section of
canal probably best serves to illustrate the
wide variety of works jointly undertaken by a
consortium made up of County and District
Councils, Manpower Services job creation
programmes, British Waterways and the
Kennet & Avon Canal Trust, who have been
at the forefront of fund raising for 25 years.
For example, Old Heale's Lock to the east and
Bull's Lock to the west have both been rebuilt
with consortium labour, while Widmead Lock
has been re-constructed to a very high
standard by outside contractors at a cost in
excess of £250,000. The many swing bridges
have either been totally rebuilt or, in some
cases, replaced by a high level structure:
Colthrop Bridge being privately funded. Old
Monkey Marsh Lock, the last remaining
example of a turf-sided lock, has been listed as
an ancient monument by English Heritage. It
is now restored with wooden piling to two feet
above low water level, turf-lined banks sloping
to the top of the lock, together with a timber
framework to delineate the actual lock
chamber when full. Elsewhere along the canal,
generous funding, be it from British
Waterways, District and County Councils or
the Kennet & Avon Canal Trust itself, has
achieved a series of impressive examples of
renewal and improvement which together
have rescued this navigation, reopened in
August 1990 by HM The Queen.

Thatcham
Berks. EC Wed. All services. The main square
of this rapidly expanding village, now almost a
suburb of Newbury, is all but dominated by
sprawling housing development. Set back
from the A4, it manages to retain some peace
which carries over into the nearby cluster of
older buildings grouped at the east end of the
pretty Victorian church and churchyard.

PUBS AND RESTAURANTS
Crickets High Street, Thatcham. Ushers
real ale and bar food.
X **White Hart** High Street, Thatcham. A
choice of real ales including Courage and John
Smith's. Good food served in both the bar and
restaurant.
X **Old Chequers** Thatcham. Comfortable
old pub serving Halls real ale. English and
continental cuisine in the restaurant. Bar food,
garden, children welcome.
Kings Head Thatcham. Courage real ale,
bar food. B & B.

Newbury

The navigation enters Newbury under a handsome new road bridge. Just beside this bridge is Newbury Wharf, where there is a stone building used by the K & A Canal Trust as an information centre and museum, and old warehouses, which have been ingeniously converted into bus station buildings. This large wharf used to be the terminus of the Kennet Navigation from Reading, before the Kennet & Avon Canal Company extended it to link up with the Avon at Bath. West of the wharf the channel gets narrower and faster until it reaches a splendid stone balustraded bridge. Just beyond is Newbury Lock, where there is a mooring site. The river cuts right through the town, and the town makes the most of it. West of the lock is the delightful, quiet West Mills area, where rows of terraced houses face the navigation. West of Newbury, the navigation again passes through extensive water-meadows before the wooded hills of Hamstead Park close in from the south.

Navigational note
The lower sill at Bull's Lock is shallow. Take care through bottom gates.

Newbury
Berks. EC Wed. MD Tue. All services. Newbury developed in the Middle Ages as a cloth town of considerable wealth, its stature indicated by the size of the church. Although the cloth trade has long vanished, the town has managed to retain much of its period charm. It is a busy shopping centre, and the shop fronts in the main streets have buried many 17th and 18thC houses. Elsewhere in the town the 18thC is well in evidence, especially in the West Mills area. There are fine almshouses, and a pretty, ornamental stone bridge over the navigation. There are also signs of the agricultural importance of Newbury: the 19thC Italianate Corn Exchange, for example.
St Nicholas Church West Mills. Borders the canal on the south bank. A large Perpendicular church, built c1500 at the height of Newbury's prosperity as a wool town. Its 17thC pulpit is most unusual.
St Nicholas School Enborne Road. By Butterfield, 1859.
Borough Museum Wharf Road. Originally built in 1626 as a cloth-weaving workshop to give employment to the poor, this is one of the most interesting buildings in Newbury. Adjoining is the corn store, once on the edge of the Kennet Wharf. The museum collection illustrates the prehistoric and Saxon history of the region, as well as the medieval and modern. Also a natural history section with an excellent display of moths and butterflies. *Closed Sun. EC Wed.*
Round Barrow Cemetery Wash Common, near the site of the 1st Battle of Newbury in 1643. Memorial stones to the victims surmount the two smaller mounds.
Newbury Fair Northcroft Lane, Northcroft. Leave canal at Kennet Bridge. Annual Michaelmas fair held since 1215. *Thur following 11 Oct.*
1st Battle of Newbury, 20 Sep 1643 Site of Wash Farm off A343. 1¼ miles south of Guyer's Lock. The Royalists were defeated by the Parliamentarians in one of the bloodiest onslaughts of the Civil War. Guyer's and Higg's Locks are named after troop commanders in the battle.
2nd Battle of Newbury, 28 Oct 1644 Donnington Castle, Donnington. 1½ miles north of Newbury Lock off the A34. The Royalists were in possession of Donnington Castle when the Parliamentarians attacked. Charles' army withdrew to Oxford, but a week later they returned and relieved the castle. There is a reconstruction model of the battle in Newbury Museum.

BOATYARDS
Ⓑ **Newbury Boat Co.** Greenham Lock Cottage, Newbury (0635 42884). Ⓡ Ⓢ Ⓦ Ⓓ Pump-out, gas, overnight mooring, long-term mooring, winter storage, books and maps, slipway, crane, boat and engine repairs, toilet.

BOAT TRIPS

Kennet Horse Boat Co. 32 West Mills, Newbury, Berks (0635 44154). Horse-drawn and motor barge. Mostly private charter. *Easter-end Sep.* Public trips on the motor barge *Sun, B. Hols, some weekdays Aug,* and also on the horse-drawn boat – ring for details. Must book.

PUBS AND RESTAURANTS

There are many pubs and restaurants in Newbury; the following are simply those closest to the canal.

⬤✕ Old Waggon & Horses 100yds east of Newbury Bridge. This comfortable pub has a pleasant terrace overlooking the river. Courage real ale, food served in both the bar and restaurant.

⬤ Bricklayers Arms 200yds south of Newbury Bridge. Courage real ale. Bar food (*not Sun*).

⬤ Catherine Wheel Cheap Street, south of Westmills Bridge. A small, town pub offering Courage and John Smith's real ale. Bar snacks. Garden, children welcome.

✕⬤ Berni Inn Riverside, Newbury, just east of Whitehouse Bridge.

Public trip boats at West Mills, Newbury, Kennet & Avon Canal. *Derek Pratt.*

Kintbury

Passing the beautiful woods of Hamstead
Park, the canal reaches Hamstead, Copse,
Drewett's and Kintbury Locks. Wooded
rolling hills flank the canal to the south as it
climbs up the locks towards Kintbury, making
this a particularly attractive stretch. The canal
enters the village beside the railway, and the
Dundas Arms, which overlooks the lock. The
centre of Kintbury is up on the hill to the
south of the lock. Leaving the wharf, the canal
follows the railway, passing the Victorian
Gothic vicarage, and then continues
westwards through pleasing open countryside.

Navigational note
Allow for river current when winding.

Kintbury
Berks. PO, tel, stores, station. A quiet village
with attractive buildings by the canal,
including a watermill and canalside pub. The
church is originally 13thC, but was restored in
1859; the railway lends excitement, and noise,
to the situation.
Hamstead Park A very fine park bordered by
the canal. There used to be a castle here and
several interesting buildings adjoin the church
on the side of the hill. There is an old
watermill by the lock. The hamlet of
Hamstead Marshall lies to the south, 1½ miles
from Hamstead Lock.

PUBS AND RESTAURANTS
▰ **Blue Ball** Kintbury. 500yds south of
Kintbury Bridge. John Smith's and Courage
real ale. Bar food *lunchtime only.* Children
welcome in garden.
▰ **Prince of Wales** Kintbury. 300yds south-
east of Kintbury Bridge. Ushers real ale. Bar
food and *Sunday lunch.* Children welcome,
garden with play area.
▰✕ **Dundas Arms** Kintbury. The river
Kennet and the canal flow on either side of
this pub, which was named after the Lord
Dundas who opened the canal in 1810. Real
ales include Adnams, Morland and Thomas
Hardy. The restaurant has an interesting
French menu and a good wine cellar. Children
welcome, garden, B & B.
▰ **Crossways Inn** Inkpen Road, Kintbury.
Bass, Marston's and Arkells real ales. Bistro
and bar snacks. Children welcome, garden.
▰✕ **White Hart** Hamstead Marshall. 1 mile
south of Hamstead Lock. Real ales include
John Smith's, Badger and Eldridge Pope.
Restaurant (*closed all day Sunday*).
▰✕ **Red House** Marsh Benham. ¼ mile
north-east of Hamstead Lock. Pub in a
thatched estate village near Benham Park.
Brakspear, Flowers and Boddingtons real ales.
Restaurant with a good menu. Garden,
children welcome. B & B.

Hungerford

The canal continues westwards through open
countryside. The railway and the River
Kennet are constantly present, the canal
leaving the river bed for the last time west of
Kintbury. Locks 77 and 76 carry the canal
past Avington, with its Norman church visible
among the trees. Pretty woods accompany the
canal to the south as it approaches
Hungerford, while to the north river and canal
run side by side through water-meadows,
separated only by a narrow ridge carrying the
towpath. As the diminutive River Kennet
accompanies the canal past Dunmill lock, the
towpath turns over to the south bank. From
the bridge there is a good view of Denford
Mill. As the canal enters Hungerford, the
Kennet swings away to the north, feeding the
trout farm that lies between canal and river.
Gardens flank the canal as it comes into the
centre of the town. Access to Hungerford is
easy by the town bridge, which leads directly
to the handsome main street.

Hungerford
*Berks. EC Thur. PO, tel, stores, garage, bank,
station.* Hungerford is built along the A338,
which runs through the town southwards from
the junction with the A4. The pleasant 18th
and 19thC buildings are set back from the
road, giving the spacious feeling of a
traditional market town. None of the
buildings are remarkable, but many are
individually pretty. Note the decorative
ironwork of the house by the canal bridge. The
manor was given to John of Gaunt in 1366,
and any monarch passing through the town is
given a red rose, the Lancastrian emblem, as a
token rent.
Hocktide Ceremonies On the *second
Tuesday after Easter*, 99 commoners (those
living within the original borough who have
the rights of the common and the fishing) are
called to the Town Hall by the blowing of a
horn. Two Tuttimen are appointed, who have
to visit the houses of the commoners to collect
a 'head penny' from the men and a kiss from
the women: they give oranges in return. All
new commoners are then shod by having a nail
driven into their shoes. This ceremony dates
from the medieval period.
Avington
Berks. The village is best approached along the
track that runs east from lock 76, although the
more adventurous can go directly across the
water-meadows, crossing the Kennet on a
small footbridge. The little church is still
wholly Norman, and contains a variety of
original work; the chancel arch, the corbels
and the font are particularly interesting.

BOAT TRIPS
Kennet & Avon Canal Trust *1½ hour* trips to
Dunmill Lock from Hungerford on *Rose of
Hungerford* on *weekends and B. Hol afternoons.*
Also longer *4-hour* trip to Froxfield. Available
for private charter, up to 50 persons. Details
from 0488 683006.

PUBS AND RESTAURANTS
🍺 **John of Gaunt** Hungerford. 16thC pub
north of the canal, serving Morland real ale.
Bar menu including take-away food. Pleasant
dining room, garden, B & B, children
welcome.
🍺 **Three Swans Hotel** Hungerford. Resort
hotel. South of canal.
🍺✕ **The Bear** Charnham St, north of canal.
Resort hotel with 13thC restaurant serving
cordon bleu menu.
🍺 **The Plume** Hungerford. South of canal.
Courage real ale. Bar food and garden.
🍺 **The Sun** Charnham St. North of canal.
Morland real ale. Bar food, garden, children
welcome.
🍺✕ **The Toad & Trout** Charnham St, north
of canal. Bistro serving Bass and Ushers real
ale. Children welcome.
🍺 **The Lamb** Charnham St, north of canal.
Bar food, garden with play area, B & B.
🍺 **Railway Tavern** 200yds south of Station
Road footbridge. Ushers real ale. Bar food.
Garden, children welcome.

Froxfield

Leaving Hungerford, the canal passes the old wharf. An original stone warehouse survives, but much of the wharf area has now been built on. West of the wooded 19thC church, the canal suddenly enters an open landscape. Water-meadows and pastureland, rich in buttercups, flank the waterway, which seems to be more river than canal. The railway is in a cutting to the south, and the quiet browsing cattle give a feeling of 18thC rural serenity. The canal is then carried on to an embankment as the wooded hills reappear on both banks, crossing the River Dun on a small brick aqueduct. The railway crosses the canal west of the aqueduct, and now hugs the north bank for several miles. The roar of the frequent diesel expresses to and from the West Country is the only interruption in the natural peace and solitude of the canal. Froxfield lies to the north, flanking the A4; the best access is from the new bridge. This was rebuilt in 1972 during a road improvement scheme using traditional methods and materials, even to the correct colour of brick. Three locks carry the canal past Froxfield, and then the spire of Little Bedwyn Church comes into view, half-hidden by trees on the north bank. The village is cut in half by the canal and the railway. In the centre the lock continues the climb towards the summit.

Navigational note
Hungerford Marsh Swing Bridge is over Hungerford Marsh lock. Boats over 30ft long (approx.) will have to swing it clear before using the lock.

Little Bedwyn
Wilts. PO, tel. Divided by the canal, the village falls into two distinct parts. North is the estate village, pretty 19thC terraces of patterned brick running eastwards to the church, half-hidden among ancient yew trees. To the south is the older farming village, handsome 18thC buildings climbing the hill away from the canal. The PO is to be found within The Harrow public house.
Froxfield
Wilts. Tel. The village is spread along the A4, which has obviously affected its development. The main feature of the village is the Somerset Hospital, a range of almshouses founded by the Duchess of Somerset in 1694, extended in 1775 and again in 1813. Facing onto the road, the hospital is built round a courtyard, which is entered by a Gothic-style gateway, part of the 1813 extension.
Littlecote 1½ miles north of Froxfield (0488 84000). A Tudor building of the 16thC. Littlecote is the most important brick mansion in Wiltshire. The formal front overlooks the gardens that run down to the Kennet. Inside, the Great Hall, the armoury and Long Gallery are particularly notable. Now extensively developed as a tourist attraction, 'The Land of Littlecote' offers a full day's entertainment for the whole family. *Open 10.00-18.00 daily Apr-Sep.*

PUBS AND RESTAURANTS
◗✕ Harrow Little Bedwyn. In the southern half of the village, serving Marston's, Hook Norton and a guest real ale. Bar food and restaurant (*no food Mon evenings*). Vegetarians catered for. Garden, children welcome. Games night *Mon.*
◗ Watermeadow Inn Froxfield. On A4. ¼ mile north of the new bridge. Ushers real ale, food, B & B, garden.

Crofton

Leaving Little Bedwyn, the canal continues through a rolling landscape towards its summit, closely accompanied by the railway. To the north is a hill fort, overlooking ridges that break up the farmland. The canal stays on the south side of the valley, a shallow side-cutting carrying it into Great Bedwyn. The village is ranged over the hillside to the north of the canal, newer houses spilling downwards towards the canal and railway station. The canal leaves the village past the church, and enters a wooded stretch that takes it up towards Crofton. The hills encroach more sharply as the summit draws nearer. Crofton appears as the canal starts a wide swing to the north west. The engine house stands on a rise above the canal, its blunt, iron-bound chimney making its purpose unmistakable. To the south lies the long expanse of Wilton Water, a natural lake from which the Crofton pumps draw their supplies. After Crofton the country opens out for a while as the flight of locks continues the final climb to the summit. Then, as the land rises steeply on both banks, it prepares itself for the short Bruce Tunnel. A wooded cutting leads towards the tunnel, taking the canal through the fringes of the Old Savernake Forest. To the north are the extensive parklands of Tottenham House, and Savernake Forest itself. The towpath climbs over the top of the tunnel.

Navigational note

Due to water supply problems, there are often restrictions to navigation between Crofton and Bath.

Wilton
Wilts. Tel. A compact village at the southern end of Wilton Water, with a pretty duck pond in the centre.

Crofton
Wilts. The scattered village is dominated by the brick pumping house with its separate chimney. It houses two 19thC steam engines, one built in 1812 by Boulton and Watt, the oldest working beam engine in the world, the other in 1845 by Harvey's of Hayle, Cornwall. Both have been restored to working order, and are steamed on several weekends in the year. The pumping house and the engines are open for viewing *every summer Sun.* For details of 'steaming' weekends, ring 0672 63498.
Wilton Windmill 1 mile south of the cnal, along footpath at lock 60.

Great Bedwyn
Wilts. PO, tel, stores, garage, station. The main street climbs gently away from the canal and the railway. It is wide, with generous grass verges; attractive houses of all periods line the street. At the top is the pub. The large church, with its well-balanced crossing tower, is mostly 12th and 13thC; inside are some interesting monuments. The road running westwards to the church passes the Bedwyn Stone Museum, an amazing establishment.
Bedwyn Stone Museum A collection of stone work of all types, showing the work of seven generations of stone masons. There are statues, tombstones, casts, even the fossilised footprint of a dinosaur. *Open daily.*

BOAT TRIPS

Kennet & Avon Canal Trust nb. *Jubilee.* 44-passenger trip boat operating from Crofton Pumping Station to Great Bedwyn. Ring 0488 82760 for details.

PUBS

☛ **Swan Inn** Wilton. ½ mile south of lock 61, on road running beside Wilton Water, serving Whitbread real ale.
☛ **Three Tuns** Great Bedwyn. Bar food and Whitbread real ale.
☛ **Cross Keys** Great Bedwyn. Offers food, and real ale from the Wiltshire Brewery. B & B.

Bruce tunnel

Wilton

Wolfhall bridge

55 Crofton top lock
Wolfhall Fields bridge

56

63-55 Crofton locks
Summit level varies
Rise approx 61' 0"

57

Crofton feeder

58 Sam Farmer lock
Freewarren bridge

59 Crofton
pumping station

N

Wilton Water 60

Roman Road

61

Crofton bridge

N

Crofton

Wilton Brail

62

63 Beech Grove lock
Beech Tree
Walk bridge

8M 13L
Pewsey
Newbury
15M 22L

Mill bridge

64 Bedwyn Church lock 7'11"

Bedwyn Church
bridge

Great Bedwyn

Bedwyn Wharf
bridge
Great Bedwyn wharf

Great Bedwyn station

65 Burnt Mill lock 7'9"
Burnt Mill footbridge

Wansdyke

66 Potters lock 7' 6"

Hill fort

Wootton Rivers

The canal emerges from the western portal of Bruce Tunnel into a deep cutting. Woods line both banks, hiding the railway, which is now on the south bank having crossed over the tunnel. The towpath passes under the railway and descends steeply to the canal. The cutting continues westwards to the high brick bridge that carries the A346, and then the landscape opens out: the rolling hills still follow the canal, but recede slightly. Immediately after the bridge is Burbage Wharf; several of the original brick canal buildings still stand, attractively converted to domestic use, and a restored wooden wharf crane hangs beside the water. Pasture and arable land flank the canal on its course to the first of the four Wootton Locks. This flight ends the short summit, and starts the long descent towards Bath. By the first lock there is a pretty cottage and garden, while the second is in the middle of Brimslade Farm, whose attractive tile-hung buildings date from the 17thC. The last two locks take the canal to Wootton Rivers; the houses stretch northwards away from the canal, which is overlooked by the church. As the country undulates, the canal maintains its level, moving alternately from low cutting to low embankment. Woods break up the hills, giving fine views to the south. New Mill is a small hamlet south of the canal where there is still evidence of a small wharf. At the end of this section the railway moves away to the south to pass through Pewsey, leaving the canal in peace at last.

New Mills
Wilts. Tel. A pretty hamlet scattered below the canal. The mill that gave it its name is now a house, with a fine garden.

Wootton Rivers
Wilts. Tel. A particularly pretty village composed almost entirely of timber-framed thatched houses, climbing gently up the hill away from the canal. Even the walls by the canal are thatched. All the houses are attractive, including the large manor by the canal. The little church with its wooden bell turret is set among trees; it was extensively rebuilt in the 19thC. The church has a most unusual coronation clock, its face having letters in place of numbers. Inside, its mechanism is equally eccentric, being assembled from a bizarre collection of cast-off agricultural implements by Jack Spratt.

Bruce Tunnel
Named in honour of Thomas Bruce, Earl of Ailesbury. 502yds with chains on the walls, with which to pull boats through.

Savernake Forest
Wilts. A small village grew up in the 19thC around the hotel and the two railway stations, to cater for an early holiday trade. Today, the stations have vanished, but the hotel, a fine example of Victorian railway architecture, still thrives on the hill above Bruce Tunnel. Timber from the forest was used to restore the handsome crane at Burbage Wharf.

BOAT TRIPS
Sarah Davey Office: 0703 266200. Boat: 0672 811075.

PUBS AND RESTAURANTS
🍺 **The Royal Oak** Wootton Rivers. A very attractive 18thC pub in the main street, serving Wadworth real ale. Extensive menu of imaginative and reasonably priced food. B & B.

🍺✕ **Savernake Forest Hotel** Savernake Forest. Mole's, Marston's and other real ales. Restaurant, buttery and bar food. The hotel has fishing rights on the canal.

🍺 **Three Horseshoes** Stibb Green. ¾ mile south west of the above hotel. Wadworth real ale and food.

Pewsey

This 15-mile long pound continues westwards towards Devizes through rolling hills. To the north, hills descend to the water's edge, and to the south the land opens out, giving fine views over the Vale of Pewsey. The canal crosses this landscape with a mixture of cutting and embankment, passing through woods from time to time. The railway lies to the south, and is now out of sight. The canal turns towards Pewsey, but still passes well outside the town, which fills the Vale to the south. Pewsey Wharf is ½ mile from the town centre, and so has developed as a separate canalside settlement, with a pub, cottages, and warehouse buildings. The canal leaves Pewsey in a low wooded cutting, swinging back to its usual westerly course. The woods continue past Stowell Park, whose landscaped grounds extend to the north. The house, built early in the 19thC, can be seen clearly from the canal. A miniature suspension bridge, the only surviving example of its kind, carries a private footpath from the park across the canal. A straight stretch leads to the first cottages of Wilcot; the rest of the village is to the south. The steep bare mound of Picked Hill dominates the canal as it passes Wilcot and enters the wooded Wide Water. In 1793 this stretch was owned by Lady Susannah Wroughton who objected to the canal cutting through her land. She was appeased by £500, the building of an elaborately decorated bridge (dated 1808 and attributed to Rennie) and the landscaping of the marshy area around it. This area is now a haven for wildlife. The canal skirts Picked Hill, giving a good view of the field terracing that is a relic of Celtic and medieval cultivation. The equally dominant Woodborough Hill now fills the north bank, while to the south open country leads to the village of Woodborough.

Wilcot
Wilts. Tel. A pretty village scattered round the green; there are several thatched houses, and a converted village school with a prominent bell. Parts of the church date from the 12thC, but it was mostly rebuilt in 1876 after a fire.
Pewsey
Wilts. EC Wed. PO, tel, stores, garage, bank, station (but very few trains stop). The little town is set compactly in the Vale of Pewsey. At its centre, overlooking the young River Avon is a fine statue of King Alfred, erected in 1911. From this all the roads radiate. There is the usual mixture of buildings; but while many are attractive, none is noteworthy. The church is mostly 13th and 15thC, but parts of the nave are late Norman: the altar rails were made from timbers of the *San Josef* captured by Nelson in 1797.
Pewsey White Horse 1½ miles south of the town. Dating from the 18thC, the horse was re-cut in 1937 by members of the Pewsey Fire Brigade, to celebrate the coronation of George VI. It is 66ft long.

BOAT TRIPS

Ⓑ *Tom Pudding* A 12-seater operated from Pewsey Wharf by the K & A Canal Trust. Ring 0380 71279 for details.

PUBS

⚐ **Golden Swan** Wilcot. A one-handed ghost is said to haunt this pub, which stands beyond the green at the far end of the village. Wadworth real ale, food, B & B.
⚐ **French Horn** Pewsey. Canalside, on the A345 by the wharf. A friendly pub serving Wadworth real ale. Interesting menu, vegetarian dishes. Garden, children welcome.
⚐ **Royal Oak** Pewsey. In the town centre. Wadworth real ale and food (including vegetarian and vegan dishes).
⚐ **Phoenix** Pewsey. In the town centre. Food, B & B.
⚐ **Coopers Arms** Pewsey. Webster's, Ushers and Ruddles real ales.
⚐ **Greyhound** Pewsey. Lively, welcoming Courage pub. Food. B & B.
⚐ **The Crown** Pewsey. Ushers, Whitbread and Wadworth real ale. Bar snacks (*not Sun*).

Honey Street

Leaving Woodborough Hill behind, the long pound continues westwards towards Devizes. To the south the land falls away, while to the north the tower of Alton Priors Church comes into view. Beyond the village can be seen the white horse, cut into the hill in 1812, a copy of the one at Cherhill. The canal passes Honey Street Wharf, where there is a canalside pub. The canal now begins to meander through the open countryside, roughly following a contour line to maintain its level. Its progress is marked by a succession of shallow cuttings and low embankments. Several villages are near the canal, all visible and easily accessible from the many bridges, but none actually approach the waterside. Their interests lie rather in the rich agricultural lands that flank the canal. Leaving Allington the canal curves round the Knoll, a major feature of the landscape to the north.

Allington
Wilts. Tel. A small agricultural village scattered round a Victorian church. East of the village is All Cannings Cross, a large Iron Age settlement.

All Cannings
Wilts. PO, tel, stores. An attractive village built round a square, with houses of all periods. To the south there is a large green, overlooked by the church with its tall central tower. Although the church is mostly 14thC, its most interesting feature is the ornamental High Victorian chancel, added in 1867.

Stanton St Bernard
Wilts. PO, tel, stores. Built in a curve of the hills, the village has one main street, flanked by pretty gardens. The best building is the 19thC manor, which incorporates relics of an earlier house. The battlemented church is Victorian.

Honey Street
Wilts. A traditional canalside village incorporating some new development.

Alton Barnes
Wilts. Tel, stores, garage. The village runs along the road northwards from Honey Street. The best part is clustered round the church. Fine farm buildings and an 18thC rectory are half-hidden among the trees. The church is essentially Anglo-Saxon, but has been heavily restored; everything is in miniature, the tiny gallery, pulpit and pews emphasising the compact scale of the whole building.

Alton Priors
Wilts. Tel. Approached along a footpath from Alton Barnes churchyard, the isolated church is the best feature of this scattered hamlet. This pretty Perpendicular building with its wide, well-lit nave contains a most interesting monument: a big box tomb is surmounted with a large engraved Dutch brass plate, dated 1590, rich in extravagant symbolism. To the east of the village the Ridgeway runs southwards towards Salisbury; this Bronze Age drover's road swings north east along the downs for 50 miles, finally joining the Thames valley at Streatley. The path is not clearly defined here, but 5 miles to the north, by the A4 crossing, it becomes a wide unmistakable track, which continues unbroken to the Thames.

PUBS

Kings Arms All Cannings. ¼ mile south of Woodway Bridge. A very comfortable and charming village pub, serving Wadworth real ale, and food *lunchtime and evenings*. Garden.

Barge Inn Honey Street. An imposing canalside pub which was once a slaughterhouse, a bakehouse, a brewery and a grocers. Courage real ale, food *lunchtime and evenings (not Tue)*. W Rowing boat hire.

Sir Hugh Stockwell
lock
BW centre
Devizes yard bridge

N

45 8'2" The Cave lock
46 8'2" A P Herbert lock
Prison bridge
47 8'2" Manifold lock 8'2"
48 8'2"
Dunkirk
49 Maton lock 8'2"

12M	37L Bradford OA
Pewsey 12M	OL

Devizes Town bridge
Devizes Castle
50 Kennet lock 8'2"
Devizes
Devizes wharf
R
Cemetery Road bridge
Park Road bridge
Roundway
London Road bridge
Brickham bridge
Coates bridge
Clay farm
Laywood bridge
Bishops Cannings
Horton bridge
Bishops Cannings swing bridge
Horton
Horton Chain bridge

Devizes

Leaving Horton, the long pound continues westwards towards Devizes. Following the contour of the land, it swings in a wide arc towards Bishops Cannings. The rolling hills climb fairly steeply to the north, while the pastureland falls away to the south. After a low cutting, the tower of Bishops Cannings church comes into view, half-hidden by trees: a footpath from the swing bridge is the quickest way to the village. At Horton Bridge, where there is a convenient canalside pub, the canal enters another short cutting. The landscape opens out again, to allow a view of the handsome Victorian barracks outside Devizes. The canal passes the barrack buildings, which are partly hidden by trees, and then enters the long wooded cutting that carries it through Devizes. Houses appear, their gardens overlooking the cutting, and the traffic noise on the busy A361 marks the return to civilisation. Several very elegant large stone bridges (many listed as ancient monuments) span the cutting. Access to the town is easy at all the bridges. At Cemetery Road Bridge the towpath turns over to the north bank for a short stretch, returning to the south at the next bridge. Between these two bridges is Devizes Wharf, where the K & A Canal Trust have a museum and shop in a converted warehouse. Beyond the wharf, the long pound ends at the first lock of the famous Caen Hill flight, preceded by the generous stone bridge with its separate towpath archway. Locks now come at regular intervals, preparing the canal for the dramatic descent down Caen Hill.

Devizes
Wilts. EC Wed. MD Thur, Sat. PO, tel, stores, garage, bank, cinema. Despite the effects of traffic, Devizes still retains the atmosphere of an old country market town. Originally the town grew up around the castle, but as this lost its significance the large marketplace became the focal point. Handsome 18thC buildings now command the square, while the market cross records the sad story of Ruth Pierce. Elsewhere there are timbered buildings from the 16thC. The two fine churches, one built for the castle and the other for the parish, tend to dominate the town, and hold it well together. Only the mount and related earthworks survive of the original Norman castle; the present building is an extravagant Victorian folly. The town's own brewery, Wadworth, in Northgate Street, fills the air with the aroma of malt and hops.

St John's Church Built by Bishop Roger of Sarum, who was also responsible for the castle, this 12thC church with its massive crossing tower is still largely original. There are 15thC and 19thC additions, but they do not affect the Norman feeling of the whole.
St Mary's Church Dating from the same time as St John's, this church was more extensively rebuilt in the 15thC; plenty of Norman work still survives, however.
Wiltshire Archaeological and Natural History Museum Long Street (0380 727369). The collections include finds from the Neolithic, Bronze and Iron Age sites in Wiltshire, the most famous being the Stourhead collection of relics excavated from burial mounds on Salisbury Plain. There are also Roman exhibits. *Open Mon–Sat.*
The Wharf Devizes (0380 721279). Kennet & Avon Canal Trust Central Offices, canal shop, theatre and exhibition.
Canal Forge Lower Wharf, Northgate Street, Devizes (0308 721759). A working forge and exhibition. *Open Mon–Fri and Sat morning.*
Tourist Information Centre Market Place, Devizes (0308 729408). *Open Easter–Sep.*
Battle of Roundway Down, 13 July 1643 Devizes was held by a Royalist army that had already tested the Roundhead forces, who were tired, dispirited and short of supplies after their defeat at Lansdown Hill, near Bath. A Royalist cavalry charge took the Roundheads by surprise, and most of the confused and battle-weary Roundheads were killed or captured. The battlefield, off the A361 north east of Devizes, is still largely

intact, and can easily be explored on foot. Mock battles are re-enacted here.

Devizes to Westminster Canoe Race The toughest and longest canoe race in the world takes place *every Easter*. The course, from Park Road Bridge, Devizes, to County Hall Steps, Westminster, includes 54 miles of the Kennet & Avon, and 71 miles of the Thames, the last 17 of which are tidal. There are 77 locks. The race grew from a background of local rivalry in Pewsey and Devizes to find the quickest way to the sea by boat; in 1948 the target was 100 hours. In 1950 the first regular annual race over the course took place; three years later the junior class was introduced. The number of entries increases every year, and is now well above 300. Anyone may enter for the race, but they would have difficulty in beating the highly-trained army and navy teams from Britain and Europe.

Bishops Cannings

Wilts. PO, tel, stores. Apart from one or two old cottages, the main feature of this village is the very grand church. This cruciform building, with its central tower and spire, is almost entirely Early English in style; its magnificence is unexpected in so small a village. Traces of the earlier Norman building survive. Inside is a 17thC penitential seat, surmounted by a giant hand painted on the wall with suitable inscriptions about sin and death.

BOAT TRIPS

Kenavon Venture Operates from The Bridge Inn, Horton. Telephone 0380 86273 for details.

PUBS

There are many good pubs and inns in Devizes. The following are simply those closest to the canal.

🍺 **Black Horse** By lock 48, on the Caen Hill flight. Well placed to refresh those exhausted by the locks. Wadworth real ale, and food *lunchtime and evenings (after 19.30 and not Sun evenings)*. Canalside garden.

🍺 **Artichoke** Bath Road, 100yds north-west of Devizes Town Bridge. Known locally as the Vegetable, it is not far from Wadworth's Brewery, and serves their beers, delivered by a dray and horses. Bar food *daily*, garden and live music on *Sun evenings*.

🍺 **Royal Oak** New Park Street, south of Devizes Wharf. A 16thC coaching inn, serving Ushers real ale, which makes a change from the excellent Wadworth ale, so readily available hereabouts. *Lunchtime* food, discos *Thur, Fri and Sat evenings*.

🍺 **Old Crown** New Park Street, south of Devizes Wharf. Wadworth real ale. Food *lunchtime and evenings*.

🍺 **Bridge Inn** At Horton Bridge. The trip boat *Kenavon Venture* operates from this welcoming pub. You can also hire rowing boats. Wadworth real ale, and *evening* bar snacks. Garden.

🍺 **Crown Inn** Bishops Cannings. A friendly village local, serving locally brewed Wadworth real ale. Extensive range of food served *lunchtime and evenings*. Garden.

Caen Hill Locks, Devizes. *Derek Pratt.*

17 8' 0"

Seend lock bridge
18 7' 10"
Seend Wharf bridge
19 7' 10"
20 8' 0"
Seend Selver bridge
21 6' 8"

Seend Cleeve

A361

A365

Rusty Lane

Rusty Lane swing bridge

Seend

Sells Green swing bridge

9M   8L
Bradford OA
Pewsey
15M   29L

Sells Green bridge

Sells Green

Martinslade bridge

Summerham Brook

A361

Summerham aqueduct

Lower Foxhangers bridge

22 8' 2"

Foxhangers foot bridge

23 8' 2"
24 8' 2"
25 8' 2"
26 8' 2"
Marsh Lane bridge
27 8' 2"

28 8' 2"

B3101

29
30
31
32
33
34
35
36
37
Caen Hill flight
130' 8"

Old Park ditch

Jack Dalby lock 38
Scaggs lock
Paul Ensor lock 40
Boto-X lock
Monument lock 42
43
Sir Hugh Stockwell lock 44
BW centre
Devizes yard bridge

45 8' 2" The Cave lock
46 8' 2" A P Herbert lock
Prison bridge
Manifold lock 8' 2" 47
8' 2" 48

A342

Dunkirk

Caen Hill

Leaving Devizes, the canal continues westwards. Ahead the landscape falls away, giving advance warning of the steep descent at Caen Hill. Locks occur at regular intervals west of Devizes, each separated by a long, wide pound. These were designed to hold sufficient water while permitting the locks to be close together to follow the slope. The towpath is in very good condition; apart from the attraction to visitors of the Caen Hill flight, the whole area is obviously used for recreation by the people of Devizes. To the south the busy A361 accompanies the canal down the hill, but it is out of sight for most of the way. At lock 44 the major flight starts; wide lock follows wide lock down the hill, each with an enormous side pound. The scale of the whole flight is most impressive. At lock 29 the Caen Hill flight ends, but the locks continue the descent, now separated once again by longer pounds. The canal passes under the B3101 road bridge, and then at lock 22 reaches the end of the long fall – 29 locks in 2 miles. At Lower Foxhangers Bridge the towpath turns over to the north bank. Water-meadows accompany the canal to the south, with views of the hills that rise in the distance. The canal turns past Sells Green in a low cutting that hides most of the village, and then strides along the valley. The hills to the south climb steeply up to the village of Seend, and to the north flat pastureland stretches away. After two swing bridges the canal reaches the first of the five Seend Locks; this is the best point for access to the village. By the third lock there is a pub, and a lane leading to Seend Cleeve village.

Seend Cleeve
Wilts. Tel. An agricultural village built on the steep slopes of the hills that overlook the canal. Some new development has merged well with the existing houses.
Seend
Wilts. PO, tel, stores, garage. Although the main road cuts the village in half, Seend is still attractive. Elegant 18thC houses flank the road, and conceal the lane that leads to the battlemented Perpendicular church.
Sells Green
Wilts. Tel, garage. A scattered main road village, the houses doing their best to hide from the traffic behind decorative gardens.

BOATYARDS
BW Centre (0380 722859).

PUBS
■ **Brewery Inn** 200yds south of lock 19. Once a brewery, now a friendly village local serving Webster's and Ruddles real ale. Meals *lunchtime and evenings*, garden, children's room.
■ **Barge** Seend Cleeve, by lock 19. Wadworth real ale in a tastefully decorated pub which was once the home of the Wiltshire Giant (8ft 4in). Excellent food *lunchtime and evenings*. Fine canalside garden. Children welcome; post box.
■ **Bell Inn** ½ mile from lock 21. Pub with a collection of canal memorabilia in an old brewhouse. Wadworth real ale and Taunton real cider. Food *lunchtime*, garden, children welcome.
■ **Three Magpies** 200yds south of Sells Green Bridge. Wadworth real ale and Taunton real cider in a comfortable inn. Meals *lunchtime and evenings*, garden, children's room.

Semington

Leaving Seend Locks behind, the canal
continues its western course, maintaining a
fairly straight line through open country. The
steep hills around Seend give way to rolling
farmland extending into the distance on both
banks. This is a quiet and secluded stretch
with no villages beside the canal; however,
farms occur regularly along the bank, each
generally with its own swing accommodation
bridge. In the distance to the north the
embankment of the disused railway follows
the course of the canal. The two Semington
Locks continue the descent towards Bath with
an attractive lock house by lock 15. Just
beyond the lock the canal is crossed by the
A350; this is the best access point for
Semington. A close examination of the north
bank just before the bridge will reveal a
bricked-up side bridge; this marks the site of
the junction with the long abandoned
Wiltshire & Berkshire Canal, which used to go
to Abingdon. Beyond the bridge the canal
curves round past Semington on an
embankment, crossing the Semington Brook
on a small stone aqueduct. A long straight
stretch now leads towards Hilperton, while to
the south the hills return to follow the canal.
To the north the River Avon draws gradually
nearer, and the two waterways begin to share
the same valley.

Semington
Wilts. PO, tel, stores, garage. Despite the main
road, Semington is a pretty village. Large
handsome houses with fine gardens run beside
the road. Several date from the 18thC. The
little stone church, crowned with a bellcote, is
at the end of a lane to the east of the village.
The old village school is beside the church,
built in the same style.
The Wiltshire & Berkshire Canal
Opened in 1810, the canal wound in a
meandering course for 51 miles between
Semington on the Kennet & Avon and
Abingdon on the River Thames. A branch was
opened in 1819 from Swindon to connect with
Latton on the Thames & Severn Canal.
Although the carriage of Somerset coal was
the inspiration for the canal, its eventual role
was agricultural. Profits were never high,
partly because the wandering line of the canal
and its 45 locks made travel very slow, and so
it suffered early from railway competition. By
the 1870s, moves were afoot to close the canal,
and, despite various efforts to give it a new
lease of life, the situation had become hopeless
by the turn of the century. Traffic finally
stopped in 1906, and the canal was formally
abandoned in 1914. Little remains of it now,
but its course can be traced with difficulty.

BOATYARDS

Ⓑ **Tranquil Boats** Lock House, Semington
(0380 870654). Electric day boat, dry dock,
slipway, DIY. B & B.

PUBS

🍺 **Somerset Arms** ¼ mile south of
Semington Bridge. Ushers and Founders real
ale and Bulmers real cider in a 400-year-old
pub. Meals *lunchtime and evenings.* Garden.

Bradford on Avon

Continuing its westerly course, the canal passes through open pastureland: the wide Avon valley, which the canal now follows, begins gradually to narrow as the hills encroach to the north and the south. The canal curves round below Hilperton; although the main village is a mile to the south, there is a convenient pub, post office and stores by the road bridge and wharf where a large new marina has been built. West of Hilperton, the canal passes the grounds of Wyke House, whose Jacobean-style towers stand among the trees; then the land to the north falls away as the canal returns to its original course on a sweeping curve. Canal and river now converge as the canal swings on a huge embankment towards the Avon, crossing the railway and the River Biss on two stone aqueducts. The classical arch over the river is particularly handsome; it is necessary to walk down the side of the embankment in order to see it properly. The view northwards across the Avon valley is very fine. For a while river and canal run side by side, the river down in the valley, the canal high above in a side cutting, shielded by trees, and then they part again to make their separate entries into Bradford. The canal stays high above the town, which fills the steep-sided valley, while the river cuts the town in two. Bradford basin appears suddenly followed by the lock, and then the canal turns to pass to the south of the town. It rejoins the course of the river, and now the two run closely together all the way to Bath. West of Bradford the canal passes through beautiful woods on the steep southern slope of the valley. From this point there are fine views of the town, spread out beyond the Tithe Barn, which is right beside the canal. Cyclists appear on the towpath, since this is part of the Wiltshire Cycleway route. The Avon rushes along the valley and beyond it the railway appears and disappears among the trees on the far side, while high above the canal pursues its more sedate course towards Bath. The thick woods often give the canal user a feeling of total seclusion. The elegant stone arches of the Avoncliff Aqueduct carry the canal high above the fast flowing river and the railway. A canal shop, and a separate canal bookshop make this a worthwhile stop. The canal then turns west again to continue its wooded course. The towpath crosses back to the south side by the aqueduct.

Avoncliffe
Wilts. Station. A hamlet clustered in the woods beside the canal. Originally it was a centre of weaving, and many traces of the old industry can be seen: weavers' cottages, and the old mills on the Avon, which falls noisily over a weir at this point. The hamlet is dominated by Rennie's aqueduct, built in 1804 to take the canal across the valley to the north side. A classical stone structure, the aqueduct suffered from casual repair work and patching in brick when owned by the GWR.

Bradford on Avon
Wilts. EC Wed. PO, tel, stores, garage, bank, station. Set in the steeply wooded Avon valley, Bradford is one of the beauty spots of Wiltshire, and one of the highlights of the canal. Rather like a miniature Bath, the town is composed of fine stone terraces rising sharply away from the river, which cuts through the centre of the town. Until the 19thC it was a prosperous centre for weaving, but a depression killed the industry and drove most of the workers away. Bradford is rich in architectural treasures from the Saxon period to the 19thC, while the abundance of fine 18thC houses make the exploration of the town a positive pleasure. The centre is very compact, and so the walk down the hill from the canal wharf lays most of it open to inspection, including the town bridge, Holy Trinity Church, the Victorian town hall, and the fine Gothic revival factory that dominates the riverside. There is also a swimming pool near the canal.

Bradford Wharf The canal wharf is particularly attractive. There is a small dock with some of the original buildings still standing, plenty of mooring space, and an old canal pub beside the lock.

Town Bridge The nine-arched bridge is unusual in having a chapel in the middle, one of the few still surviving in Britain. Parts of the bridge, including the chapel, are medieval, but much dates from a 17thC rebuilding. During the 17th and 18thC the chapel fell out of use, and was turned into a small prison, serving as the town lock up.

Holy Trinity Church Basically a 12thC building with additions dating over the next three centuries. Inside are some medieval wall paintings, and fine 18thC monuments.

Saxon Church of St Lawrence Founded in 705, this tiny church was enlarged in the 10thC. Since then it has survived essentially unchanged, having been at various times a school, a cottage and a slaughterhouse. The true origins and purpose of the building were only rediscovered in the 19thC, and so it remains one of the best-preserved Saxon churches in England.

Great Tithe Barn Standing below the canal embankment, this great stone building is one of the finest tithe barns in England. It was built in the 14thC by the Abbess of Shaftesbury. Its great length (168ft) is broken by two porches, with massive doors that open to reveal the beamed roof. Maintained by the Department of the Environment the barn now contains a collection of old agricultural implements, and is *open to the public at all reasonable times.*

Westwood Manor 1 mile south west of Bradford. This 15thC stone manor house contains much original Jacobean plaster and woodwork, although much was lost when the manor became a farm in the 18thC. Skilful restoration by the National Trust has returned the manor to its former glory. *Open: Wed afternoons Apr-Sep.*

Staverton
Wilts. Tel, stores. The village lies north of the canal, spreading down to the bank of the Avon, where there is a small Nestlé factory. A small isolated part of the Avon is navigable here, and is used by a few pleasure boats. In the village are terraces of weavers' cottages, a sign of what was once the staple trade of the area.

Hilperton
Wilts. PO, tel, stores, garage. A scattered village that stretches away from the settlement by the

canal wharf. Wyke House stands to the west of the village. This very ornate Jacobean mansion was in fact built in 1865, a replica of the original house. House *not open to the public.*

BOATYARDS

Ⓑ **Hilperton Marina** Hilperton Wharf, Hammond Way, Trowbridge (0225 765243). Ⓡ Ⓢ Ⓦ Ⓓ Pump-out, gas, slipway, overnight mooring, long-term mooring, chandlery, books and maps, boat and engine sales and repairs, toilets, BW licences.

Ⓑ **Wessex Narrowboats** Wessex Wharf, Hilperton Marina, Trowbridge (0225 769847). Narrowboat hire, day hire craft, books and maps, boat building, engine repairs, shop, double wet dock.

BOAT TRIPS

Patricia II An electric replica of an Edwardian launch available for private charter; 12 seats for picnic trips from Hilperton Wharf. Gibsons Boat Services, 9 Boreham Road, Warminster (0985 212094).

Nb. Ladywood operated by the K & A Canal Trust. Pleasure and charter trips from Bradford Wharf. Ring 022 16 6135 for details.

PUBS

⚓ **Cross Guns** Fine 17thC inn by south side of Avoncliff Aqueduct, with a good choice of real ales. Riverside garden, meals *lunchtime and evenings.*

Canal Tavern Bradford Wharf. Basic locals pub with strong K & A Trust connections. Wadworth real ale and Bulmers real cider, snacks *lunchtime (not Sun)* and garden. Children welcome.

⚓ **Barge Inn** Bradford Wharf. Comfortable one bar pub. Ushers and Founders real ale and Bulmers real cider, *lunchtime* food, garden and accommodation.

⚓ **Beehive** Widbrook Bridge, Bradford on Avon. Popular stone built pub dispensing Ushers real ale and Bulmers real cider. Meals *lunchtime and evenings (not Sun evenings)*, garden.

⚓ **Old Bear** Staverton, ⅓ mile north west of Hilperton Bridge. 300-year-old inn serving Bass, Marston's and Wadworth real ale along with *lunchtime* food. Garden.

⚓ **Kings Arms** 100yds south of Hilperton Wharf. A renovated pub with a 6ft 5in tall ghost, offering Ushers and Webster's real ale and food *lunchtime and evenings (not Sun evenings)*. Garden.

Avoncliff Aqueduct, where the Kennet & Avon crosses over the River Avon. *David Perrott.*

Claverton

Leaving the Avoncliff Aqueduct, the canal
continues westwards through the woods above
the River Avon. The valley gets steeper and
narrower as it approaches Bath and thick
woods cover both sides as the river and canal
run side by side. The canal passes Limpley
Stoke, scattered over the southern valley side.
The country opens out slightly, to allow views
across the valley as the canal approaches the
Dundas Aqueduct, perhaps the best known
feature of the Kennet & Avon. Emerging from
the woods, the canal turns suddenly onto the
aqueduct, which carries it across the Avon
valley and the railway to the south side. At the
southern end of the aqueduct is a small wharf
and basin, with an old crane standing over the
water. Here was the junction with the
Somersetshire Coal Canal, which, until its
closure in 1904, ran south from the Kennet &
Avon Canal towards Paulton. Beyond the
basin the towpath turns over to the north
bank, where it remains until Bath is reached.
The canal enters another thickly wooded
stretch, a side cutting taking it towards
Claverton. The woods soon give way to allow
fine views to the north, across rolling country
and the railway and River Avon in the valley
below. Claverton flanks the canal, but it is
hidden by the folds of the land to the south.
Access is easy, and both the village and
Claverton Manor are worth a visit. Claverton
Ram, a water-powered pump which lifts water
up from the Avon to feed the canal has been
restored by the Kennet & Avon Canal Trust,
with help from engineering students from
Bath University. The more open country
continues, allowing views across the valley to
Warleigh Manor, now a college, and to
Bathford church. The canal follows the
contours of the land as it turns towards Bath,
maintaining the level of the 9-mile pound that
runs from Bradford to Bath Top Lock.

Claverton
Somerset. Tel. Although devoid of all facilities,
Claverton is well worth a visit. It is a manorial
village of stone houses, surrounding the 17thC
farm, and in early days clearly dependent
upon Claverton Manor. The main road misses
the village, increasing the peace and seclusion.
Claverton Manor The American Museum in
Britain. The manor was built in 1820 by Sir
Jeffry Wyatville in the Greek revival style. It
now houses a museum of American decorative
arts from the late 17thC to the mid 19thC.
Open Apr-Oct, Tue-Sun afternoons.
Claverton Pump The waterwheel pump at
Claverton is the only one of its kind on British
canals. Designed by John Rennie, the pump
was built to feed the 9-mile Bradford-Bath
pound, and started operating in 1813. The
two undershot breast wheels, each 15ft in
diameter and 11ft wide, then powered the
pumping machinery until a major breakdown
in 1952 prompted its closure, and
replacement by a temporary diesel pump. The
original machinery has now been restored, and
'pumping weekends' are organised – details
0272 515954. New electric pumps now do the
day-to-day work, raising water from the Avon
47ft below.
Dundas Aqueduct
Built in 1804, this three-arch classical stone
aqueduct is justifiably one of the most well-
known features of the canal, and stands as a
fitting monument to the architectural and
engineering skill of John Rennie. It is
necessary to leave the canal and walk down
into the valley below to appreciate the beauty
of the aqueduct, and see it in the context of the
narrow Avon valley into which it fits so well.
Somersetshire Coal Canal Opened in
1805, this narrow canal was sponsored by the
Somerset Coal owners, who wanted a more
efficient means of moving their coal to Bath,
Bristol and the rest of England. Originally
surveyed by Rennie in 1793, the canal was to
run from Limpley Stoke to Paulton, with a
branch to Radstock. There were steep
gradients to overcome at Midford and Combe
Hay, and these plagued the canal throughout
its life. The Radstock Arm was never

completed and tramroads were built over the difficult stretches. The canal was never profitable, and was sold to the Somerset & Dorset Railway in 1871. The main line was completed throughout, but not before some remarkable solutions to the problems of the Combe Hay gradient had been tried out. First there was Robert Weldon's caisson lock; a watertight caisson, large enough to hold a narrowboat and crew, was pulled up and down an 88ft-deep water-filled cistern by means of a rack and pinion. This terrifying device was soon replaced by an inclined plane, which in turn was replaced by a conventional flight of locks. Once open, the canal carried a large tonnage of coal throughout the 19thC: it served 30 collieries more directly than the railway. However, by the end of the century the inevitable competition was taking away the traffic, which finally stopped in 1898. The canal was officially abandoned in 1904. The first ¼ mile has now been restored and is used by a boatyard, and for moorings. A stop lock at the entrance restricts its use to craft of 7ft beam only.

Limpley Stoke
Avon. PO, tel, stores. Built on the side of the valley overlooking the river, Limpley Stoke is a quiet village, a residential outpost of Bath. The little church includes work of all periods, from Norman to the 20thC: inside is a collection of carved coffin lids.

Freshford
Somerset. PO, tel, garage. Although not on the canal, Freshford is well worth the ½-mile walk south from Limpley Stoke. It is a particularly attractive village, set on the side of the steep hill that flanks the confluence of the rivers Avon and Frome. At the top of the hill is the church, and terraces of handsome stone houses fall away in both directions, filling the valley below, and crowding the narrow streets. At the bottom of the hill is the river, crossed by the medieval bridge.

BOATYARDS
ⓑ **Bath & Dundas Canal Co.** (Anglo Welsh) The Boatyard, Monkton Combe (0225 722292). At the end of the Somersetshire Coal Canal, where boats up to 62ft can turn, BUT do not bring your boat in without first walking along the main road to the office to check if space is available. Ⓢ Ⓦ Ⓓ Pump-out, gas, narrowboat hire, day hire craft, long-term mooring, slipway, dry dock, books and maps, boat sales, ices, drinks.

PUBS
▶ **Viaduct Hotel** Monkton Combe. Moor west of Dundas Aqueduct, the pub is 400yds south of the A36. Courage real ale, food *lunchtime and evenings.* Garden, children welcome.
▶ **Hop Pole** Limpley Stoke. Moor at Limpley Stoke Bridge, walk down to railway bridge and turn left to find this popular oak-panelled pub. Courage real ale, meals *lunchtime and evenings*, children's room, garden.
▶ **The Inn** Freshford. An attractive pub overlooking the river. Ushers real ale and bar food. Garden, children welcome.

Cleveland House, standing over the canal in Sydney Gardens, Bath. *Derek Pratt.*

Bath

Following the course of the River Avon, the canal turns west towards Bath, leaving behind Bathford church on the opposite side of the valley. Groups of houses appear more frequently scattered among the trees of the Avon valley; these form the outposts of Bath, whose suburbs are now visible to the west. The canal passes through Bathampton, on a low embankment above the school and church, and then continues on a straight course, closely flanked by the railway, which is in a cutting below. On the south bank there are gardens running down to the water, which accompany the canal into Bath. The entry into Bath is magnificent. The canal sweeps round the south of the city, cut into the side of the hill, and so there are extensive views across Bath. From this point it is possible to pick out many of the features of the city, and the Georgian terraces can be seen spread out over the far side of the valley. As the buildings fill the valley, canal and River Avon part, to make their separate entries into Bath. The first Georgian buildings flank the canal as it reaches Sydney Gardens. A short tunnel with a fine Adamesque portal takes the canal under a road, and then it passes two pretty cast iron bridges, both dated 1800. A cutting carries the canal through this attractive part of Bath, and so the houses seem to hang over the water. Another ornamental tunnel actually carries houses over the canal, among them Cleveland House, the old canal company's headquarters. The towpath turns over briefly to the south side, returning to the north at the next bridge. The cutting then ends, once more allowing magnificent views of the lock of the Widcombe flight. This flight of six locks takes the canal down to join the Avon. Locks 8 and 9 were merged together as part of a road-building scheme, making one new lock with a fall of over 19ft. The canal joins the Avon immediately beyond Bath Lower Lock (number 7) in the middle of the industrial quarter of Bath. The railway station is opposite the junction of canal and river, and factories and warehouses flank the Avon as it leaves Bath. The fine Georgian city surrounds the unnavigable Avon to the east. The junction is the best point of access for Bath as a whole. A long belt of industry accompanies the river out of Bath but access to the towpath is always easy. There are several footbridges across the river, some of them private, and a disused railway crosses twice as the river meanders in long, gentle curves. As the industry gradually falls away, the river divides; the right fork leads to Weston Lock, the left to a weir, as the river continues its fall to the sea.

Navigational notes
1. Restrictions on the Widcombe flight should be checked with BW.
2. Due to water supply problems, there are often restrictions to navigation between Bath and Crofton.

Navigating the Bristol Avon
Pleasure boats should always give way to barges, and should let them use the locks first. In general, downstream traffic has right of way, especially through bridges. All the locks are accompanied by weirs, so take great care to turn into the lock cuts, and avoid the weir channel. Remember that a river always has a current, and is liable to change in speed and level of flow. When mooring, allow enough slack on lines. Do not moor in lock cuts or near weirs. All pleasure boats should moor up at night, and show a white light. With the exception of Hanham, the locks are not manned. Boats should always be held by ropes while the locks are being operated.

Bath
Avon. EC Thur. MD Wed. All services. Bath was first developed by the Romans as a spa town and resort because of its natural warm springs. They started a trend of bathing and 'taking the waters' which survives today. There are extensive Roman remains to be seen in the city, not least the baths themselves.

The city grew further during the medieval period, when it was a centre of the wool trade; the fine abbey dates from this time. But the true splendour of Bath is the 18thC development, when the city grew as a resort and watering place that was frequented by all levels of English society, from Royalty downwards. Despite heavy bombing in the 1939-45 war, Bath is still a magnificent memorial to the 18thC and Neo-classicism generally. The terraces that adorn the steep northern slope of the Avon valley contain some of the best Georgian architecture in Britain. Much of the city was designed by John Wood the Younger, who was responsible for the great sweeping Royal Crescent. Other architects include Thomas Baldwin, who built the Guildhall, 1766-75, and the Pump Room, 1789-99, and Robert Adam, whose Pulteney Bridge carries terraces of shops across the Avon. Plagued by traffic, Bath is best seen on foot, for its glories and riches are far too numerous to list. Visitors should not fail to try the waters, which gush continuously from a fountain outside the Pump Room.

Bath Abbey Set in an attractive piazza, the abbey is a pleasingly uniform Perpendicular building, founded in 1499. Twin towers crown the west front, decorated with carved angels ascending and descending ladders. Inside, the abbey is justly famous for its fan vaulting, which covers the whole roof of the building but is not all of the same date. Inside also is a wealth of memorials of all periods, an interesting indication of the vast range of people who, over the ages, have come to die at Bath.

Holburne of Menstrie Museum Great Pulteney Street, Bath (0225 466669). Housed in an 18thC Palladian building that was designed as part of the Sydney pleasure gardens, it contains collections of silver, ceramics and 18thC paintings and furniture. *Open daily mid Feb-mid Dec (closed Mon Feb-Easter).*

Museum of Costume Assembly Rooms (02225 461111). Display of fashion from the 17thC to the present day; one of the largest collections of costume in the world. *Open daily.*

Bath Roman Museum Abbey Churchyard, Bath (0225 461111). The great bath buildings with their dependent temple were the centre of Roman Bath. Much of these survive, incorporated into the 18thC Pump Room. The museum, attached to the bath buildings, contains finds excavated from the site. *Open daily all year.*

1 Royal Crescent A typical mid-18thC house, complete with original furniture and fittings. *Open Mar-Oct weekdays and Sun afternoons.*

Victoria Art Gallery Bridge Street, Bath (0225 248144). Collection of 18thC and modern paintings, prints and ceramics. Visiting exhibitions. *Open Mon-Sat.*

Tourist Information Centre Abbey Churchyard, Bath (0225 462831).

Bathampton
Avon. PO, tel, stores, garage. The centre of the village surrounds the canal and is still compact and undeveloped, but new housing around the village has turned it into a suburb of Bath. The church is mostly 19thC.

BOATYARDS

ⓑ **T.J. & K. Knill** By Holcombe Swing Bridge, Bathampton (0225 466634)Ⓦ Pump-out, long-term mooring, books and maps, refreshments.
ⓑ **John Rennie** Sydney Wharf Road, Bath (0225 447276). Ⓦ Ⓓ Pump-out.

BOAT TRIPS

John Rennie A large and well equipped restaurant boat available for private charter from Sydney Wharf Road, Bath. Details from 0225 447276.
K & A Canal Trust Trips from Bath Top Lock. Details from 0225 462313.

PUBS AND RESTAURANTS

Bath is well-endowed with distinguished restaurants, lively wine bars and excellent real ale pubs. The following is a selection of real ale pubs nearest to the canal.
🍺 **Dolphin** On the Western Cut. Flowers real ale. Pub food (*not Tue or Sun evenings*). Garden. Children welcome.
🍺 **Golden Fleece** 1-3 Avon Buildings, Lower Bristol Road. One bar local 50yds south of the river, serving John Smith's, Courage, Exmoor plus guest real ales. Bar food *lunchtimes only* (*not Sun*). Vegetarians catered for.
🍺 **Windsor Castle** Upper Bristol Road. Bass and Worthington real ale. Bar food (*not Sun*). Children's room. Barbecue, live music, bar games.
🍺 **New Esthall** Upper Bristol Road, opposite large children's play park. Marston's and Border real ale. Food (*not Sun evenings*), vegetarians catered for. Bar games, garden.
🍺 **Hop Pole** Upper Bristol Road. Ushers and Butcombe real ale. Food *lunchtime only.* Barbecues in *summer*. Vegetarian food. Bar games. Live music *last Sat in month.*
🍺 **Golden Fleece** 150yds down footpath from lock 11. Newly refurbished pub serving Flowers and Whitbread real ale. Bar food (*not Mon evenings*). Barbecues *at weekends during summer.*
🍺 **Ram** 150yds south of lock 8. Friendly local catering for jazz enthusiasts. Ruddles and Ushers real ale. Bar food *lunchtime, weekdays only.*
🍺 **Ring o'Bells** 100yds south of lock 8. Ruddles and Webster's real ale. Bar food. Live music *Sun evenings.*
🍺 **White Hart** South of lock 8. Spacious lounge and basic public bar where you can enjoy Flowers and Marston's real ale. Bar food *Mon-Sat lunchtime, Mon-Fri evenings.* Live music *Wed, Fri, Sat, Sun.* B & B.
🍺 **Royal Oak** 100yds down footpath from lock 11. Comfortable pub serving Gibbs Mew real ale. Bar food. Live music *Tuesdays and first Sunday in month.*
✗ ❗ **Bathampton Mill** 400yds north of Bathampton Bridge. A Beefeater restaurant serving Flowers real ale and meals. Garden.
🍺 **George Inn** Bathampton Bridge. Family pub with a canalside garden serving Courage real ale and bar meals.

Claverton Pumping Station near Bath, Kennet & Avon Canal. *Derek Pratt.*

Saltford

The River Avon at last leaves behind the industries of Bath, and enters a wooded stretch. The railway closely follows the south bank, vanishing at one point into a tunnel. As the river continues its wide, wandering course westwards, the valley opens out, and rolling hills and pastureland flank both banks. A disused rail bridge is followed by the elegant single stone arch of New Bridge, carrying the A4. At this point the towpath crosses to the south bank, although, as on all river navigations, its position is never well-defined. After New Bridge there is a small boatyard, and a line of moored craft along the north bank. The river passes Kelston Park in a series of gentle bends, against a background of wooded hills to the north. The disused railway crosses the Avon for the fourth time, an indication of the river's winding course. The river straightens as it approaches Kelston Lock, where the stream again divides. Navigators should take the right fork to the lock, and avoid the weir on the left. Saltford can be seen among the trees on the south bank. Mooring is possible by the lock, and this is the best access point for boaters visiting the town. The towpath continues along the north bank, as the river curves towards Saltford Lock. At one time there was a horse and passenger ferry near the lock that allowed the towpath to cross to the south bank. By Saltford Lock is Saltford Sailing Club where there is a riverside pub. At Saltford the lock is on the left. The river then turns past Saltford Mead towards Swineford, passing a large factory on the low-lying land to the south. At Swineford the river again divides, the left fork leading to the particularly attractive lock.

Swineford
Avon. PO, tel, stores. Although bisected by the A431, the settlement by the river is still attractive; old mill buildings overlook the weir.
Saltford
Avon. EC Wed. PO, tel, stores, garage. Although Saltford has been developed as a large-scale dormitory suburb, the older parts by the river are still pretty and secluded.
Saltford Manor Situated by the church, the manor is one of the oldest inhabited houses in England. Much of the building is still original Norman work, behind a 17thC façade.

BOATYARDS
Ⓑ **Bristol Boats** by Saltford Lock, Mead Lane, Saltford (0225 2032). Boat building, boat sales and repairs, inboard and outboard engine sales and repairs, slipway, chandlery, gas. *Closed Sun in winter.*
Ⓑ✕ **Saltford Marina** The Shallows, Saltford (0225 2226). Ⓡ Ⓦ Ⓓ Overnight mooring, engine repairs, slipway, crane. Restaurant and bar.
Ⓑ✕ **Bath Marina** Newbridge, Bath. Ⓡ Ⓦ Ⓓ Ⓢ Pump-out, engine repairs, overnight mooring. Restaurant and bar.

PUBS AND RESTAURANTS
✕ **Swan** near Swineford Lock. 200-year-old stone built cottage pub, dispensing Courage real ale. Good pub food served in the bar and restaurant. Garden, children welcome.
 White Hart Bitton. Courage real ale. Varied menu including vegetarian dishes. Garden, children welcome.
✕ **Jolly Sailor** By Saltford Lock. A delightful pub dating back to 1727. An original painting of the lock and its activity hangs above the fire-place, whose surround is scarred with holes, where newly promoted skippers thrust a red-hot poker into the oak lintel before buying a florin's worth of ale for those assembled. Courage, John Smith's and Butcombe real ale are available. Gazebo restaurant; barbecues at *weekends during the summer.* Children welcome.
 Bird in Hand Saltford. A beautifully kept village local which offers Courage and Wadworth real ale, and Taunton real cider. Good bar food (*not Sun or Mon evenings*). Large garden and terrace. Children welcome.

Keynsham

As the river passes Bitton it reaches another disused railway bridge. Low-lying pasture and arable land continue to flank the river in its meandering course towards Keynsham. After passing a vast brick and stone factory complex, dated 1881, which dominates the south bank, the river starts a long horseshoe bend that leads to Keynsham. The river divides, the right fork leading to the lock. Keynsham lies well to the south of the river, but is easily accessible. There is a small settlement round the lock, rather over-awed by the industry that surrounds it. As the valley narrows, steep wooded hills return to follow the north bank of the river as it twists and turns. After a particularly sharp bend, the southern hills approach as well, and Hanham Lock appears. Again the river divides, the left fork leading to the lock. This is lock 1, the last lock between Reading and Bristol, the end of BW's jurisdiction, and the beginning of the Port of Bristol Authority area. There is a small hamlet on the north bank, overlooking the weir, and two pubs, side by side. From here the river Avon continues through a steeply wooded valley to Bristol; a canal takes boats through Bristol harbour and then the navigation rejoins the river which flows down to join the Severn estuary at Avonmouth, having passed the Clifton Suspension Bridge and the Avon gorge.

Navigational note
The river is tidal below Keynsham Lock. Do not navigate in tidal waters without charts, tide-tables, anchor etc. Ensure your craft is suitable. Seek expert advice if in any doubt (the lock keepers are extremely helpful).

Keynsham
Avon. All services. Keynsham has grown steadily along the Bristol road, and so is now a vast shapeless suburb. However, the centre still retains a feeling of independence, and has many traces of Keynsham's past. An Augustinian abbey was founded here in 1170, and there are a few surviving remains in Abbey Park. Elsewhere in the main street are a few 17th and 18thC houses, but bungalows and modern shops predominate. The main feature of interest is the large church. Originally 13thC, the interior is now attractively Victorian, after the restoration of 1861. The ornamental west tower was built in 1734, after the earlier tower was blown down in a storm. There is a fine 16thC monument to Sir Henry Bridges.
Bitton
Avon. PO, tel, stores, garage. Although a main-road village, Bitton's heart survives intact south of the road. Here is a fine group formed by the church, the grange, and the 18thC vicarage, all built around the churchyard. The church is very splendid; it has a long Saxon nave with Norman details, a 14thC chancel, and a magnificently decorative late 14thC tower. On the main road is an attractive early 19thC Wesleyan chapel.

BOATYARDS

BW Hanham Lock Toll office (0272 862550). K & A windlasses.
ⓑ **Port Avon Marina** Bitton Road, Keynsham (0272 861626). Ⓡ Ⓢ Ⓦ Ⓓ Ⓔ Gas, overnight mooring, winter storage, slipway, chandlery, books and maps, boat sales, engine sales and repairs, toilets, showers.
ⓑ **Jondeblin Marine** Broadmead Lane, Keynsham (0272 866066). Ⓡ Ⓢ Ⓦ Ⓓ Pump-out, overnight mooring, winter storage, crane, chandlery, repairs, toilets.

PUBS AND RESTAURANTS

☞ **Old Lock and Weir** Hanham. Riverside, overlooking the lock. Once used as a boatyard, this pub retains the simplicity of the old cottage which it occupies. Whitewashed walls and flagged floors contribute to the atmosphere. Ruddles, Smiles, Marston's and Ushers real ales. Bar food and barbecues. Pleasant riverside garden.

☞✕ **Chequers** Hanham, riverside. A sharp contrast to its neighbouring pub although under the same ownership, the Chequers offers refreshment in very plush surroundings. Courage, Marston's and Ushers real ale and Taunton real cider. Bar food and carvery. Riverside garden, children welcome. [R] [W].

☞ **Lock Keeper** Keynsham Lock (0272 862383). Unpredictable flood waters forced many a crew to stay the night at the Lock Keeper. Courage real ale and bar food. Garden. Children welcome.

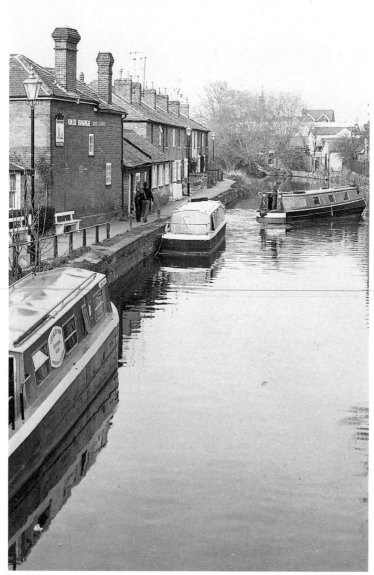

The River Lee Navigation at Hertford. *Derek Pratt.*

LEE & STORT

Maximum dimensions

River Lee
Bow to Ponders End
Length: 88'
Beam: 18'
Headroom: 6' 9"
Draught: 4' 6"
North of Ponders End
Length: 85'
Beam: 15' 9"
Headroom: 6' 9"
Draught: 4' 6"

Low Bridges *check tides or flood water*
conditions if close to maximum headroom
Northern Outfall Sewer Bridge (100yds below
Old Ford Locks)
Lea Bridge Road
Enfield Lock Road Bridge
Ware Town Bridge

River Stort
Length: 85'
Beam: 13'
Headroom: 5' 9"
Draught: 3'

Low Bridges (check flood water conditions
if close to maximum headroom)
Roydon Bridge
Burnt Mill Bridge

Manager
(0992) 764626

Mileage

River Lee

LIMEHOUSE BASIN TO
Old Ford Locks: 2¾
Lea Bridge: 4¾
Pickett's Lock: 10
Enfield Lock: 13
Waltham Abbey: 14
Broxbourne: 18½
FEILDE'S WEIR (junction with River Stort):
20½
St Margaret's: 22½
Ware Bridge: 25
HERTFORD, head of navigation, 27¾

Locks: 19

River Stort

FEILDE'S WEIR (junction with River Lee) to
Roydon station: 1½
Burnt Mill: 4½
Harlow Lock: 6¾
Sawbridgeworth: 8¾
BISHOP'S STORTFORD, head of
navigation: 13¼

Locks: 15

Lee Valley Park

Parts of the River Lee (often known as 'Lea': the spelling is optional) were used as navigations in Roman times, and much of the river was navigable before the reign of Elizabeth I. The first major attempt to speed up traffic by means of an artificial cut was made under the powers of an Act of 1571. In the same year an early pound lock was built at Waltham Abbey, using two sets of mitred gates, a principle that then became a standard feature of lock design. In the 17thC the Lee was established as a source of water supply for London, a role it still fulfils. The navigation was steadily improved throughout the 18th and 19thC, under the direction of various well-known engineers. During and immediately after the 1914-18 war enlargements were carried out to allow 130-ton boats to reach Enfield, and 100-ton boats to Ware and Hertford. In the 1930s further canalisation was carried out and more recently locks have been mechanised and duplicated. Timber had always been the main support of the Lee navigation, a trade that sadly does not survive today.

The River Stort has never been a very significant navigation commercially, and has not in fact carried any traffic for some years. The navigation as such dates back over 200 years, and has been owned by a series of individuals and companies, including Sir George Duckett; but it would have prospered far more if the ill-fated scheme to build a canal from Bishop's Stortford to Cambridge and the Fenland waterways had ever succeeded.

In making the Lee Valley a regional park (the first area in Britain to be so designated) the Authority has realised the need of a rapidly increasing population for an expanse of open space where leisure time can be both utilised and enjoyed. An amazing factor of the park is its sheer size; it runs from Eastway (A106) in the south to Ware in the north.

The Authority caters for all types: young, old, beginners, experts, teams and individuals. Outdoor and indoor sports, social centres, cultural activities and play centres have all been built.

This ambitious scheme has not been, of course, without its difficulties; there was serious danger of flooding, which has since been alleviated by the construction of drainage channels; massive areas of soil have had to be moved from one area to another; and natural vegetation has largely disappeared except for the woodlands north of Waltham Abbey. As one of the chief aims of the Authority is to make the Park visually pleasing, trees and other vegetation have been planted (especially in areas where pylons march conspicuously across the landscape), and buildings of historical interest within the park, many of which are mentioned in the text, have been preserved.

For more information and a brief guide, the address of the Lee Valley Park Authority is Middleton House, Bulls Cross, Enfield, Middx (0992 717711).

Bow

The River Lee is navigable from London up to Hertford. The River Stort, which joins the Lee at Feilde's Weir, is canalised as far as Bishop's Stortford. Entrance to the river navigation can be made from three places:
>   From the Regent's Canal via the Hertford Union Canal
>   (recommended)
>   From the Thames via Limehouse Basin
>   From the Thames direct up Bow Creek, and through Bow Locks

The Hertford Union Canal is a short (1¼ miles) canal built in 1830 by Sir George Duckett (hence it is often referred to as 'Duckett's') as a useful junction between the Regent's Canal and the Lee Navigation. It is straight, has three locks, and borders the attractive Victoria Park for most of the way. The route up into the River Lee from the Thames is through the new ship lock into Limehouse Basin (1½ miles below Tower Bridge), then east through the new short cut and along the Limehouse Cut to Bow Locks and Old Ford. The other entrance to the Lee Navigation is by way of Bow Creek, whose mouth is 5 miles down the Thames from the Limehouse Basin entrance. Bow Creek is a tidal river – it is in fact the mouth of the River Lee. It is very twisting, 2 miles long and only navigable around high tide. The Three Mills at Bow still remain from the 18thC, although they were modified some years later. Nearby is the Abbey Mills Pumping House of Gothic-Byzantine style designed in 1868 by Bazalgette, who was also responsible for the Thames embankments. Hackney Marsh on the east bank of the canal is a footballer's delight: there are many pitches here by the Eastway Sports Centre.

The Reservoirs of the Lee Valley

Navigational notes
1 The rebuilt Limehouse Basin Ship Lock can accommodate craft 98' x 25' 4". It is *open daily 08.00-17.00 (no access 1 hour either side of LW)*. Ring 071-895 9930 to check.
2 Bow Locks are *open from four hours before high water until two hours after high water Mon-Sat, and from two hours before high water until two hours after high water on Sun and B. Hols.* They can accommodate craft 88' x 18'. Ring 071-987 5661 to check. (High water times can also be obtained from this number).
3 All locks can be used at all times. For Tottenham and Ponders End locks a BW key is needed for the key operated lock. Old Ford and Stonebridge manual locks are no longer operational and a BW key is essential.
4 The towpath of Limehouse cut is not fully open along its entire length. Access to Blackwell Tunnel Approach Road is with a BW key.

PUBS AND RESTAURANTS
King's Head ¼ mile north of Lea Bridge Road (A104), E14. Canalside. Welcoming family pub with garden bar, outside seating and play area. Ruddles real ale and food *always available*. Barbecue for customers' own use. Disco *Fri and Sat*. Children and dogs welcome. Resident rabbit.
Ship Aground Lea Bridge Road, E14. Canalside. Bass real ale. Food *lunchtime and evenings (not Sun)*. Outside seating area.
Prince of Wales Lea Bridge, E14. Canalside. Comfortable pub serving Young's real ale. Food available *lunchtime and evenings (not Sun evenings)*. Bar billiards and darts.
Royal Cricketers Regent's Canal, immediately south of junction with Hertford Union Canal. Canalside pub serving Whitbread real ale, snacks and sandwiches on an inviting waterside patio.
Freemason's Arms Salmon Lane, E14. ¼ mile north of Limehouse Basin, midway between Regent's Canal and Limehouse Cut. A friendly pub offering Tetley's real ale and snacks *lunchtime and evenings (not Sun)*. Garden.
The House They Left Behind Narrow Street, E14. ¼ mile east of Limehouse Lock. The only building left standing in a demolished terrace, this shored up pub offers a warm and friendly welcome and serves an appetising range of home cooked food, *lunchtime and evenings (not Fri and Sun evenings)*. Vegetarians catered for. Webster's and Ruddles real ales. Outside seating area.
Grapes Narrow Street, E14. ¼ mile east of Limehouse Lock. Beautifully kept one bar pub behind an inviting traditional façade, serving Taylor Walker real ale. Restaurant upstairs.
Barley Mow 44 Narrow Street, E14. In the original Dockmaster's office, at the entrance to Limehouse Dock. Set on the site of the original Taylor Walker brewery this splendid new waterside pub serves Tetley's and Young's real ale together with Taylor Walker. Carvery and *summer* barbecue.

1 King George's reservoir (fishing)
2 King George's reservoir (fishing and sailing)
3 William Girling reservoir (fishing at selected spots only. Nature reserve)
4 Banbury reservoir (fishing and sailing) Banbury Sailing Centre (081-531 1129). Courses to all RYA standards
5 Lockwood reservoir (fishing and nature reserve)
6 High Maynard reservoir (fishing and nature reserve)
7 Low Maynard reservoir (nature reserve)
8 Fishing and nature reserve
9 Fishing
10 Nature reserve
11 Nature reserve
12 Warwick east reservoir (fishing and nature reserve)
13 Warwick west reservoir (fishing and nature reserve)

Tottenham

The river now begins to follow the wider sweeping course that is typical of this navigation. The Walthamstow reservoirs close in from the east, blocking off the river with their high embankments bordering the navigation, while the river begins to adopt the bleak, stark appearance that characterises it for miles ahead. Racing 'fours' and 'eights' emanate from the occasional rowing club, but riverside life is sparse for the next 15 miles and there is little to see. It is inadvisable to venture up any of the side creeks feeding into the river; they are usually heavily silted up. At Walthamstow, ¼ mile north east of the Lee Valley Marina, is the old Copper Mill built c1800 to process the copper that was brought from the port of London along the Lee.

Walthamstow Reservoirs Alongside the east bank of the navigation: an important part of London's water supply, controlled by Thames Water. Access is allowed only for bird-watching or fishing by permits obtained from Thames Water (081-808 1527). There is a variety of land and water birds, including great crested grebes and yellow wagtails, as well as two thriving, long-established heronries on islands in reservoirs 1 and 5. The stock of fish in the reservoirs is being steadily increased and the reservoirs where fishing is permitted may vary each year; details can be obtained from TW.

BOATYARDS
ⓑ**Springfield Marina** Springhill, Clapton (081-806 1717). ⓇⓈⓌⒹⒺ Pump-out, gas, overnight mooring, long-term mooring, winter storage, slipway, boat lift (36ft), toilet, showers.

BOAT TRIPS
Pride of Lee Public trips at *weekends*, and private charter for up to 52 persons. Ring 081-806 1717 for details.

PUBS AND RESTAURANTS
🍺✗**Cook's Ferry Inn** Edmonton. Canalside. A busy family pub serving Boddingtons, Flowers and Marston's real ale. Food available *lunchtime and evenings* in the bar and Beefeater restaurant. Outside seating and play area.
🍺 **Narrowboat** ¼ mile south of Tottenham Lock. Canalside. Incorporated into a row of modern maisonettes this pub serves a range of real ale including Younger, Greene King and Theakston, together with at least two guest beers. Sandwiches and snacks *always available*. Garden. Disco *Fri* and *summer* barbecues.
🍺 **Robin Hood** High Hill Ferry, Upper Clapton. Canalside. Basic family pub serving Whitbread and Ruddles real ale. Bar food available *Mon–Sat*. Children's room and outdoor play area. Garden and barbecue *B. Hols and summer weekends*. Mooring.
🍺 **Anchor and Hope** High Hill Ferry, Upper Clapton. Canalside. Tiny, one bar pub serving Fuller's ale.

Enfield

Straight as a die for over a mile, the river passes Pickett's Lock, where the Regional Park Authority has built a large covered leisure and sports centre, as well as a golf course. The King George & William Girling reservoirs accompany the navigation (fishing on these reservoirs is restricted to clubs); so do vast power lines, which stride along as purposefully as the river. Ponders End Locks provide canal interest in this rather bleak area, with a handy wine merchant situated in a converted warehouse on Columbia Wharf, close by. Enfield Lock signals the end of nearly 4 miles of reservoirs and north of here the landscape opens out. Near Enfield Lock there are plenty of shops and pubs.

Enfield
Middx. All services. Interesting features in this town include the Church of St Andrew in the market place; the chancel window is 13thC. Gentlemen's Row, which probably dates from the early 18thC, is completely preserved from numbers 9 to 23. (Charles Lamb stayed at no. 17 in 1827).

Pickett's Lock Centre
Edmonton (081-803 4756). All sorts of sports activities, including squash, yoga, swimming, golf and many others. Sauna, solarium. *Open daily.*

Chingford
Essex. All services. Uninteresting town except for All Saints Church, which is medieval. To the north of the town, which is east of the river along the A110, is a pole obelisk on a 300ft hill 1½ miles from Ponders End Locks. It was erected in 1825 as a North mark for Greenwich Observatory. 1 mile east of the obelisk is Queen Elizabeth I's hunting lodge – a timber-framed, three-storeyed building from where the hunting could be viewed, now housing a local museum. The 10 square miles of Epping Forest lie to the north east of Chingford: the forest is remarkable for the large number of hornbeams and a diminishing herd of deer.

BOATYARD

BW Enfield Yard Ordnance Road, Enfield Lock (0992 764626). No services.

PUBS

⬤ **Greyhound** Enfield Lock. Canalside pub serving McMullen real ale. Bar food *Mon-Fri lunchtime.* Children welcome *Sat & Sun lunchtime only.* Patio.

⬤ **Rifles** Enfield Lock. Canalside. Bar food *Mon-Fri lunchtime only.*

⬤ **Railway** Ponders End station. Webster's and Ruddles real ale are served together with *lunchtime* food (*not Sun*). Garden.

⬤✕ **Churchills** Wharf Road, Ponders End Lock (081-443 4051/4106). Smart bar and restaurant in converted electricity power house, serving Webster's real ale. Food *lunchtime and evenings (not Sun, or Mon evenings).* Adjacent disco.

Waltham Abbey

Waltham Town Lock is the first of four locks in this section. Waltham Abbey is a fine old town where the ancient abbey, an architectural gem, looks down unperturbed on attractively pedestrianised streets. The intermittent glinting of glasshouses around shows that this is a market gardening area. North of here the navigation runs into a massive water parkland with sailing clubs on the worked out gravel pits.

Cheshunt
Herts. EC Thur. PO, tel, stores, station, take-away. The Church of St Mary's was built in 1418-48 by the then rector of Cheshunt and is an example of the Perpendicular style. Of Cheshunt House not much remains: only one wing of a courtyard house. There is a carnival every *Jul.*

Waltham Cross
Herts. EC Thur. PO, tel, stores, station, cinema. The Eleanor Cross, 1 mile west along the A121, is one of the 12 crosses (of which only three survive) erected by Edward I to commemorate the resting places of his dead queen, Eleanor of Castile, on her last journey from Leicestershire where she died, to Westminster Abbey. The Cross was built in 1291, but was greatly restored in Ketton stone in the 19thC.

Waltham Abbey
Essex. EC Thur, MD Thur, Sat. PO, tel, stores, station. The history of the town goes back to before the Norman Conquest when King Harold chose it for development as a centre of learning and religious instruction. Local museum in Sun Street.

Abbey Church Founded in 1030 as a collegiate church of secular canons. In 1184 it was nominated a mitred abbey and was soon one of the most prosperous and important in the country. Today's building is largely 19thC, but the Norman nave and aisles still stand. The south chapel is 14thC and the west tower, 16thC. The Jesse window at the east end is a fine example of Burne-Jones, 1861. Within the abbey grounds and just outside to the north are several interesting archaeological remains.

BOATYARD
Hazelmere Marina S W Slipway, pump-out, gas.

PUBS
Windmill West of Cheshunt station. Serves Ind Coope (Burton) real ale. Food. Garden.
Red Cow West of Cheshunt station. Well appointed pub serving Greene King real ale together with guest beers. Food. Garden.
Maltsters West of Cheshunt station. A smart pub serving McMullen real ale. Food. Vegetarians catered for.
Old English Gentleman Waltham Town Lock. Canalside. Serves McMullen real ale. Food. Garden.
Welsh Harp Market Square, Waltham Abbey. Town pub serving McMullen real ale. Bar snacks and basket meals available *lunchtime and evenings (not Sun evenings).* Vegetarians catered for. Children welcome.
Green Dragon Market Square, Waltham Abbey. Meals and snacks available *lunchtime (not Sun).* Children welcome at *meal times only.* Music and discos *Fri and Sat nights.*
Angel Sun Street, Waltham Abbey. The landlord of this cosy pub is an ex-marine and keen amateur pilot as the framed pictures fixed to both the ceilings and walls testify. He also sports an interesting collection of mugs and an array of coins glued to the canopy above the bar. Real ales are from Benskins, Tetley's, Ind Coope and Greene King as well as a guest beer, with at least one 'on offer'. Good food is served *lunchtime and evenings (not Sun evenings).* Vegetarians catered for. Games room. Interesting garden area.
Queens Arms Market Square, Waltham Abbey. Serves Webster's real ale and food at *lunchtime (not Sun).* Children welcome. Garden.

Broxbourne

At Feilde's Weir the beautiful River Stort flows in from the north east and the Lee bears round to the north west to Stanstead Abbots, an attractive old town with all useful facilities. Already one feels that the character of the river is changing dramatically – it is smaller, shallower and in every way more attractive than further south, and the pylons, which have relentlessly dogged the river since the outskirts of London, at last recede. Boaters should be extremely careful when ascending the Stanstead Lock: the top paddles are, unusually, on the *gates*: the unexpected rush of water into the lock chamber can cause great harm to the unwary, as can the swing bridge *over* the lock, which should be swung out of the way.

Stanstead Abbots
Herts. EC Thur. PO, tel, stores, garage, station.
A picturesque village with the Church of St James, interesting particularly because of its 15thC open timber south porch and 16thC brick north chancel chapel. Stanstead Bury nearby was originally a 15thC manor house at the west end of the village and dates from 1752.
Rye House Plot During the reign of Charles II, Rye House (the building, not the village) was owned by Rumbold, an ex-officer of the Parliamentarian army. It was here that he and a group of other discontented conspirators decided to ambush the King and his son James, heir to the throne. The plot failed miserably because the royal party passed by sooner than expected.
Hoddesdon
Herts. EC Thur. MD Wed. PO, tel, stores, station. St Monica's Priory was the manor house of Marmaduke Rawdon from 1622. A clock tower stands in the centre of the town from where the two main streets of Hoddesdon begin. A fair is held in *Jun.*
Broxbourne
Herts. EC Wed. PO, tel, stores, station. The church is entirely 15thC and 16thC. In the High Street there are several timber-framed 17thC Georgian brick houses. Broxbourne Lido is a beautiful indoor heated pool, by the river. Ring 0992 442841. *Open daily.*

BOATYARDS

Ⓑ **Stanstead Abbots Marina** South Street, Stanstead Abbots (0920 870499).
Pump-out, overnight mooring, long-term mooring, winter storage, crane, boat building, engine sales and repairs, toilets, showers.
Ⓑ **Broxbourne Boat Centre** Old Nazeing Road, Broxbourne (0992 462085)ⓇⓈⓌ ⓇⓈⓌⒹ Pump-out, narrowboat hire, day hire craft, overnight mooring, toilets, gifts.

BOAT TRIPS

Lady of Lee Valley 85-seater available for functions. Ring 0992 462085/440235.

PUBS AND RESTAURANTS

🍺 **Jolly Fisherman** Stanstead Abbotts. Riverside. Notable for its fisherman's breakfast served *daily between 07.30 and 10.30.* Also McMullen real ale and bar food *lunchtime and evenings (no food Sun).* Vegetarians catered for. Children welcome.
🍺 **Rye's** Hoddesdon. Riverside. Essentially a young people's pub with *weekend discos.* Food always available together with Webster's real ales. Garden with bowls and play area.
🍺 **Fish and Eels** Dobbs Weir, Broxbourne. Riverside. This family pub with large garden area beside the river has an attractive setting opposite the weir. It serves Benskins, Tetley's and Ind Coope real ale together with food *lunchtime and evenings (not Sun evenings)* from a small though varied and inexpensive servery menu. Vegetarians catered for. In the summer the fish are ground baited for amusement.
🍺✕ **Crown Inn** Broxbourne. Riverside. Another well kept pub with garden and children's play area overlooking the river. Food is always available together with Bass real ale. Separate restaurant and grill room.

Hertford

Leaving Stanstead Lock, the navigation runs dead straight for 1½ miles north west, flanked by beautiful green, uncluttered water-meadows contained by the nearby wooded hills. A lovely old branch railway line once ran from Stanstead Abbots to Buntingford – it now forms part of the Amwell Walkway to Easneye Woods. The river turns west into Ware, the 'granary of London', where the river bisects this fine old town. There are some remarkable 18thC summer houses along the riverfront and Ware Lock is surrounded by beautifully maintained flower beds. Above this lock, the river wanders along one side of the valley, with water-meadows on one side and wooded parkland on the other. The river enters Hertford via a deep lock, then passes a marina used for pleasure-boat moorings. A weir in the centre of the town prevents further progress, but craft may wind beyond Mill Bridge, overlooked by a fine wooden warehouse.

Hertford
Herts. EC Thur. MD Mon. PO, tel, stores, garage, stations. A large and mostly attractive county town with a long history. Two of its medieval parish churches still stand, and other buildings in the town bear witness to the Middle Ages. A new relief road through the town has destroyed many interesting and attractive houses; but it has ensured the survival of the compact old town centre, which is now a delightful place to stroll around in. In the 9thC the area was invaded with great regularity by the Danes; they were eventually seen off by King Alfred the Great. Dane End, 3½ miles north of Hertford, marks the northern limit of their incursions into this region.
The Castle Built in 1100, the castle belonged to the Cecil family after Prince Charles, son of James I, sold it. King John of France and David Bruce of Scotland were both imprisoned here; and it was here that Bolingbroke drew up charges against Richard II that led to Richard's dethronement in 1399. A few medieval structures remain, including a 12thC curtain wall. The lawns and trees which extend to the river make an attractive setting. The 15thC gatehouse was extensively altered about 1800. Those houses in Water Lane numbered 4 to 16 are thought to have been outhouses of the castle. Several buildings in Castle Street itself are noteworthy, and also those in Fore Street, including Shire Hall, built by James Adam (brother of Robert) in the 18thC. The castle now belongs to the Council and contains the Tourist Information Centre.
Hertford Museum 18 Bull Plain, Hertford (0992 582686). Local archaeology, history, geology and natural history. *Open Tue-Sat 10.00-17.00.*
Ware
Herts. EC Thur. MD Tue. PO, tel, stores, garage, station. There is much evidence of a former medieval town here, while other buildings with their projecting upper storeys show the importance of through-traffic during the coaching days.
Ware Priory Priory Street. Built from the remains of a Franciscan friary founded by Thomas Wake, Lord of the Manor, in 1338.
St Mary's Church Church Street. Its battlemented clock tower is surmounted by a spire. There is a fascinating story connected with the oak railings enclosing the children's corner.
New River
Opposite Ware Park is the intake from the River Lee of the New River, which continues 24 miles south, terminating at Stoke Newington. It was a great feat of engineering designed by Sir Hugh Myddelton in the 17thC to bring a fresh water supply from Amwell Springs, which have since run dry, to north London to replace the polluted supply obtained from the Thames. Work started on this remarkable plan in 1609 and the original 44-mile course, including several large wooden aqueducts, was completed within four years. As Amwell Springs had ceased to flow

by the end of the 19thC, most of the water in the New River is now drawn from the River Lee. A monument, overhung by weeping willows and a yew tree, commemorating Myddelton's great achievement, can be seen on an island at the foot of the slope below Great Amwell church, ¼ mile west of the iron footbridge half way between Hardmead and Stanstead Locks.

BOATYARDS

ⓑ **Lea Valley Narrowboat Co.** Lock-keeper's Cottage, Stanstead Lock, Amwell Lane, Stanstead Abbots (0920 870068). Ⓓ Ⓔ Pump-out, gas, long-term mooring, chandlery, books and maps, boat sales.

BOAT TRIPS

Jonas Fosbrooke Widebeam boat available for private hire. 60 persons. Ring 0920 870068.

PUBS AND RESTAURANTS

🍺 **Woolpack** Near Mill Bridge, Hertford. Small town pub serving McMullen real ale. Bar food and Sunday roasts.

🍺✕ **Salisbury Arms Hotel** Fore Street, Hertford (0992 583091). Restaurant and bar food together with McMullen real ale. B & B.

🍺 **White Hart Hotel** Salisbury Square, Hertford (0992 583605). Bars with cosy pub atmosphere dispensing McMullen real ale. Food is on offer from an exciting French bistro style menu at very reasonable prices. The family owned McMullen brewery, established in the town in 1827, is not far away. B & B.

🍺 **Three Tuns** Brewhouse Lane, Hertford. A wide range of real ales including Tetley's, Wadworth, Ind Coope (Burton) and McMullen are here to be enjoyed.

🍺 **Old Barge** The Folly, Hertford (0992 581871). A canalside pub run by a real ale enthusiast and offering an extensive menu, at reasonable prices, served in a separate dining area lunchtime and evenings (not Sun evening). Vegetarian food vailable. Real ales might include Ind Coope (Burton), Tetley's, Marston's, Greene King, Wadworth and Adnams. Waterside patio.

🍺 **Saracen's** Ware. Modern riverside pub serving McMullen real ale together with bar food.

🍺 **Bell** High Street, Ware. Well kept town pub serving Greene King, Boddingtons and Flowers real ale. Food is available *all day*.

🍺 **Old Punch House** High Street, Ware. Comfortable pub set in the centre of the town serving Greene King real ale and bar food. Garden.

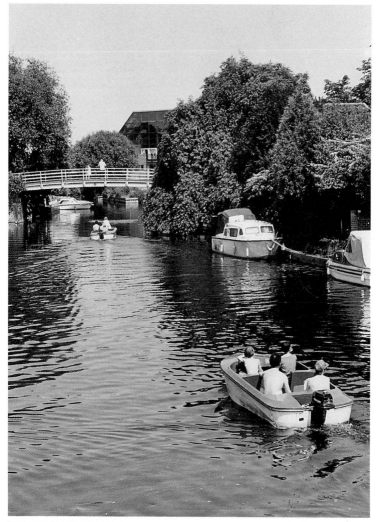

Broxbourne, River Lee. *Derek Pratt.*

Roydon

The River Stort joins the Lee at Feilde's Weir. It is instantly different from the Lee: narrow, winding, totally rural along almost its entire length, and very beautiful. There is no longer any commercial traffic on the river, which with its winding course, shallow draught and slightly narrow locks (about 13ft wide), became financially uncompetitive long ago. Water mills are seen at many of these locks: the attendant clapboarded buildings are a handsome feature of this navigation. Low bridges are also common, and when the river is swollen by excessive rainwater, the headroom under the bridges is even further reduced.

Starting at Feilde's Weir, the Stort follows a line of hills past Lower Lock and Brick Lock to Roydon. Roydon Mill is now the centre of a large caravan site, and contains a useful grocery and laundry facilities. (Southbound boats should turn left under the bridge before the mill.) Roydon village itself stretches up a hill away from the river, which is crossed by the railway on an extremely low bridge (less than 6ft headroom) and followed by Roydon Lock. East of Roydon the river flows through quiet water-meadows to Hunsdon Mill Lock, with Briggens Park up to the left an enchanting area.

Roydon
Essex. EC Wed. PO, tel, stores, chemist, station. Roydon Mill is the headquarters of a large residential and holiday caravan site. The pleasantness of the village itself is enhanced by the bold modern housing estate on the waterfront. The church is small but attractive and dates from the 13thC. Note the shield of Sir George Jackson, later Duckett (a former owner of the Stort Navigation) on the lock cottage.

PUBS AND RESTAURANTS
New Inn Roydon. Cosy village pub serving Ind Coope (Burton) and Tetley's real ale. Food served in both the bar and restaurant *lunchtime and evenings (not Sun)*. Children welcome. Garden.

Crusader Roydon. Smart pub offering food in separate restaurant area *lunchtime and evenings (not Sun and Mon evenings)*. McMullen real ale.

White Hart Roydon. Bar food available at all times with restaurant open in the *evenings*. Real ales include Greene King, Tetley's, Boddingtons and Wadworth. Outside area for the family.

White Horse Roydon. Friendly, inviting pub at the top of the village. Old-world interior with low beams, horse brasses and inglenook fireplace surrounds a bar serving Courage real ale. Imaginative menu served in restaurant area *lunchtime (not Sun) and evenings Wed-Sat*.

Sawbridgeworth

Leaving Eastwick to the north, the navigation passes the attractive Little Parndon Mill, then Burnt Mill; perhaps the name explains its absence (rowing boat hire, café and children's boating lake). South of the railway lies Harlow New Town; it does not intrude on the navigation. Winding on north eastwards up the valley, one comes to Harlow Mill. There are usually skiffs and dayboats for hire at the lock. Walkers should note that the towpath changes side at this point – do not be deceived by the path continuing up the west bank. Passing under the A11, the river continues to wind tortuously through water-meadows past Pishiobury Park. Sheering Mill Lock is a good point from which to enter the very attractive town of Sawbridgeworth. A little further north is Sawbridgeworth Lock and Mill.

Sawbridgeworth
Herts. EC Thur, Sat. PO, tel, stores, garage, station. An attractive town with houses from the 16th to the 19thC, including many white clapboarded ones. The large 14th and 15thC church is rich in monuments and brasses, and has a collection of 18thC gravestones of great elegance. The town is well shielded from the A11, but makes the most of the Stort; the group of clapboarded mill buildings are particularly pretty. There is an impressive array of maltings near the river.
Hyde Hall East of the Stort, 1 mile from town centre. Built in 1806 by Sir Jeffrey Wyatville in Tudor style, the mansion stands in a wooded park of 300 acres.
Pishiobury Castellated mansion rebuilt in 1782 by James Wyatt from earlier Tudor house. Still retains some Tudor and Jacobean work inside. Park and lake by Capability Brown.

Harlow
Essex. EC Wed. MD Tue, Fri, Sat. PO, tel, stores, garage, station, cinema. Harlow Old Town, which contains several 18thC houses, a Norman chapel at Harlowbury and the site of a Romano-Celtic temple, has been swallowed up by Harlow New Town, set up in 1947 as a balanced area for London's overspilling population. Frederick Gibberd masterminded the plan, and the New Town is now well known as an important breakthrough in town planning.
Harlow Town Pets' Corner Harlow Park. Animals roaming free in the park. Also aquarium, vivarium and aviaries. *Open daily, school holidays and week-ends; afternoons during term-time.*
Parndon Mill at Parndon Lock, Harlow (0279 415063). A fine tall wooden watermill now housing offices.

BOAT TRIPS
Lee & Stort Waterbus Co (0920 487999). Trips on their boat, *The Wind in the Willows.*

PUBS
🍺 **King William IV** Fairgreen, Sawbridgeworth, ¼ mile west of Sheering Mill Lock. Old pub opening onto a courtyard and serving Courage real ale. Bar snacks and sandwiches available *lunchtime (not Sun).* Patio area.
🍺✕ **Market House Hotel** Sawbridgeworth. Set on the crossroads, at the heart of the village, this 400 year old hotel provides both bar snacks and an à la carte menu in the restaurant (*not Sun evenings and all day Mon*) as well as afternoon teas. Vegetarians are catered for. Real ales served include Banks and Taylor together with Adnams. Children welcome. B & B.
🍺✕ **Churchgate Manor Hotel** Churchgate Street, Harlow (0279 420246). Smart hotel offering accommodation and a wide selection of food available from two restaurant menus. Leisure centre available for guests only.
🍺 **Dusty Miller** ¼ mile north of Burnt Mill Lock. On the outskirts of Harlow. Serves McMullen real ale. Bar food *lunchtime and evenings (not Mon evenings or all day Sun).* Disco *lst Sat of month.* Garden.

Bishop's Stortford

Leaving Sawbridgeworth and its riverside
malthouses, the river passes a very low railway
bridge and wanders round to Tednambury
Lock. Just to the north of this an arm leads off
to Little Hallingbury Mill in its attractive
setting at the bottom of a hill. Walbury Camp
is half a mile upstream beside Spellbrook
Lock, but there is little about the camp to
interest the layman. Twyford House, Mill and
Lock form a very attractive group in the water-
meadows that flank the river; then a final
sweep of the river past trees and fields brings
the outskirts of Bishop's Stortford. A petrol
station adjoins the towpath before the river
reaches the town centre. The navigation
almost reaches the middle of the town, but
navigators are not advised to proceed further
than the car park, where the river divides:
there are only a few inches of water beyond
this junction, and most boats tend
immediately to get stuck.

Bishop's Stortford
*Herts. EC Wed. MD Thur, Sat. PO, tel, stores,
garage, station.* A thriving market town that has
retained much of its old-world atmosphere.
Many of the inns are centuries old. St
Michael's Church has a Norman font, which
survives from an earlier church built on the
same site.
Rhodes Memorial Museum South Road,
Bishop's Stortford (0279 51746). Contains a
collection illustrating Cecil Rhodes' life,
particularly in relation to his activities in
Rhodesia. The old vicarage where Rhodes was
born contains descriptive maps, pictures and
documents devoted to him. *Open Mon-Sat.
Closed first 2 weeks in August.*
Local History Museum Cemetery Lodge,
Apton Road (0279 722557). *Open Sun
afternoons May-Sep & Fri afternoons in summer.*
Corn Exchange corner of Market Square
and High Street. Built by Lewis Vulliamy:
Neo-Classical façade with Ionic columns and
pediments.
Town Trail Details on 0279 722557. Route
through medieval town centre.
Tourist Information Centre 2 The
Causeway, Bishop's Stortford (0279 655261).
Waytemore Castle Bridge Street. Only the
foundations of the rectangular keep remain.
What used to be the bailey is now a pleasure
garden.
Thorley
Herts. The church retains its Norman south
doorway, and a west tower from the 15thC, in
spite of extensive restoration in 1854 by
Vulliamy. Thorley Hall, nearby, is a 15thC
farmhouse which was modernised in the
18thC.
Little Hallingbury *Essex. Tel.* The church
has a Norman doorway made with Roman
bricks; the south porch is of timber. Note also
the pretty timber-framed house behind the
little pond by the church.

PUBS AND RESTAURANTS

🍺 **George Hotel** Bishop's Stortford. In the
centre of the town and serving Ind Coope
(Burton) real ale and bar snacks. B & B.
🍺 **Black Lion** Bishop's Stortford. Lively
town pub serving bar food and Benskins real
ale. Weekend discos and live bands *Wed and
Thur.* B & B.
🍺 **Falcon** Station Road, Bishop's Stortford.
Bar snacks and Benskins real ale.
🍺 **Old Bull's Head** London Road, Bishop's
Stortford. Riverside. Bar snacks and Benskins
real ale.
🍺 **Tanner's Arms** Station Road, Bishop's
Stortford. Riverside. Cosy pub serving a
varied menu *lunchtime and evenings (not Tue
and Sun evenings)* together with McMullen
real ale. Vegetarians catered for.
🍺✗ **Three Horseshoes** ¼ mile north of
Spellbrook Lock. An interesting squat timber-
framed building, thatched and dating from
1449. Restaurant.

MONMOUTHSHIRE & BRECON

Maximum dimensions

Length: 44' 3"
Beam: 8' 6"
Headroom: 5' 6"
Draught: 2'

Manager
(0873) 830328

Mileage
PONTYPOOL to
Goytre Wharf: 6
Llanfoist: 11½
Gilwern: 14½
Llangattock Bridge: 18
Talybont: 26½
BRECON: 33¼

Locks: 6

In 1792 the Act of Authorisation for the Monmouthshire Canal was passed. This gave permission for a canal to be cut from the estuary of the River Usk at Newport to Pontnewydd, north of Pontypool. In addition to this 11-mile main line, there was to be an 11-mile branch from Malpas to Crumlin. The canal was designed to connect with a large network of tramways that were to be built to serve the iron ore, limestone and coal mines of the area. Thomas Dadford was appointed engineer, and the canal was opened in 1796, with many of the tramways still to be built.

The close relationship between canal and tramway from the start of the scheme was a feature of South Wales. The promoters of the canal saw these embryo railways as a means of increasing their revenue, without suspecting that they were encouraging the development of a means of transport that later was to cause the downfall of the canals.

When the Act for the Brecknock & Abergavenny Canal was passed in 1793, it was conceived in very similar terms to its southerly neighbour. The canal was planned to connect Brecon with the River Usk at Caerleon, to serve as a link between the various tramways and the Usk Navigation. The directors of the Monmouthshire Canal persuaded the promoters of this rival venture to alter their plans to include a junction with their own canal, whose construction was well under way by this date. And so the Brecknock & Abergavenny Canal, with Thomas Dadford again as engineer, was cut from Brecon to Pontymoile Basin, where it joined the Monmouthshire Canal. Construction was begun in 1797. It progressed slowly because the company's first priority was the building of the tramways, a more immediate source of revenue. The canal was only to be built when all the tramways were in operation, to serve as a keystone for the whole system. After the usual delays caused by shortage

of money, the Brecknock & Abergavenny Canal was opened throughout in 1812.

For a while the two canals were profitable, because the iron and coal cargoes justified the use of both canal and tramway. However, the greater speed and efficiency of the railways soon became apparent, and by the 1850s there were many schemes to give up the canals and rely entirely on the rail system. Some were put forward by the canal companies, in order to protect their interests as best they could. In 1865 the Monmouthshire and the Brecknock & Abergavenny Canal Companies amalgamated, becoming the Monmouthshire & Brecon Canal Company; but already it was too late for the merger to be effective. Revenues were dropping fast as the railway tentacles reached through the South Wales coalfields. Later the whole system was bought by the Great Western Railway, and by the turn of the century only a few boats were still using the canal. Bit by bit the original Monmouthshire Canal was closed, but the Brecon line was kept open as a water channel. In 1962 the network was formally 'abandoned', and parts were filled in.

However, with the development of the Brecon Beacons National Park, the amenity potential of the Brecon line was realised. In 1964 the slow task of restoration was begun by BWB, with the help of Brecon and Monmouth County Councils. The locks were restored, and soon boats were once more able to cruise from Pontymoile to Talybont. In 1970 the low fixed bridge at Talybont was replaced with a new lifting bridge, and once again navigation was open all along the old Brecknock & Abergavenny Canal. The Monmouthshire line from Pontymoile to the Usk at Newport may never be reopened in its entirety, for stretches have vanished completely; but parts have been restored as far south as Cwmbran, where it is proving a valuable asset to the developing new town.

Natural history

A diversity of interesting and colourful wild plants and animals can be seen along the Monmouthsire & Brecon Canal. For much of its length the canal is tree-lined, mostly by alders, which can be recognised by their smooth, roundish leaves with jagged edges and their clusters of little cones. Interspersed with the alders, or in small copses nearby, is a variety of other trees such as oak, ash and sycamore. Between Llanfoist and Govilon fine beech trees clothe the hillside and reach down to the canal, and in spring wild cherries are conspicuously beautiful in blossom between Llangynidr and Crickhowell.

The smaller aquatic plants grow best in less shady places. Rooted in the mud at the bottom of the canal, and completely submerged in water, are the true aquatics like the feathery-leaved water milfoil and Canadian pondweed. The latter, a North American plant, spread rapidly after its introduction into this country halfway through the last century. Other water plants to be seen include bur-reeds, with long ribbon-shaped leaves floating on the surface, and water plantains, with oval leaves thrust above the water and tiny pink or white three-petalled flowers.

Bordering the canal grow many gaily coloured marsh plants, in bloom from July until autumn. Especially conspicuous are the tall 'codlins and cream', with rose flowers, and hemp agrimony with fluffy heads of pink flowers. The sweetly scented, feathery clusters of cream meadowsweet contrast effectively with the lovely blue of water forget-me-not. Marsh woundwort with its lilac flowers is frequent and here and there along the banks the blue trumpets of skullcap can be seen.

The animal life is also rich and varied, although it has lately suffered considerably from predation by wild mink. The kingfisher with its scintillating blue-green plumage is always an exciting sight. Fortunately it is now fairly frequent again along the canal. Another bird which comes to fish is the tall grey heron, which flaps away on slow wingbeats when disturbed. The largest bird likely to be encountered is the mute swan; a family party including four or five cygnets may often be seen near Brecon. Moorhens can be observed at several spots, either swimming along in their inimitable jerky style or walking about on the banks in search of food. Where the canal overlooks the River Usk as at Llanhamlach or crosses it via Brynich Aqueduct, the dipper – a dark, tubby, thrush-sized bird with a white front – may be seen bobbing up and down on stones in the river. Although its main habitat is the fast-flowing river, it may forsake this for the canal on occasions and be seen on the towpath. In summer, from bramble thickets and hedgerows along the towpath issue the songs of whitethroats and garden warblers. Many small birds such as tree creepers, nuthatches and tits feed in the overhanging trees, and in winter the alders are sometimes thronged with twittering parties of siskins, searching the cones for seeds.

Of the wealth of smaller animal life along the canal, the dragonflies are perhaps the most noticeable, as they patrol to and fro over their particular stretch of water. Occasionally the female dragonflies may be seen dipping their long abdomens into the water at intervals to lay eggs on the submerged water plants. Pond skaters are the numerous small dark insects with long legs that dart away over the surface of the water at your approach. On marsh plants like the fragrant water mint, beautiful beetles with a greenish metallic lustre may be found. During May and June, orange-tip butterflies are on the wing along the banks, where the females (with grey, not orange-tipped wings) lay eggs on milkmaid plants, on which their caterpillars feed. Later in summer, speckled wood butterflies may also be seen flying or basking in sunny glades.

Brecon Beacons National Park

The Park covers 519 square miles of mountain and hill country, embracing parts of the old counties of Herefordshire, Monmouthshire, Breconshire and Carmarthenshire. Apart from a great variety of fine scenery, the Park also includes three nature reserves, a forest reserve, opportunities for fishing, caving, pony trekking, sailing and boating, and several towns of interest to tourists, notably Brecon, Crickhowell, Talgarth and Hay-on-Wye; in addition, Abergavenny, Llandovery and Llandeilo are just outside the Park boundary.

Virtually all the canal is within the Park – a factor that greatly strengthened the case for its restoration and reopening. The canal is an excellent introduction to the Park, crossing it roughly from south-east to north-west; in several places there are foot and bridle paths leading away into the mountains from the towpath. Various main roads cross the Park, and so access by car is easy, but the whole area is best explored on foot. A good place to start any exploration is the Mountain Centre, 1000ft up on Mynydd Illtud, above the village of Libanus, 4 miles south west of Brecon. There are rest and refreshment rooms, car parks and picnic sites overlooking the Brecon Beacons, and the wardens at the Centre give lectures to visitors and youth groups on the Park and the use of the countryside.

Pontypool

Before the closure of the Newport section, the old Monmouthsire & Brecon Canal used to run from Brecon to the estuary of the River Usk at Newport, and thus to the sea. After a quarter of a century of decay, the upper section, from Pontypool to Brecon, was restored and reopened to craft in 1970. The limit of navigation is just below Crown Bridge (number 48). The town centre is about one mile to the north west, through the lovely Pontypool park. After a few canalside gardens, all traces of the town are left behind, and the canal starts its meandering contour course towards Brecon. The character of this canal is quickly apparent; it twists and turns, clinging to the hillside on the west, while to the east wide views open up across the rolling pastures and woods of the Usk valley. The winding course, and the frequent stone bridges make the canal interesting, for every bend offers a different view of the steep hills to the west and the valley to the east, while the canal itsef remains entirely quiet, rural and isolated. Navigators should look out for the cast iron mile posts, which survive irregularly along the length of the canal. There are no villages by the canal in this section, but services and pubs are never more than a short walk away, at Pontymoile, at Mamhilad and at Penperlleni. Provisions are available at Ty-bach, west of bridge 62. Main roads also keep their distance, although they are generally clearly visible in the valley below the canal. After passing the long tunnel-like Saron bridge (no.74), the seclusion is interrupted by long lines of moored boats, which are the prelude to Goytre Wharf. Old lime kilns can be seen by the wharf, indicating the agricultural nature of the canal in its heyday. The wooded hills sweep down to the wharf, giving it a most attractive setting.

Penperlleni
Gwent. PO, tel, stores, garage. Main road village useful for supplies.

Mamhilad
Gwent. Tel. A little hillside hamlet scattered round the church. Overshadowed by massive yew trees, the pleasantly over-grown churchyard has fine views across the valley.

Pontypool
Gwent. EC Thur. MD Wed, Fri, Sat.
Pontypool has been an industrial town since Roman times, concentrating on the production or iron. This reached a peak in the 18th and 19thC, but has declined in recent times. In 1720 tinplate was produced here for the first time in Britain, and in the 19thC the town was a centre for japanning – the coating of objects with an extract of oils from coal, so producing a black varnish similar to Japanese lacquer. Coal mining has also been important. Despite this industrial heritage, Pontypool has always remained a farming centre, and so the hard industrial elements are softened by the traditions of a rural market town. The steep walls of the Lwyd valley have also limited the growth of the town, and made the centre very self-contained.

Pontypool Park Originally the seat of the Hanburys, the famous iron and steel family, this Georgian mansion is now a school. The park, which contains the Torfaen Trust Museum and a Leisure Centre, is open to the public. The magnificent wrought iron entrance gates at Pontymoile (by bridge 53) were given to John Hanbury by Sarah Churchill, Duchess of Marlborough.

BOATYARDS
Ⓑ **Red Line Boats** Goytre Wharf, Pontypool, Gwent (0873 880516). Ⓡ Ⓢ Ⓦ Pump-out, gas, narrowboat hire, day hire craft, overnight mooring opposite, long-term mooring, winter storage, slipway, chandlery, books and maps, boat sales, engine sales and repairs, toilets, showers, café.

PUBS

◖ **Goytre Arms** Penperlleni. ¼ mile east of bridge 72. Food, garden, real ale, children welcome.
◖ **Horseshoe Inn** Goetre Fawr. ¼ mile north of bridge 65.
◖ **Star** Mamhilad. 200yds east of bridge 62. Food, real ale, children welcome.

◖ **Horse & Jockey** Pontymoile, on A472. 100yds east of bridge 55.
◖ **Bell Inn** High Street, Pontypool.
◖ **Forge Hammer** High Street, Pontypool.
◖ **Open Hearth** Sebastopol. Canalside, between bridges 48 and 49, south of Pontymoile Basin. Food, garden, children welcome.

Llangattock, Monmouthshire & Brecon Canal. *Derek Pratt.*

Abergavenny

Beyond Goytre Wharf, the canal continues its meandering course northwards, passing through a thick wooded cutting before returning to the pattern set in the previous section: steep wooded hills to the west, the wide valley rolling away to the east. The canal clings to its contour line high on the side of the hills, at times making horseshoe bends to avoid any change in level. At the apex of each such bend, there is generally a small stone aqueduct taking the canal over a stream that tumbles noisily down towards the valley. In several places these streams serve as feeders for the canal, half their water joining the canal, half passing beneath an aqueduct. 200yds west of bridge 76, in Pen-groes-oped, there is a good general store, a post box and a telephone. After the first horseshoe bend, set among thick woods, the canal passes Llanover Park to the east; the house is out of sight, shielded by trees, but the village can be seen nestling in the hillside. The next bend is much wider; looking back, the course of the canal along the side of the hill can be clearly seen. After the bend there is a long straight for over a mile, which carries the canal through the trees above Llanellen. The River Usk is coming nearer all the time, and its course into Abergavenny is visible below. To the west the hills are now very steep, rising sharply to over 1800ft, at times almost vertically away from the canal. From its elevated position there is an excellent view of Abergavenny, laid out like a model in the valley below, nearly a mile from the canal. In the 19thC the hills to the west were heavily mined and quarried, and many tramways constructed to carry the coal, iron ore and limestone down to the canal to be loaded into boats. There are sometimes still traces of these tramways; often their course into the hills can be followed from the canal bridges. A good example leaves the canal at Llanfoist, by the boathouse. The loading wharves, cut into the steep hillside, can also be seen in many places along the canal.

Abergavenny
Gwent. EC Thur. MD Tue. All services.
Abergavenny lies beside the fast flowing River Usk, surrounded on all sides by mountains and hills; the Sugar Loaf, Blorenge and the Skirrids overlook the town, a dramatic natural wall ranging up to 2000ft. Abergavenny enjoys this magnificent setting, living up to its reputation as the gateway to Wales. Primarily a market town, it contains the traditional mixture of buildings of all periods and styles, from the Tudor houses in the main street to the red stone of the 19thC Gothic town hall.
Abergavenny Castle The mound of the castle dominates the town. Built in the 11thC, the castle was the scene in 1177 of a treacherous massacre of several notable Welsh leaders; invited to the castle to dine by William de Braose, they were put to death with no warning. In this violent way William made sure of his control over the surrounding lands. Parts of walls, towers and a gateway survive. Ruins and grounds *open daily.*
St Mary's Church Originally the chapel of the Benedictine priory, the church was extensively rebuilt in the 14thC, after the destruction of the priory. It contains fine wooden 14thC choir stalls, a wooden figure of Jesse, and rich monuments in the Herbert chapel.
Abergavenny and District Museum Situated in the castle precincts, the museum contains items of local interest, Roman coins, tools and examples of local crafts. *Open daily.*
Sugar Loaf A conspicuous landmark 2 miles north west of Abergavenny, so named because of its shape. 2130 acres, including the 1955ft summit, are owned by the National Trust.
Rural Crafts Museum Llanvapley. 4 miles east of Abergavenny, on B4233. 500 tools, rural and farm equipment and implements, domestic bygones. *Open Sun afternoons.*
Llanellen
Gwent. PO, tel, stores. Although modern housing has greatly extended Llanellen into a suburb of Abergavenny, it is still an attractive village, especially by the three-arch stone bridge over the Usk. The 19thC church is pleasantly set among woods.

Llanover

Gwent. PO, tel. The famous bell Big Ben in Westminster was named after the politician Benjamin Hall (Lord Llanover), who was responsible for the construction of the tower whilst Chief Commissioner of Works. He also initiated the tramway from Buckland House Wharf to Rhymney Ironworks, east of Talybont reservoir. The estate village is particularly elegant; stone cottages and terraces all built in the same style, pleasingly laid out with generous grass verges and trees.

BOAT TRIPS

Owain Glyndwr 46-seater water bus operated by B & M Charters and based at bridge 76 near Goytre (0291 690201). Licensed bar.

PUBS

Many pubs and restaurants in Abergavenny.

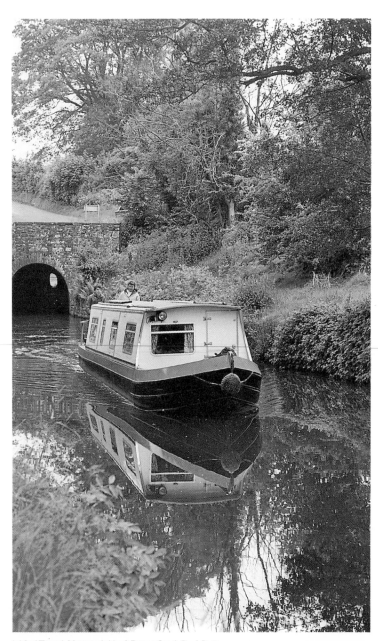

Ashford Tunnel, Monmouthshire & Brecon Canal. *Derek Pratt.*

Govilon

The canal continues to follow its contour
course northwards, cut into the steep, rocky
sides of the hill. With Abergavenny spread out
in the valley below, and the wooded slopes
climbing up from the water, it is a very
dramatic stretch. Llanfoist comes into view,
partly hidden by the trees. The old wharf
buildings, originally built for the tramway that
ran up into the hills from the canal, are now a
boatyard and hire cruiser base. The boatyard
bridge is the best place to leave the canal on
foot for Abergavenny.

Leaving Llanfoist, the canal continues
through the wooded side-cutting. As the
course of the long abandoned railway swings
in to join the canal, the towpath changes sides
to the west, where it remains until Govilon.
The village is huddled beneath the canal; the
wharf buildings are now used by Govilon Boat
Club, who restored them. The BW section
office is also here. A butcher's shop by bridge
98 sells milk and eggs. After the big skewed
rail bridge (now disused) the canal makes
another horseshoe bend, crossing a stream on
an aqueduct. As it approaches Gilwern, the
presence of the Heads of the Valley road
becomes more obvious, close to the eastern
bank. The canal passes above Gilwern, which
spreads down the hill to the east, and then
turns sharply before Gilwern Wharf. This area
has now been landscaped, and it is worth
stopping the boat to inspect the information
board between bridges 104 and 105, opposite
the lime kilns, which illustrates how the area
looked before 1850, when it served the
Clydach Ironworks, situated up the gorge.
The road and the hills swing away to the west,
leaving the canal to pass through a thickly
wooded stretch in comparative quiet.

Gilwern
Gwent. PO, tel, stores. The village is built along
one main street, which falls steeply away from
the canal; there are fine views of the country
running down to the River Usk.

Govilon
Gwent. PO, tel, stores, garage. The canal passes
above the village, and little can be seen from
the water.

Llanfoist
Gwent. PO, tel, stores, golf course. The
boatyard, housed in the old stone wharf
buildings, has given the little village a new
lease of life. There is a good walk from the
boathouse into the mountains, following the
course of the old tramway.

BOATYARDS
ⓑ **Castle Narrowboats** Church Road Wharf,
Gilwern (0873 830001). Ⓦ Pump-out,
narrowboat hire, day boat hire.
ⓑ **Road House Holiday Hire
Narrowboats** Main Road, Gilwern (0873
830240). Pump-out, gas, narrowboat hire.
BW Govilon Yard (0873 830328). Ⓡ Ⓢ Ⓦ
Slipway by arrangement, toilets.
ⓑ **Beacon Park Boats** The Boatyard,
Llanfoist (0873 858277), bookings 0222
484677). Narrowboat hire.

BOAT TRIPS
Ohmega is a 40-seater electric boat available
for charter from Gilwern. Ring 0873 830001.

PUBS
🍺 **Beaufort Arms** Gilwern. Food. B & B.
🍺 **Bridgend** Gilwern. Canalside at bridge
103. A welcoming pub offering a good choice
of real ales, food and a garden. Children
welcome.
🍺 **Corn Exchange** Gilwern. Food, garden,
real ale, children welcome.
🍺 **Navigation** Gilwern. Canalside at bridge
103. Fine picture of a navvy and his tools on
the sign. Food, garden, children welcome.
🍺 **Bridge End** Govilon, below the aqueduct.
Food, real ale, garden, children welcome.
🍺 **Bridge Inn** Llanfoist.
🍺 **Llanfoist Inn** Llanfoist. Food, garden,
children welcome.

121 Llwyncelyn bridge
Glen Usk Park
N
Baylis bridge **120**

119 Folly bridge

Ffawyddog
Quarries
Workhouse bridge **118**
B4558
River Usk
Golf course
117 Dan-y-garth bridge
Llangattock wharf
116 Ffawyddog bridge
Aqueduct
115 Upper Yard bridge
SW
114 Lower Yard bridge
Llangattock Park
Crickhowell
113 Llwmus bridge

16M 6L
Brecon
Pontypool
17¼M 0L

112 Park bridge
A40(T)
111 Wooden bridge
110 Pen-pedair Heol bridge
109 Dark bridge

107 Dan-y-graig bridge

106 Haunted House bridge
A4077
River Clydach

105
Sand bridge
River Clydach
Gilwern
104 Auckland bridge

Crickhowell

Continuing north west, the canal clings to its contour on the side of the hill, which separates it from the River Usk for a while. As the canal passes the old army camp laid out in parkland to the east, the hills become less dramatic. The approach to Llangattock is through flatter country, but trees still surround the canal, hiding the extensive parkland that falls away to the east. Llangattock is set below the canal, best approached from bridges 114 and 115 where there are toilets and showers (BW key); beyond it lies Crickhowell, the fine houses rising out of the valley over the river. Llangattock Wharf is just beyond bridge 115; now a busy mooring site overlooked by the old stone wharf buildings, which include a range of lime kilns. This is a good base for exploring the Brecon Beacons; there are opportunities for caving in the surrounding hills, and horses can be hired in Crickhowell for trekking. Leaving Llangattock, the canal crosses a small aqueduct, and is then quickly back among the hills, whose steep wooded slopes fall sharply to the water's edge. As the River Usk and the canal close together again, there are fine views to the east across the valley. One of the best is across the golf course, which comes right up to the towpath. A short straight then takes the canal to Glen Usk Park, through woods that get progressively thicker.

Llangattock
Powys. PO, tel, stores. This little village, just down the lane from bridge 116, was once famous for its weaving and its lime kilns. It also has a 12thC church, founded in the 6thC. With a handsome square tower, it is worth a visit. The hills behind the village are riddled with limestone caves and quarries. One cave, Agen Allwedd, has 11 miles of underground passages. The entrance is in the Craig-y-Cilau Nature Reserve, but exploration should only be undertaken by experienced cavers. Permits for rock climbing, and for specimen collecting, must be obtained from: Nature Conservancy, Plas Gogerddan, Aberystwyth, Dyfed.
Crickhowell
Powys. EC Wed. MD Thur. PO, tel, stores, garage, bank. The road down through Llangattock leads to the 13-arch medieval stone bridge over the Usk, the imposing entry to Crickhowell. This fine market town, once a centre for the production of Welsh flannel, is spread over the northern slopes of the Usk valley. The town is compact and elegant, with terraces of 18th and 19thC houses, and some handsome inns. In the centre are the scant remains of the Norman castle. Once controlling a large area, the castle was destroyed during the 15thC, and only the motte and bailey, parts of the curtain wall and a small tower survive. The 14thC parish church contains interesting stained glass. Crickhowell has long been a famous holiday centre, a role it still enjoys today. Apart from hill walking, there are opportunities for fishing and pony trekking.

PUBS AND RESTAURANTS
🍺 **Horse Shoe** Llangattock. 200yds from bridge 114 or 115. Food, garden, real ale, children welcome.
🍺 **Bridgend Inn** Crickhowell. Well worth the one mile walk from either bridge 114 or 116 to this fine old inn overlooking the medieval bridge. Bass, Worthington and Hancocks real ale, food, riverside garden. Good collections of jugs and chamber pots, and a cosy fire in cold weather.
🍺✕ **Bear Hotel** Crickhowell (0873 810408). Food. B & B.
🍺 **Six Bells** Mill Street, Crickhowell. Davenports real ale, food, garden.

Llangynidr

Leaving the wooded Glen Usk Park behind, the canal continues its north-westerly course along the Usk valley. Among the trees to the east can be seen the Italianate towers of Gliffaes. As the canal approaches Llangynidr, it begins to meander more, leaving the hills and woods behind; river-like, it wanders through open rolling pastureland beside the Usk, passing to the south of the village. Bridge 129 is the best access point for Llangynidr. The small settlement by bridge 131 includes a shop, telephone, tennis courts, and a garage. As this is left behind, the canal reaches the first lock of the Llangynidr flight of five; this, the first lock on the navigable section of the canal, ends the 23-mile-long pound; the short climb to the summit at Brecon starts here. Leaving Cwm Crawnon, where there is a pub and restaurant, the canal turns sharply over an aqueduct and reaches the second lock. On the old wharf beyond the lock is a toll house, now used by BW, and a sanitary station. Hire craft operate from here. Thick woods now flank the canal as the steep hills return on both sides. The Usk valley has narrowed, and so canal and river flow close together through the hills; the canal is still high above the river. In the middle of the woods are the final three locks of the flight, following closely upon each other. The surrounding woods and hills make this one of the most beautiful settings on the canal system. Each lock is fitted with two ladders, so you can motor straight in, when ascending.

Navigational note
Llangynidr locks should be left empty with the bottom gates open.

Cwm Crawnon
Powys. Clustered round the canal as it climbs the Llangynidr locks, this hamlet is famous for the Coach & Horses pub, with its French cuisine.
Tretower Court and Castle 2½ miles north west of Crickhowell on A479. Ruins of a late 14thC fortified manor house, which was built to replace a Norman castle whose remains still exist nearby. The ruined cylindrical keep is unusual.
Llangynidr
Powys. PO, tel, stores (open every day). Spread out over a plateau, this farming village is scattered round the pretty 19thC church. The grandest house in the village is the old rectory, whose grounds run almost to the canal bank.

BOATYARDS
BW Llangynidr Yard By bridge 134. R S W

PUBS AND RESTAURANTS
🍺 **Coach & Horses** Cwm Crawnon. Llangynidr. Canalside at bridge 133. Food, garden. Ushers real ale, children welcome.
🍺✕ **Red Lion** Llangynidr (0874 730223). Food. B & B. Local trout and salmon served in 16thC surroundings.

- Pencelli wharf
- 154 Pencelli bridge
- 153 Cross Keys bridge
- **Pencelli**
- 152 Castle bridge
- River Usk
- B4558
- 151 Penawr bridge
- 150 Penawr lift bridge
- 149 Gethinog lift bridge
- **Cross Oak**
- 148 Cross Oak lift bridge
- 147 Cross Oak bridge
- 146 Chilson bridge
- 145 Beniah bridge
- 144 Talybont lift bridge
- Aqueduct
- River Caerfanell
- Talybont wharf
- 143 White Hart bridge
- W
- Pipe bridge
- **Talybont**
- Talybont wharf
- 142 Graiglas bridge

6¼M 1L Brecon
Pontypool 26½M 5L

- B4558
- ROMAN ROAD
- Ashford tunnel 375 yards
- River Usk
- 141 Wenallt upper bridge
- 140 Wenallt lower bridge
- Snake bridge
- 139 Llanddetty bridge
- River Usk
- 138 Parsons bridge
- 137 Dany Graig bridge
- 136 Workhouse bridge
- Tots Lock bridge 135

Talybont

Leaving the Llangynidr locks behind, the canal continues through thick woods passing the three cottages by bridge 135, once a workhouse. The narrow Usk valley pushes the two waterways close together, although the canal stays high above the river. The thick wooded walls of the valley fall steeply on both sides. The minor road that has accompanied the canal all along the valley is still much in evidence, although traffic is luckily very light. The valley starts to open out, and as the hills recede, rolling pastureland flanks the canal as it enters the slight cutting that precedes the short Ashford Tunnel. The tunnel, 375yds long, seems particularly small as it has no portals to speak of; a round hole disappears into the side of a low hill, looking more like a large culvert than a tunnel. The towpath goes over the top, following the line of the tunnel and the B4558. Leaving the tunnel behind, the canal goes straight to Talybont through a low cutting. Passing an old wharf where there is a pub on the road beside the canal, bridge 142, and the disused rail bridge, the canal goes through the village on an embankment, crossing the fast flowing Caerfanell river on an aqueduct. From bridge 142 the remains of a Roman road run to the hill fort above the village. The wharf was used by the Bryn-Oer tramway, which brought limestone down from the quarry above. Lime kilns are much in evidence by the canal. Its course can still be followed. Talybont stretches along the road below the canal, seemingly a typical canal village. At the end of the village is a lift bridge. It is electrically operated and instructions are clearly posted. Leaving the village, the canal enters a different landscape. Pasturelands still roll steeply away to the west, but to the east there are wide flat lands; the canal is carried on a low embankment which continues irregularly for the next 3 miles. Three newly built conventional lift bridges cross the canal. These are sometimes fixed in the open position to stop livestock crossing the canal; navigators should always leave them as they find them. A very wide towpath accompanies the canal along this stretch, while on the west side the steep wooded slopes conceal the minor road. A sharp bend takes the canal into the village of Pencelli; the mound of the old castle dominates the village and the canal. There is a slipway just beyond bridge 154.

Pencelli

Powys. This little village was at one time the head of a medieval lordship: but the only indication of this today is the castle mound.

Talybont

Powys. PO, tel, stores (right by the canal), garage. When the railway and canal were both operating commercially, Talybont must have been a busy village. Today it is a quiet holiday centre with facilities for fishing, pony trekking and hill walking, although there is still a busy livestock market. The large wharf overlooks the village, which is clustered round the Caerfanell Aqueduct. The river falls rapidly from Talybont reservoir in the hills to the south, to join the Usk.

Llangorse Lake

3½ miles north of Talybont is the largest natural lake in South Wales, 502 acres given over to pleasure and recreation. Wildlife is abundant, and the goosander is a frequent visitor. The legendary town of Mara is supposed to lie submerged in the lake, and in fact a crannog, or lake dwelling set on stilts, has been found near the lake's outlet.

PUBS

- **Star Inn** Talybont. Canalside by the aqueduct. Food, garden, real ale, children welcome.
- **White Hart** Talybont. Canalside at bridge 143. Fine traditional pub with an open fire offering Bass and Felinfoel real ale. Food, children welcome.
- **Travellers' Rest** Talybont. Canalside at bridge 142. Food, garden, children welcome.

Brecon

Leaving Pencelli, the canal starts on a long horseshoe bend that carries it through flat wooded country towards the crossing of the Usk. After the last lift bridge, a low embankment carries the canal across marshy ground towards Llanfrynach, but it never goes near the village. The best access point is the B4558 bridge. Before this bridge, a small aqueduct takes the canal over the Nant Menascin. Beyond the aqueduct there is an old mill, housing the Waterfolk Canal Centre (*open daily 10.00-17.30. Closed Fri*). A trip boat operates from here. The canal completes the long curve back, well above the fast flowing Usk. Llanhamlach lies across the river. In addition to its 13thC church, the area is rich in prehistoric remains. The Usk now stays in sight all the way to Brecon, apart from one small interruption. Bridge 162 takes the towpath to the west bank, where it remains to the terminus, and then the canal turns sharply on to the Brynich aqueduct. This four-arched stone structure takes the canal across the Usk to the east side of the valley. To the west can be seen the old bridge that takes the B4558 across the river. Immediately beyond the aqueduct is the last lock. The canal now goes straight to Brecon, passing through a tunnel-like bridge under the A470. The final mile of the route is high on the hillside, overlooking the Usk all the way. Although all of the canal is very clean, the stretch into Brecon is remarkably clear and free of weed. The canal follows the road to the outskirts of the town, passing the barracks, and then swings slightly to the west, along the backs of the houses. The entry into Brecon is attractive, with many pretty houses and gardens flanking the canal. Originally the canal went almost to the town centre, turning sharply into a right-angled basin, but now it stops short, just beyond bridge 166. The course of the canal to the old terminus can still be traced, although it has vanished beneath a car park and a builder's yard. A big brick warehouse, dated 1892, marks the old head of the navigation.

Brecon
Powys. EC Wed. MD Fri. PO, tel, stores, garage, bank, cinema, swimming pool. Built at the confluence of the Usk and Honddu rivers, Brecon has long been the administrative centre and market town for the Breconshire uplands. It dates back to the Roman period, and although little remains, the narrow streets that surround the castle give an idea of medieval Brecon. Today the town is famous as a touring centre, its cathedral and generous 18thC architecture making it seem more English than Welsh. The Usk waterfront is especially attractive, dominated by the old stone bridge. Sarah Siddons and her brother Charles Kemble lived in the High Street.
Brecon Cathedral Originally the Priory Church of St John, founded by Bernard Newmarch, it was given cathedral status in 1923. Most of the building is 13thC, although the nave is a century later. There is some fine glass, and side chapels dedicated to various medieval trade guilds.
Brecon Castle Most of the remains of the 11thC castle now stand in the grounds of the Brecon Hotel, and permission to view must be obtained from the hotel. A large motte and bailey, parts of the walls and two towers survive. The destruction of the castle during the Civil War was hastened by the inhabitants of Brecon, who did not want either side to occupy it.
Brecknock Museum Glamorgan Street, Brecon (0874 624121). The collections include local history, natural history and a large archaeology section, from pre-Roman to medieval times. The prize exhibit is a dug-out canoe found in Llangorse Lake. *Open Mon-Sat 10.00-13.00, 14.00-17.00 (Sun Apr-Sep only).*

Museum of the South Wales Borderers and the Monmouthshire Regiment The Barracks, Brecon (0874 623111). History of two famous regiments over 280 years. *Open Mon-Sat Apr-Sep (closed Sun); Mon-Fri Oct-Mar (closed Sat & Sun).*
Tourist Information Centre Cattle Market, Brecon (0874 622485). *Closed in winter.*
Llanfrynach
Powys. An attractive village built in a square round the pretty church. Nearby is the site of a Roman bath house. The white-painted pub dates from the 13thC.

BOATYARDS

Ⓑ **Cambrian Cruisers** Ty Newydd, Pencelli, Brecon (0874 665315). Narrowboat hire.

PUBS

Many pubs and restaurants in Brecon, including:
- **Wellington** Bulwark, Brecon.
- **Boars Head** Watergate, Brecon. Real ales, garden, *lunchtime* food.
- **Gremlin** The Watton, Brecon.
- **Old Ford** Llanhamlach. On A40. ½ mile east of bridge 160. Welcoming pub serving Felinfoel real ale. Food.
- **White Swan** Llanfrynach. ¾ mile from bridges 158 or 157. Food, garden, real ale, children welcome.

Monmouthshire & Brecon Canal. *Derek Pratt.*

OXFORD

Maximum dimensions

Oxford to Napton
Length: 72'
Beam: 6' 10"
Headroom: 6' 6"
Braunston to Hawkesbury
Length: 72'
Beam: 7'
Headroom: 6'

Manager
(0926) 812882

Mileage

OXFORD (River Thames) to
Duke's Cut: 3
Thrupp: 7½
Lower Heyford: 14¾
Aynho Wharf: 20¼
Banbury: 27
Cropredy: 31½
Fenny Compton Wharf: 37¾
Napton Bottom Lock: 48
NAPTON JUNCTION (Grand Union
Canal): 49¼
BRAUNSTON TURN (Grand Union Canal):
54¼
Hillmorton Bottom Lock: 61¾
Rugby Wharf Arm: 64½
Stretton Stop: 69¾
HAWKESBURY JUNCTION (Coventry
Canal): 77

Locks: 43

This was one of the earliest and for many years one of the most important canals in southern England. It was authorised in 1769, when the Coventry Canal was in the offing, and was intended to fetch coal southwards from the Warwickshire coalfield to Banbury and Oxford, at the same time given access to the River Thames. James Brindley was appointed engineer; he built a winding contour canal 91 miles long that soon began to look thoroughly out-dated and inefficient for the carriage of goods. Brindley died in 1772, and was replaced by Samuel Simcock; he completed the line from Longford, where a junction was made with the Coventry Canal, to Banbury in 1778. After a long pause, the canal was finally brought into Oxford in 1790, and thereafter through-traffic flowed constantly along this important new trade route.

In 1780, however, the Grand Junction Canal opened (excepting the tunnel at Blisworth) from London to Braunston, and the Warwick & Napton and Warwick & Birmingham canals completed the new short route from London to Birmingham. This had the natural – and intended – effect of drawing traffic off the Oxford Canal, especially south of Napton Junction; but the Oxford company protected itself very effectively against this powerful opposition by charging outrageously high rates for their 5½-mile stretch between Braunston and Napton, which had become part of the new London–Birmingham through route. Thus the Oxford maintained its revenue and very high dividends for many years to come.

By the late 1820s, however, the Oxford

Canal had become conspicuously out of date with its extravagant winding course; and under the threat of various schemes for big new canals which, if built, would render the Oxford Canal almost redundant, the company decided to modernise the northern part of their navigation. Tremendous engineering works were therefore carried out that completely changed the face of the canal north of Braunston. Aqueducts, massive embankments and deep cuttings were built, carrying the canal in great sweeps through the countryside and cutting almost 14 miles off the original 36 miles between Braunston Junction and the Coventry Canal. Much of the old main line suddenly became a series of loops and branches leading nowhere and crossed by elegant new towpath bridges inscribed 'Horseley Ironworks 1828'. Now most of these old loops are abandoned and weeded up, although their twisting course can still be easily traced.

This very expensive programme was well worth while. Although toll rates, and thus revenue, began to fall because of keen competition from the railways, dividends were kept at a high level for years; indeed a respectable profit was still shown right through to the 20th century. Now, there is no trade on the canal – but this beautiful waterway has become one of the most popular canals in Britain for pleasure cruising, fishing and walking. However, water shortages on the long top pound have always presented problems during the dry summer months and can lead to restricted lock opening times on the Claydon and Napton flights. BW are working towards a progressive improvement in the situation.

Oxford

The Oxford Canal can be reached from the
Thames in two places; one, via Duke's Cut, is
convenient but by-passes Oxford altogether;
the other, via a backwater under the north end
of Oxford station to the canal at Isis Lock, is
more enjoyable. A railway swing bridge here
was once a notorious obstruction, but this is
now left open. Past this bridge, boats continue
for 50yds along the backwater and should then
join the canal by turning sharp left into Isis
Lock. The canal continues southwards for ¼
mile past Worcester College to its terminus
near Nuffield College where there are 3-day
visitor moorings. Isis Lock, with its pretty iron
turnover bridge, is wooded and secluded,
despite its nearness to the centre of Oxford.
The canal goes northwards, flanked by houses
to the east whose gardens run down to the
water. This is an attractive stretch of urban
canal. After passing several wharves the
houses give way to industry, while Port
Meadow lies to the west. At bridge 240 there is
a PO, stores and off-licence, also swings for
children. The first Oxford Canal lift bridge
appears followed by an electric lift bridge,
opened by push button controls during
working hours, and left open at other times.
Beyond the railway bridge is Wolvercote,
where the canal starts the long climb up to the
Midlands. After a series of main road bridges,
carrying the A40 and the A34, Duke's Cut
branches off to the west to join a backwater of
the Thames, and the canal moves into open
country, leaving Oxford behind. Those joining
the River Thames from the canal should
obtain a copy of the *Nicholson/Ordnance Survey
Guide to the River Thames* and obtain a licence
from the National Rivers Authority, 2nd
Floor, King's Meadow House, Reading, Berks
RG1 8DQ (0734 535000).

Wolvercote
Oxon. PO, tel, stores, garage. Oxford spreads
north along the Woodstock and Banbury
roads, making Wolvercote inseparable from
the city. There is little of interest, although it is
useful as a supply centre, and there are swings
for children. The concrete footbridge that
crosses the canal and railway in one span is
impressive.
Oxford
*Oxon. EC Thur. MD Wed. PO, tel, stores,
garage, station, cinemas, theatres, university.*
Oxford was founded in the 10thC and has
been a university town since the 13thC. Its 39
colleges can be visited, but those noted here
have been selected as particularly
representative of their periods.
Merton College dates from 1264 and is one
of the earliest collegiate foundations that is
almost unrestored. Typical of the
Perpendicular and Decorative periods. The
Grove buildings are by Butterfield.
New College Founded by William of
Wykeham, Bishop of Winchester, in 1379.
The Perpendicular chapel was greatly restored
by Sir George Gilbert Scott in the 19thC.
Keble College Built by Butterfield in 1870
entirely in the Victorian Gothic style.
Sheldonian Theatre Broad Street. Built by
Sir Christopher Wren in the 17thC under the
auspices of Gilbert Sheldon, Archbishop of
Canterbury, who disapproved of the annual
performances of plays in St Mary's Church.
University degrees are awarded here. It has an
attractive ceiling by Robert Streeter.
Ashmolean Museum Beaumont Street.
Outstanding collection of Near Eastern and
European archaeology, the Farrer collection
of 17th and 18thC silver, a display of early
coins and some drawings of Michelangelo and
Raphael. *Open weekdays and Sun afternoons.*
Christ Church Gallery Christ Church. Built
by Powell and Moya in 1967, it contains
drawings by Michelangelo, Veronese and
Tintoretto, and 14th-18thC paintings, mainly
Italian. *Open afternoons.*
Museum of Modern Art Pembroke Street.
Gives unusual art exhibitions – anything from
environment to architecture, graphics and
photography. *Open Tue-Sat and Sun
afternoons.*

University Museum Parks Road. A high Victorian Gothic building by Deane and Woodward. Natural history, including the head and claw of a dodo. *Open weekdays.*

Christ Church Meadows Approach from St Aldate's. A path leads down to the Thames, where the rowing eights are to be seen.

University Botanic Garden High Street. Oldest botanic garden in Britain, founded by Henry Danvers, Earl of Danby. In the 17thC the garden was intended for the culture of medicinal plants, but today it fosters extensive collections of rare plants for research and teaching. The gateway is by Inigo Jones.

Tourist Information Centre St Aldate's (0865 48707).

BOATYARDS

Ⓑ **Orchard Cruisers** Castle Mill Boatyard, Cardigan Street, Oxford (0865 54043). ⓇⓈⓌⒹ Pump-out, gas, narrowboat hire, overnight mooring, long-term mooring, winter storage, dry dock, chandlery, boat building, boat and engine sales and repairs, toilets, gift shop.

Ⓑ **College Cruisers** Combe Road Wharf, Oxford (0865 54343). ⓇⓌⒹⒺ Pump-out, gas, narrowboat hire, day hire craft, overnight mooring, long-term mooring, winter storage, books and maps, boat building, boat sales, engine sales and repairs, toilets, 24hr breakdown service (*evenings* ring 0491 34155).

PUBS AND RESTAURANTS

There are many fine pubs, restaurants, wine bars and snack places in Oxford.

🍺 **Red Lion** Lower Wolvercote. Popular local serving Tetley's and Ind Coope (Burton) real ale. Basic bar snacks (*not Sun evenings*). Garden.

🍺 **White Hart** Lower Wolvercote. Bar snacks and meals *lunchtime and evenings*. Tetley's and Wadworth real ale. Patio.

🍺✕ **Plough** Upper Wolvercote. A collection of old red telephone boxes identifies this canalside pub from a distance. Real ales include Morrells, Bass and Felinfoel. Food is available *lunchtime and evenings*. The restaurant, previously the local morgue, now serves an exciting seafood menu.

🍺✕ **Trout Inn** on the Thames near Godstow Lock (10 mins walk from canal bridge 235). Dating from the 12thC, the pub commands a beautiful setting overlooking the river. Meals are served *lunchtime and evenings* in both the bar and restaurant (*not Sun evenings*), each catering for vegetarians. During the summer months there is a weekend barbecue. Bass real ale.

🍺 **Gardener's Arms** Plantation Road, Oxford. A small friendly pub serving Morrells real ale. It attracts locals from the pretty cottages nearby. Meals are served in the garden room *lunchtime and evenings.*

🍺 **Turf Tavern** 4 Bath Place, (off Holywell Street). Surprisingly secluded from the bustle of the city this pub is one of the most distinctive in Oxford. Made famous through Hardy's 'Jude the Obscure', the 13thC tavern has become popular with both students and tourists and is consequently expensive. Large choice of real ales. Bar meals and snacks. Garden, children welcome.

Oxford from the air. *Aerofilms.*

Kidlington

Continuing northwards the canal runs
through lightly wooded fields and meadows to
Kidlington, which is hidden from the canal by
a low cutting. Keeping Kidlington in the
distance, it then swings north east to join the
Cherwell valley at Thrupp. From Thrupp the
canal closely follows the Cherwell and adopts
the meandering characteristics of a contour
canal. Much of the canal is tree-lined, while its
shallow banks and close relationship with the
villages make it seem very river-like. At
Shipton Weir Lock, whose modest rise is
made up by its great width, the Cherwell and
the canal merge and share a common course
for the next mile (this stretch can be hazardous
in times of flood). The tall chimney at the
quarry and abandoned cement works on
Bunker Hill dominate the valley for several
miles. The Cherwell swings away west under
an elegant iron bridge before Baker's Lock,
but soon returns to run parallel to the canal.
Wooded hills now determine the course of the
canal, which passes plenty of villages and
places of interest. Only Thrupp yard and the
moored maintenance boats, the bridges and
the occasional locks give away the fact that this
is a canal. The railway follows the canal: the
A423 crosses by Thrupp and the A4095 by
Bunker Hill. A delightful stretch of rural
canal.

Hampton Gay

Oxon. A deserted village. The church stands
by itself, overlooking the River Cherwell, it
can only be approached on foot, its seclusion
and peace rather disturbed by the railway that
almost runs through the churchyard. To the
east, half-hidden by trees, are the romantic
ruins of the manor: gaunt broken stone walls,
windows open to the sky. The whole is well
worth exploration, but is difficult to approach
owing to the presence of the River Cherwell.
Leave the canal at bridge 220 and walk east.

Shipton-on-Cherwell

Oxon. PO box, tel. A magnificent situation: the
wooded church overlooks the bridge and the
canal, which curls round the foot of the church
yard. Behind, the grey stone manor and farm
look out over rolling fields to the west. The
well-concealed A423 does not intrude.
Shipton Bridge, ¼ mile to the east of the
village, was the scene of a railway disaster on
Christmas Eve 1874. Nine carriages fell from
the Bridge on to the frozen canal below and 34
people were killed. In the 1860s the thigh-
bones of an immense dinosaur, cetiosaurus
oxoniensis, were found in the nearby Enslow
quarry. They are now in the University
Museum, Oxford.

Blenheim Palace

Oxon. 3 miles west of
Shipton, at Woodstock. The English
Versailles, built by Sir John Vanbrugh in 1722.
Seat of the Dukes of Marlborough and
birthplace of Sir Winston Churchill, who is
buried in the nearby village of Bladon.
Grounds restyled by Capability Brown
include a large lake: altogether a superb
setting. Fine furniture, paintings, tapestries.
Open daily mid Mar-31 Oct 10.30-17.30.

Thrupp

Oxon. PO box, tel. A fine canal village, terrace
houses running along beside the towpath, with
a pub at one end and a BW yard at the other.
The quality of the village makes it an unusual
survival of early canal prosperity.

Kidlington

Oxon. PO, tel, stores, garage. The canal skirts
round Kidlington, an extended suburb of
Oxford. Parts of an older village survive to the
north around the tall-spired church, including
Sir William Morton's 17thC gabled
almshouses. Nearby is the Oxford Air
Training School, one of only 20 such places in
the world training airline pilots. The town is
most easily reached from bridge 228.

BOATYARDS

Ⓑ **BW Thrupp Yard** Kidlington (0865 2222). Ⓡ Ⓢ Ⓦ Moorings, toilets.

PUBS AND RESTAURANTS

🛶 **Rock of Gibraltar** Canalside at bridge 216. Henry Baker, once landlord of this pub and a contractor during the building of the canal, has a nearby lock named after him. Food *lunchtime and evenings* from the servery in this well-kept establishment. Ruddles, Ushers and Bass real ale as well as a good selection of wines. Garden.

🛶 **Boat Inn** Thrupp. Canalside near bridge 221. A popular pub with boaters serving Morrells real ale. Food *lunchtime and evenings.*

🛶✕ **Jolly Boatman** Thrupp, by bridge 223. A smart pub which was originally two cottages, now serving food *lunchtime and evenings* in both the bar and restaurant. Morrells real ale.

🛶 **Wise Alderman** Kidlington. Canalside at bridge 224. Comfortable town pub with a canalside garden dispensing Hook Norton, Wadworth and Tetley's real ales. Food *lunchtime and evenings.*

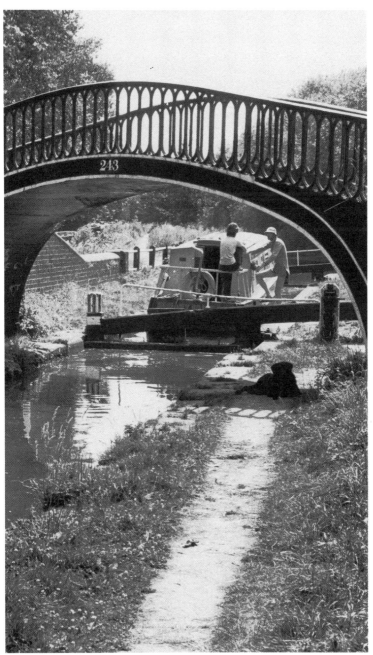

Isis Lock, with its pretty iron turnover bridge. *David Perrott.*

Lower Heyford

The canal continues to follow the Cherwell,
winding its way through wooded undulating
scenery. The canal does not intrude at all, in
fact it is so well landscaped as to be often
invisible from the hills on either side. At first
the woods are thick, the overhanging trees
forming a tunnel through which the canal
passes, bounded by old stone walls. Pigeon's
Lock marks the centre of the woods, which
gradually diminish to reveal rolling farmland
to the east and the water-meadows of the
Cherwell to the west. The canal passes over
the route of Akeman Street, and then the trees
and the isolation return to conceal the canal
from the grounds of Rousham House. As it
reaches Lower Heyford the landscape opens
out. The locks continue the rise towards
Claydon. Kirtlington and Tackley are set up
on ridges away from the canal, but Lower
Heyford actually reaches its banks. Here the
wharf is now a hire boat base. The railway
follows the canal very closely: Heyford station
is very convenient. The B4030 crosses here.

Lower Heyford
Oxon. PO, tel, stores, station. Built among
woods along the south bank of the Cherwell,
and hence the canal. The church, with fine
stained glass, overlooks the canal from a slight
hill that conceals many of the cottages in a
village where motor cars still seem intruders.
To the north is a fine and very ancient water
mill, screened by a line of willow trees.
Rousham House Steeple Aston. A lively
picture of fighting during the Civil War is
conjured up by the shooting holes made in the
doors, which are preserved from the time
when a Royalist garrison used the house. It
dates from 1635 and was enlarged and its
gardens landscaped in 1730 by William Kent.
*Open Wed, Sun & B. Hol afternoons Apr–Sep.
Gardens open daily.*
Northbrook Bridge The stone canal bridge
adjoins a much earlier packhorse bridge that
crosses the Cherwell to the east.
Tackley
Oxon. PO, tel, stores, garage. 1 mile north west
of Pigeons Lock across the Cherwell. (Access
from the canal is by the footpath and a bridge
leading from Pigeons Lock. It is a pleasant
walk.) A residential stone village, spreading
down towards the canal to include Nethercott
where there is a small station, Tackley Halt.
The church, set on a hill to the south, contains
fine monuments.
Kirtlington
Oxon. 1 mile east of Pigeons Lock. *PO, tel,
stores.* Stone village laid out around a green.

BOATYARDS

ⓑ **Oxfordshire Narrowboats** Canal Wharf,
Lower Heyford (0869 40348). Ⓡ Ⓦ Ⓓ
Pump-out (*Mon–Fri*), narrowboat hire, overnight mooring, long-term mooring, dry dock,
chandlery, books and maps, boat building,
boat sales, engine repairs, boat hoist, gifts.
ⓑ **Boat Maintenance Services** Canal
Wharf, Lower Heyford (0860 577480,
evenings 0867 53885). *24 hour* breakdown
service and engine sales and repairs.

PUBS AND RESTAURANTS

🍺 **Red Lion** Steeple Aston. Follow the path
north from bridge 205.
🍺 **White Lion** Steeple Aston. Morrells real
ale is served in this friendly village local. Hot
and cold bar food available *lunchtime and
evenings*. Garden. Pub games. B & B.
🍺 **Bell** Market Square, Lower Heyford.
🍺 **Gardiner Arms** Tackley. Aylesbury,
Tetley's and a guest real ale are served in this
pleasant pub. Bar food *lunchtime and evenings*,
vegetarians catered for. Garden. Pub games.
Children welcome.
🍺 **Kings Arms** Tackley. Morrells real ale and
bar snacks. Garden. Children welcome.
🍺 **Dashwood Arms** Kirtlington. An
attractive pub overlooking the village green
serving Halls real ale. Food.
🍺✕ **Oxford Arms** Kirtlington (0869
50208). Halls real ale. Food available in both
the bar and restaurant.

Somerton

Continuing north along the Cherwell valley, the canal wanders through water-meadows, the high towpath hedge often obscuring the fine views across the valley. As it curves towards Somerton the canal enters a short cutting and then moves out into open pastureland. Somerton climbs up the hillside to the east, altogether a very attractive situation. Throughout this stretch the canal is isolated in the middle of the landscape, the locks are generally remote, and set among trees, a pattern only broken at Heyford Common Lock. However, the open country continues after Somerton Deep Lock, and the canal pursues a straighter course towards Banbury. After Somerton two railways run side by side to the east of the canal, before joining at Aynho.

Aynho
Northants. EC Tue. PO (a.m. only), tel. The village is 1 mile east of Aynho Wharf, but must be seen. A self-contained village square sheltered from the road, very unchanged, very complete in rich stone. New houses have been carefully blended with the old. Note the peach trees that have been trained along the walls of many of the cottages. On the other side of the road is the formal classical facade of Aynho Park, a 17thC mansion rebuilt by Sir John Soane in the late 18thC. The house is large but restrained, and does not look out of place in a village street. Fine paintings, furniture and Venetian glass. *Open Wed & Thur afternoons May–Sep.* The church beside the house was classicised at the same time: the strange facade added to the nave wall makes it a charming folly.

Clifton
Oxon. PO box, tel. Small village, overlooking the canal.

Somerton
Oxon. PO box, tel. A straggling grey stone village winding up the hill to the east of the canal. On the highest point is the church with its decorated tower: there are good 16thC tombs inside. In all the villages along the Cherwell valley the churches are placed on mounds or higher ground, overlooking the valley.

Upper Heyford
Oxon. PO, tel. A main street of thatched stone cottages falls steeply to the canal, with views across the valley to Steeple Aston. The huge USAF Heyford airfield, to the east, makes its presence felt. F-111s fly from here.

BOATYARDS
Ⓑ **Anglo Welsh Narrowboats** Aynho Wharf, Banbury (0869 38483). Ⓡ Ⓢ Ⓦ Ⓓ Pump-out, narrowboat hire, gas, wet dock, engine repairs, overnight mooring, toilets, provisions, canal shop. *Facilities available Mon–Fri.*

PUBS AND RESTAURANTS
◖ **Great Western Arms** Aynho Wharf. The interior of this popular pub is devoted to memorabilia of the GWR. Hook Norton real ale. Bar meals are available *lunchtime and evenings Easter–Oct (not Sun in winter).* Family room. Garden.
◖ **Cartwright Arms** Aynho.
◖✕ **Duke of Cumberland's Head** Clifton. 'Filthy ale and disgusting food' are advertised by the somewhat eccentric landlord at this attractive pub. Good food is available in both the bar and the popular restaurant (*not Sun evenings*) but service can be erratic. A well-kept selection of real ales including Hook Norton, Ruddles and Jennings. Garden. Children welcome. B & B.
◖ **Barley Mow** Upper Heyford. A plush village local serving Fuller's real ale. Bar food. Garden. Children welcome.
◖ **Three Horseshoes** Upper Heyford. Basic local. Food available *lunchtime and evenings.*

King's Sutton

The canal continues through wooded open
country with a background of hills to the east.
The Cherwell crosses the canal at Aynho Weir
Lock before continuing parallel to it and
forming a large loop lined by trees as it
approaches King's Sutton. Then the tall spire
of the church comes into view. Locks continue
the rise to Banbury: the very narrow Nell
Bridge, where the B4100 crosses the canal, is
one of the oldest, having survived the various
road-widening schemes. The railway follows
the canal to the east. This pleasant rural
stretch of the canal along the Cherwell valley is
well punctuated by the characteristic wooden
lift bridges: luckily most of these are nowadays
left open (raised). Railway and motorway now
bracket the canal intruding into its rural peace.
In parts the skilful sinking of the motorway
into deep cuttings has helped to lessen its
impact upon the countryside, but the steady
drone of the traffic is still discernible. At
Twyford bridge is Banbury Lawnmower
Repair Service. *Open all week from dawn till
dusk* this useful outfit also supplies water, sells
groceries, calor gas and diesel and will even
run you to the local pub.

King's Sutton
Northants. PO, tel, stores, garage, station. An
attractive village of narrow streets that wander
in every direction. The centre is round a
green, at the top of a hill, where rows of
thatched cottages, two pubs and the church
stand in quiet harmony. The church is superb:
beautifully proportioned with a tall, slender
spire. The Saxon font, found buried in the
churchyard in 1923, has been linked with the
baptism in 662 AD of St Rumbold who was
born at nearby Walton Fields. It is estimated
that it is about 1000 years old. The River
Cherwell makes access to this village difficult
from the canal; the only practicable access is
by walking south east for 1½ miles from bridge
177.
Adderbury
Oxon. EC Wed. PO, tel, stores, garage. West of
bridge 177. The large expanse of village green
surrounded by splendid houses and overlooked by the old coaching inn gives
Adderbury an air of affluence. The church was
fortunate in benefiting from the experience of
the medieval master mason Richard
Winchcombe and is one of the finest examples
of Decorated and Perpendicular architecture
in the country. Sadly the building was
neglected and had to be restored in the 19thC.
The graceful spire is one of the famous three
that stand in line across the countryside in full
view of the Oxford road.

PUBS AND RESTAURANTS
🍺 **Three Tuns** King's Sutton. Cosy and
friendly local serving bar snacks. Garden.
Children welcome.
🍺 **Butcher's Arms** King's Sutton. A lively
family pub serving Hook Norton and Flowers
real ale. Food available *lunchtime and evenings*.
Garden and play area. Pub games. Quiz night
Tue.
🍺 **White Horse** The Square, King's Sutton.
🍺✕ **Red Lion Hotel** Adderbury.
Overlooking the village green this fine old
coaching inn has been beautifully restored.
Features discovered during the restoration
work indicate that this ancient Royalist
hostelry dates from before the civil war. Hook
Norton, Flowers and Wadworth real ale.
Reasonably priced food is available in both the
bar and restaurant *lunchtime and evenings (not
Sun)*. Vegetarians catered for. Garden.
Children welcome. B & B.
🍺 **Coach and Horses** Adderbury. An
attractive little pub offering an interesting
menu at reasonable prices. Children welcome.
🍺 **Bell Inn** Adderbury. It is worth the walk
down the village street to find this little pub
dating back to 1779. Varied choice of real ales
including Hook Norton, Flowers, Fuller's,
Bass, plus a guest beer.

Banbury

Continuing north west along the Cherwell
valley the canal enters Banbury through
housing estates and an industrial area. North
of Banbury the factories continue but
gradually give way on the east to open fields.
Your nose may tell you there is a General
Foods Company factory west of bridge 162.
To the west a main road follows the canal,
accompanied by power lines and disused
railways. Hardwick Lock marks the end of
Oxford countryside. The canal swings north
east and hills rise on the west. Locks
continue the steady rise throughout this stretch; north
of here all the locks feature double bottom
gates, which make for lighter work. The
railway follows the canal but crosses to the
west after Banbury. The A422 crosses at
Banbury.

Little Bourton
Oxon. ½ *mile west of bridge 158. PO box, tel,
stores, garage.* Quiet residential village to the
west of the beautifully kept Little Bourton
Lock and cottage. Stores at the garage open
each day till late.

Banbury
*Oxon. EC Tue. MD Thur, Sat. PO, tel, stores,
garage, cinema, station.* The view of Banbury
from the canal is not really fair to the town; it
is far more attractive than the dismal industry
and housing estates imply. Originally a wool
town, the castle was pulled down by
Cromwell's forces in 1646 and no trace
remains. The ancient cross of nursery rhyme
fame in the town centre was pulled down in
1602, and the present cross is a 19thC replica.
The church was built in 1793 by S. P.
Cockrell. The original bake house, which
produced the spiced Banbury cakes, was
demolished in 1968.

Tourist Information Centre & Museum
8 Horsefair, Banbury (0295 259855). *Open all
year Apr-Sept 10.00-17.00 Mon-Sat, Oct-
March 10.00-16.30 Tue-Sat.*

Broughton Castle
Broughton. 3 miles south
west of Banbury, on B4035. Mainly moated
Tudor castle with fine period fireplaces,
ceilings and panelling. Collection of Civil War
relics. *Open mid-May to mid-Sep Wed and Sun
afternoons only. Also Thur afternoons during
July/Aug.* Admission charge.

Sulgrave Manor
Sulgrave. 8 miles north east
of Banbury. Small Elizabethan manor house
completed in 1560 by Lawrence, direct
ancestor of George Washington. The design of
arms, consisting of three stars and two stripes,
which are found in the main doorway.
Contemporary furniture, portraits and
personal possessions of George Washington.
The Great Kitchen contains a range of
impressive antique equipment. *Open every day
except Wed. Closed Jan/Feb.*

BOATYARDS
Ⓑ **Morse Marine** Factory Street, Banbury
(0295 261221). Ⓡ Ⓦ Ⓔ Gas, long-term
mooring, dry dock, chandlery, books and
maps, boat building, boat sales, engine sales
and repairs, *24 hour* breakdown service.
Ⓑ **Sovereign Narrowboats** Banbury Canal
Centre, Compton Road, Banbury (0295
275657). Ⓡ Ⓢ Ⓦ Ⓓ Ⓔ Pump-out, gas,
narrowboat hire, long-term mooring, winter
storage, dry dock, chandlery, books and maps,
engine repairs, toilets.

PUBS
🍺 **Bell Inn** Great Bourton. 1¼ miles west of
bridge 153.
🍺 **Ye Olde Reindeer Inn** Parson Street,
Banbury. Dating from 1570, this pub offers
Hook Norton real ale. Bar food. Outside
seating area.
🍺 **Flying Horse** Parson Street, Banbury.
Ruddles real ale is served in this dark, low-
ceilinged pub.
🍺 **Muswell's** Bridge Street, Banbury. A
continental bar and café attracting young
people. Food available *lunchtime and evenings*.
Children's menu and drinks.
🍺 **Woolpack** Horsefair, Banbury. Cosy pub
serving Ruddles and Webster's real ale.

Cropredy

Continuing north along the Cherwell valley the canal enters Cropredy, whose stone cottages and wharf have been visible for some time. The village flanks the canal on the west bank, and all services are beside Cropredy Bridge. After the village the high towpath hedge conceals the open fields beyond, although there are views across the valley to the west. Milk, eggs and sometimes vegetables can be bought at Forge Farm. Around here the old ridge and furrow field patterns are very pronounced. Claydon comes into sight – here five locks take the canal to the summit level. Light woods border the canal, which is both shallow and very narrow in places. Near the second lock the remains of old stabling for boat horses can be seen; after the locks the canal twists and turns, swinging north west towards Fenny Compton. Hills and trees close in, preparing for the cutting that marks the course of the old tunnel. The feeder from Boddington reservoir, 2½ miles to the east, enters the canal through the towpath bridge 142. The railway, which moved to the west after Cropredy, reappears beside the canal. Bridge 141 is the last that the north-bound traveller sees of the very attractive wooden lift bridges that are such a well known feature of this canal.

Claydon
Oxon. PO, tel. Set in a rolling open landscape to the west of the canal. Claydon is an old-fashioned brown-stone village; in spite of some new development it preserves a quiet unpretentious charm. The curiously irregular Church of St James the Great provides a focal point – parts of it date from before the 12thC and the tower, which has a saddle back roof, contains a clock. There is no face, but the hour is chimed. Clattercote Priory, just to the south, still remains.
The Granary Museum Claydon. Andrew Fox's fascinating museum of local relics continues to grow and never fails to entrance visitors. Children love to handle the objects, and his recreation of a 19thC cottage kitchen is remarkably atmospheric. Well-stocked gift shop. Modest admission charge.
Cropredy
Oxon. PO, tel, stores, garage. Quiet village of wandering streets of old brick houses. There is no real centre, but the whole village is very close to the canal, especially the garage and stores. The stately sandstone church contains fine woodwork; the slow swing of the clock pendulum in the belfry seems to echo the sleepy nature of the village, which only bursts into life during the annual Folk Festival, now Europe's largest. It is held on the second weekend in August, ticket details on 0869 37142. It all began in 1979, when 'Fairport Convention' held their farewell concert here.
Battle of Cropredy 29 June 1644.
Cromwell's forces under Waller attacked Cropredy Bridge in an attempt to open a way to Oxford. Despite greatly inferior numbers the Royalist cavalry managed to scatter Waller's army and capture his artillery.

PUBS AND RESTAURANTS
🍺✕ **Brasenose Inn** Cropredy. Hook Norton and Bass real ale. Taunton draught cider. Extensive menu for both the bar and restaurant including children's menu and vegetarian dishes *lunchtime and evenings (not Tue evenings)*.
🍺 **Red Lion** Cropredy. Tetley's, Wadworth and Boddingtons real ale is served in this attractive pub, which has stone walls and flagged floors. Good straightforward food at reasonable prices. Children welcome.

Fenny Compton

The canal continues along the Fenny Compton 'tunnel', a steep, thickly wooded cutting which ends as it swings in a wide loop eastwards towards Fenny Compton Wharf. The hills retreat for a while, although their influence is still present in the extravagantly indirect course taken by the canal: Brindley seems to have had a horror of straight lines. The long winding route involves a large number of brick arch accommodation bridges and many are now un-numbered – it is easy to become disorientated here. The canal first runs west before doubling back on itself and running east to Stoneton Manor, where a steep ridge causes it to resume a north-westerly direction towards Napton. Fenny Compton and Wormleighton are both about a mile from the canal; Priors Hardwick is nearer, across the fields, but has no supplies. The railway disappears to the west after Fenny Compton Wharf; the A423 crosses twice by Fenny Compton. Although the towpath is in a poor state of repair on this section, short sections having eroded away entirely, BW has plans for improvement along the whole of the remote top pound.

Priors Hardwick
Warwicks. East of bridge 124. PO box, tel. Approachable from the canal by a footpath (all gates along the way must be left closed). A small, partly deserted village much of which was pulled down by Cistercian monks in the 14thC. The squat stone church is partly 13thC while the little cottage opposite the former school looks as if it were straight out of a picture book.

Wormleighton
Warwicks. Tel. A manorial village that still retains a feeling of privacy. Its 13thC brown stone church contains a Perpendicular screen and Jacobean woodwork. Further up the road from the canal (leave at bridge 135) is the early 16thC brick manor house that must once have been very impressive. South of the house is a grand stone gatehouse dated 1613. A row of Victorian mock-Tudor cottages completes the village, which is well worth a visit for its feeling of unity and self-reliance.

Fenny Compton
Warwicks. PO, tel, stores, garage. 1 mile west of the wharf. A scattered brown stone village, whose attractiveness is rather marred by a large housing estate near the canal. The church is partly 14thC and partly Victorian, with a curious offset tower; alongside is a fine brick rectory of 1707. Most of the village follows the road, which forms a central square containing the most interesting buildings and shops. All the houses are graced by well-laid out gardens. Fenny Compton Tunnel is no more, having been converted into a cutting in 1868.

BOATYARDS
Ⓑ **Cowroast** Fenny Marina, Fenny Compton (0295 770461). Ⓡ Ⓢ Ⓦ Ⓓ Pump-out, gas, overnight mooring, long-term mooring, slipway, dry dock, chandlery, boat building, boat sales, repairs, toilets, grocery shop, books and maps. *Please, no winding (turning) here.*

PUBS
🍺✕ **Butchers Arms** Priors Hardwick. A very smart establishment with a fine restaurant and extensive wine list. Worth visiting to enjoy the exquisite 4½ acre garden which has been created by the Italian owners.
🍺✕ **George and Dragon** Fenny Compton Wharf. Canalside pub serving Bass real ale. Cold buffet and basket meals in the bar. Restaurant open *evenings only.* Children's play area. Ⓦ
🍺 **Merrie Lion** Fenny Compton.

Napton

The canal continues northwards through rolling open farmland, the view to the west concealed by the towpath hedge. At Marston Doles the country opens out and the windmill on top of Napton Hill comes into view. Here the summit level ends and the canal starts the fall towards the junction that continues through this heavily locked section.

The arm to the east, now used for private moorings, leads to the site of the former pump house. The canal swings to the west of Napton Hill, passing Brickyard Bridge and then turns east to meet the Grand Union at the junction. Marston Doles is a typical canal settlement, but Napton is set to the east on the side of the hill. There are moorings available at Napton Bottom Lock.

Napton-on-the-Hill
Warwicks. PO, tel, stores, garage. Rising to over 400ft, Napton Hill dominates the immediate landscape. The village is scattered all over the hill, climbing steeply up the sides. The shops and pubs are at the bottom, however, and so only those wishing to enjoy the view or visit the 13thC church need climb to the top. Legend has it that the church was to be built on the village green but the devil persisted in carrying the building stones to the present site where the church was eventually built. Seven counties can be seen from this high vantage point. Near the church is the restored windmill alone on the hilltop. The canal wanders round the base of the hill, by-passing the village except for the wharf alongside Brickyard Bridge.

Holt Farm Between Marston Doles and Napton by Green's Lock (092 6812225). Farm shop, souvenirs, off-licence and moorings. See signs for opening hours.

Marston Doles
Warwicks. Tel. Tiny settlement that owes its existence to the canal. Towing horses used to be stabled here. To the north, at the end of an arm, are the remains of a pumping house.

BOATYARDS
Ⓑ **Calcutt Boats** Calcutt Top Lock (on the Grand Union), Southam (092 681 3757). R S W D Pump-out, gas, slipway, narrowboat hire and building, repairs, long-term mooring, winter storage, crane, dry dock, chandlery, toilets and provisions.

Ⓑ **Napton Narrowboats** Napton Marina, Stockton (092 681 3644). R S W D Pump-out, gas, narrowboat hire, overnight mooring, long-term mooring, winter storage, slipway, crane, groceries, chandlery, books and maps, boat building, boat sales, wet dock, engine sales and repairs, toilets, gifts.

PUBS AND RESTAURANTS
■✕ **Kings Head Inn** 200yds south of bridge 109 (092 681 2202). Ind Coope (Burton) real ale, food, games room, garden.

■✕ **Napton Bridge Inn** Napton. Canalside at bridge 111. (092 681 2466). A justly famous pub serving Davenports real ale and food in the bar or in the restaurant.

■ **Crown** Napton. ½ mile east of bridge 113 with PO and stores nearby. Friendly local with garden area to the rear. Banks's real ale. Bar snacks. A large horse chestnut tree planted to commemorate the coronation of George V provides a shady drinking area on the green.

■ **Folly** Napton. Next to bridge 113. A welcoming family pub dispensing an interesting choice of real ales. An unusual menu offers up to 19 different pies, including vegetarian. Garden area, children welcome.

■✕ **Hollybush** Priors Marston. 1½ miles east of bridge 119. 15thC inn serving Theakston, Marston's and Hook Norton real ale. Food available in the bar and restaurant *lunchtime and evenings (not Sun).* Play area and children's room.

■ **Falcon** Hellidon Road, Priors Marston. An exciting choice of real ales is served from behind the bar of this fine 15thC pub including Bishop's Finger, Falcon, Pendle Witch's Brew and Old Grumble. Interesting but expensive food *lunchtime and evenings.*

Map labels

108 Nimrod bridge

A425

OXFORD (GRAND UNION) CANAL

GRAND UNION CANAL

Napton Junction

continued page 65 GRAND UNION CANAL

5M   0L
Braunston
Oxford
49¼M   39L

Ⓑ

Ⓑ

N ←

Coventry Road bridge 109

Stockton road bridge 110

A425

111 Napton bridge

N ↑

Napton Brickyard
112 Brickyard bridge

olly turning point

113 The Folly bridge

Napton on the Hill

W RS

Napton bottom lock

114 Gilkes bridge

115 Shut bridge

Napton locks 49' 1"

116 Green's lock

Holt Farm

OLD ENGINE HOUSE ARM

117 Old Engine House bridge

118 Twenty Acre bridge

Marston Doles

119 Marston Doles bridge

Napton top lock (50')

B W Oxford Canal offices

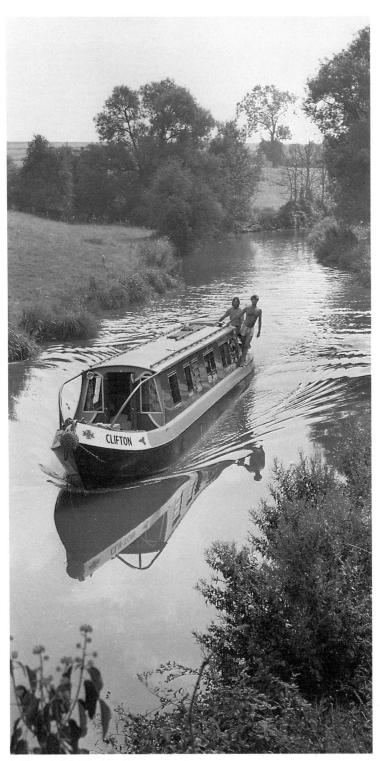

Cruising on the Oxford Canal. *Derek Pratt.*

The map on the left shows the canal route with the following labels (top to bottom):

- OXFORD CANAL
- N 89
- GRAND UNION CANAL page 64
- B
- W
- 91 Castle bridge
- A45(T)
- 90
- RSW
- Braunston Turn
- 94 & 93
- 95 Turnover bridge
- Braunston puddle banks
- 96 aqueduct
- 97
- Wolfhampcote Hall
- 98 Ivy bridge
- 99 Hargreaves bridge
- 100 Chambers bridge
- 2¼M 0L Braunston / Napton 2¾M 0L
- 101 Nethercote bridge
- 102 Flecknoe road bridge
- OXFORD/GRAND UNION CANAL
- New bridge 103
- Jacksons bridge 104
- A425
- 105
- Lower Shuckburgh
- 107 Garners bridge

Braunston

Leaving Napton, the canal runs north east to Braunston Turn. This stretch of the Oxford Canal was used jointly by the Grand Junction Company, and as a result the Oxford charged excessive toll rates in an attempt to get even with their rival, whose more direct route to London had attracted most of the traffic. Proceeding through open country with a background of hills to the south, the canal is quiet and empty after the activity around Napton. The land is agricultural, with few houses in sight: the surviving medieval ridge and furrow system on the south bank reveals the age of the landscape, Note how the canal cuts the system at right angles. There are no locks, no villages and few bridges: a very pleasant stretch of rural canal. The A425 crosses through Lower Shuckburgh and the A45 in Braunston. The Oxford Canal bears off to the north at Braunston Turn: the Grand Union heads south east at this point, passing through the canal centre of Braunston. Boaters will find almost everything they are likely to need here. There are good temporary moorings either side of bridge 91.

Lower Shuckburgh
Warwicks. PO box. A tiny village along the main road. The church, built in 1864, is attractive in a Victorian way, with great use of constrasting brickwork inside. The farm, west of bridge 104, sells eggs.

Braunston
Northants. PO, tel, stores, butcher. Set up on a hill to the north of the canal, so that the spire of Braunston church dominates the valley for miles around. The village is really a long main street, with houses of all periods that give the feeling of a spacious market town. The village is a very well known canal centre, and as such is no less significant today than when the Oxford and Grand Junction Canals were first connected here.

BOATYARDS

Ⓑ **Braunston Boats** Bottom Lock, Braunston (0788 891079). Ⓦ Ⓓ Pump-out, gas, narrowboat hire, long-term mooring.
Ⓑ **Braunston Marina** The Wharf, Braunston (0788 891373). Under the fine bridge dated 1834. Ⓡ Ⓢ Ⓦ Ⓓ Gas, pump-out, overnight mooring, long-term mooring, winter storage, dry dock, wet dock, chandlery, boat building, engineering – all services. Toilets.
Ⓑ **Boatserve** The Wharf, Braunston (0788 891971).
Ⓑ **Midland Chandlers** Canalside, Braunston (0788 891401).
Ⓑ **Union Canal Carriers** Canalside, Braunston (0788 890784). Ⓢ Ⓓ Pump-out, gas, narrowboat hire, overnight mooring by arrangement, long-term mooring, books and maps, boat building, boat sales, engine sales and repairs. 24hr breakdown service (ring 0788 812156 *evenings*).

PUBS AND RESTAURANTS

Ⓟ✕ **Boatman** Braunston (0788 891313). Once the Rose & Castle, now a comfortable and friendly modern hotel/restaurant/pub. Ruddles and Wilson's real ale. Interesting bar menu at reasonable prices. Children's room, canalside garden with swings and overnight moorings for patrons.
Ⓟ **Old Plough** High Street, Braunston. Imposing 17thC pub of great character, serving Ind Coope (Burton) and Ansells real ale, and food *lunchtime and evenings*. Garden.
Ⓟ **Wheatsheaf** The Green, Braunston. A locals' pub with a striking red bar, dispensing Courage, Webster's and Ruddles real ale. Snacks.

Willoughby

North west from Braunston the canal runs
through wide open country, backed by bare
hills to the east. At bridge 87 the medieval
ridge and furrow patterns are in evidence.
Skirting round Barby Hill, the canal swings
north east towards Hillmorton and Rugby.
The railway and the A45 run to the west of the
canal, and the M45 crosses after Barby Hill.

Willoughby
Warwicks. PO, tel, garage, transport cafe.
Mellow red-brick village to which new
buildings have been unobtrusively added. The
small church is dominated by a fine 18thC
rectory.

BOATYARDS

The Boat Shop (0788 891310). This started
on board a boat moored at Braunston Turn,
now a shop by Braunston bottom lock selling
chandlery, coal, groceries, fruit and vegetables
and canal ware. *Open 08.00-20.00 June-Sep,
08.00-18.00 Oct-May.*

PUBS

🍺 **Rose Inn** Willoughby. An attractively
maintained thatched village pub, offering John
Smith's real ale. Bar meals *lunchtime and
evenings (not Sun evenings)*. Outside seating
and play area. Children welcome.

Hillmorton

After running north east for 2 miles, the canal swings in a wide arc round Rugby. To the east the radio masts dominate the landscape. The canal descends Hillmorton Locks, a flight of three paired narrow locks, and passes the attractively sited BW maintenance yard and hire craft base. There is an excellent all-purpose grocer's shop at bridge 71. The railway accompanies the canal through Hillmorton and the A428 crosses south of the town. The little brick footbridge at the bottom locks is delightful.

Hillmorton
Warwicks. PO, tel, stores, garage, take-aways, but all a fair distance from the canal. Its church dates from c1300, but there have been additions as late as the 18thC. There is an interesting medieval cross in the centre of the village, but the independence this implies has long since been swallowed up by Rugby.

BOATYARDS
ⓑ **Hillmorton Lock Services** The Locks, Hillmorton (0788 578661). Ⓡ Ⓢ Ⓦ Dry dock, boat re-painting, engineering services, signwriting, boat covers. *24 hour* boat emergency breakdown call out.
ⓑ **Clifton Cruisers** Clifton Wharf, Vicarage Hill, Clifton on Dunsmore (0788 543570). Ⓡ Ⓦ Ⓓ Pump-out, gas, narrowboat hire, long-term mooring, groceries, chandlery, books and maps, boat building, engine repairs, off-licence, gifts.
ⓑ **Club Line Cruisers** Hillmorton Wharf, Crick Road, Rugby (0788 577300). Ⓢ Ⓦ Ⓓ Pump-out, mooring, chandlery, gift shop, dry dock, engine repairs, toilets. *Closed Sat.*

PUBS
🍺 **Clifton Inn** Clifton Road, Rugby. South of bridge 66. Popular locals' pub with mock Tudor façade. Pleasant lounge, basic bar and leaded windows. Ansells and Ind Coope (Burton) real ale, snacks, garden.
🍺 **Stag & Pheasant** School Street, Hillmorton. Good basic pub offering Ansells real ale and snacks.
🍺 **Old Royal Oak** Canalside at bridge 73. A substantial brick pub with a very tidy garden. Marston's real ale and bar meals *lunchtime and evenings.* Children's room and play area. Mooring for patrons.

Rugby

Continuing the swing round Rugby, the canal enters a side cut embankment whose tall towpath hedge hides the town from view. There are shops to the south of bridge 59 and a picnic area below bridge 58, with a huge Tesco supermarket nearby. The River Avon is crossed by an aqueduct, and the Rugby Arm branches to the west; there is a boatyard on the arm. A short open stretch and then another deep cutting take the canal to Newbold, where the short tunnel and thickly-wooded cutting lead the canal into open countryside. The iron bridges over the various arms reveal the course of the old canal.

Harborough Magna
Warwicks. PO, tel, stores. Quiet red-brick village 1 mile to the north of the canal from bridges 43 or 48. The 14thC church has an interesting stained-glass window.

Newbold on Avon
Warwicks. PO, tel, stores, garage, fish & chips. A pleasant village with an interesting 15thC church and attractive cottages.

Newbold Tunnel
This 250yd long tunnel was built during the shortening of the Oxford Canal in the 1820s. The old route was at right angles to the new, and the old tunnel mouth can be seen from the south by Newbold church. The new tunnel was cut wide enough to allow for a towpath on both sides, a luxury at that date.

Rugby
Warwicks. EC Wed. MD Mon/Fri/Sat. PO, tel, stores, garage, station, theatre, cinema, leisure centre. A settlement for 2000 years, which has grown in turn as an agricultural centre, market town (since 1255), seat of learning and railway centre. More recently the heavy electrical industry has become established here. St Andrew's parish church dates from the 14thC, but in 1879 Butterfield added a nave and a tower, making it probably the only church in England to have a double peal of bells. Butterfield's work is also much in evidence in Rugby school, which also gave its name to rugby football. A granite plaque commemorating the 'exploit of William Webb Ellis' in 1823 which gave birth to the game can be seen in the grounds. Nearby in St Matthew's Street are the James Gilbert Museum of Rugby Football and the tourist Information Centre at Rugby Library, where the Exhibition Gallery and Museum have regular displays. There is a pedestrianised shopping centre, a leisure centre and an open market with a town crier. Look out for Miranda's Shop in Chapel Street, reputedly the oldest building in the town. The Monday livestock market is one of the largest in the area. Information boards and town maps will be found near bridges 30, 50 and 66.
Tourist Information Centre Rugby Library, St Matthew's Street (0788 71813).

BOATYARDS
ⓑ **T F Yates** East of bridge 44 (0788 569140). Ⓓ Repairs.
ⓑ **Willow Wren Hire Cruisers** Rugby Wharf, off Consul Road, Leicester Road, Rugby (0788 562183). Ⓡ Ⓢ Ⓦ Ⓓ Pump-out, narrowboat hire, overnight mooring, long-term mooring, wet dock, books and maps. *Closed Sun & Mon.*

PUBS
🍺 **Old Lion** Harborough Magna, on the B4112. Quiet lounge with beamed ceiling and giant handpumps for mature drinkers, separate room for the younger set. Marston's real ale, food *lunchtime and evenings,* including vegetarian dishes.
🍺 **Boat** Newbold Wharf. A pub of great character, with one long room with cosy alcoves and a fire. Bass and Greenall Whitley real ale. Extensive home cooked menu, including vegetarian, *lunchtime and evenings (not Sun evenings).* Garden, children welcome.
🍺 **Barley Mow** Main Street, Newbold. Canalside pub with two small bars and a pleasant garden. M & B real ale and food *lunchtime and evenings.*

Brinklow

Continuing north west, the canal runs through fine farming land, and passes All Oaks Wood, where good moorings have been provided. By Brinklow the canal passes over an embankment, which was originally an aqueduct; the arches have long been filled in. Brinklow Arm to the west is unnavigable. The long embankment continues through Stretton Stop and past Stretton Arm, used for mooring. Open, rolling fields follow, and then the canal enters a deep cutting, spanned by the new motorway. The M6 cuts through this stretch, and has greatly altered the landscape. The elegant iron bridges that occur periodically mark the course of the old Oxford Canal, prior to the 1829 shortening. The railway follows the canal to the east. The A4114 crosses through Brinklow.

Brinklow
Warwicks. PO, tel, stores, garage, fish & chips. A spacious pre-industrial village built along a wide main street, the A4114. The church is alongside the earthworks that mark the site of the castle built to defend the Fosse Way, and is unusual in having a distinctly sloping floor which climbs 12 feet from west to east.

BOATYARDS

Ⓑ **Rose Narrowboats** Brinklow Marina, Stretton Stop, Rugby (0788 832449). Ⓡ Ⓢ Ⓦ Ⓟ Ⓓ Ⓔ Pump-out, gas, narrowboat hire, day hire craft, overnight mooring, long-term mooring, slipway, groceries, chandlery, books and maps, boat building and painting, boat sales, engine sales and repairs. Gift shop, art gallery, pottery.

PUBS

🍺 **Railway** Canalside at Stretton Stop. Davenports and Marston's real ale in an open-plan lounge. *Lunchtime* food.
🍺 **White Lion** Broad Street, Brinklow. A welcoming local pub. Plush lounge, old fashioned bar. Banks's real ale, bar snacks *lunchtime Mon–Fri.* Garden, Children's room. B & B.
🍺 **Bulls Head** Broad Street, Brinklow. Marston's and Whitbread real ale in a sprawling, smartly furnished Brewers Fayre pub. Food, including vegetarian, available *lunchtime and evenings.*
🍺 **Raven** Broad Street, Brinklow. A friendly family pub at the top of the village, with Banks's and Marston's real ale. Extensive range of bar meals, *lunchtime and evenings.* Traditional Sunday lunch.
🍺 **Dun Cow** Coventry Road, Brinklow. Locals' pub with food available *lunchtime and evenings.* Children welcome in the lounge. Garden.

Hawkesbury Junction

Continuing north west, the canal leaves the cutting and crosses a long embankment, which is shared by the railway. The open landscape continues to Ansty, although the motorway is never far away. After the village the first signs of Coventry appear, with views of pylons and housing estates. The new Wyken Colliery Arm leaves to the west: it was built to replace the old one eaten up by the motorway which comes alongside the canal at this point. Sharp bends then lead to the stop lock before Hawkesbury Junction, the end of the Oxford Canal where it joins the Coventry. The last stretch of the Oxford is characterised by the 1820s shortenings; the straight cuttings and embankments obviously date from this period, while the cast-iron bridges mark the old route. The railway turns away before Ansty.

Ansty
Warwicks. Tel, garage. Tiny village that grew up along the canal, now disturbed by the A46. To the north are the church and Hall together; the Hall is mostly 18thC. This area has been much altered by motorway construction.

Shilton
Warwicks. PO, tel, stores, garage. ½ mile north of bridge 17. Main road village left bewildered by the railway and the A46.

PUBS AND RESTAURANTS

🍺✕ **Greyhound** Hawkesbury Junction. A fascinating pub beside the junction, decorated with canal and rugby memorabilia, together with an immense collection of Toby jugs. An imaginative selection of food, especially pies and salads, is served in the bar or restaurant *lunchtime and evenings, but not Sun or Mon evenings.* Real ales include Bass, Banks's, Stones and Highgate mild. Canalside garden and safe children's play area.

🍺 **Elephant & Castle** Canalside, by bridge 4. M & B real ale, food.

🍺✕ **Old Crown** Aldermans Green Road. A cosy pub with carved woodwork, beams, brasses, and snug settees, south of Tusses Bridge 4. Ruddles and Webster's real ale, food *lunchtime and evenings (not Sun evenings).*

🍺 **Rose and Castle** Ansty. A new pub. Food *lunchtime and evenings.* Children welcome, play area.

🍺 **Shilton Arms** Opposite the church, Shilton. Greenall Whitley and Tetley's real ale. Garden with play area.

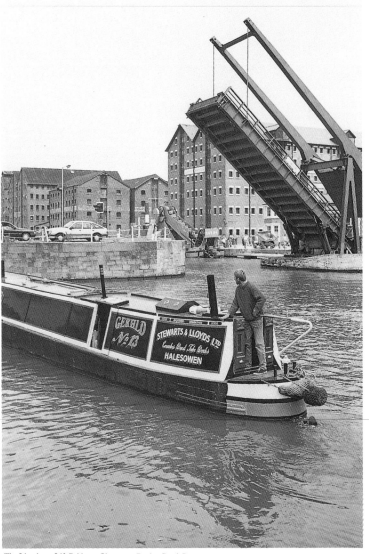

The Llanthony Lift Bridge at Gloucester Docks. *Derek Pratt*.

GLOUCESTER & SHARPNESS RIVER SEVERN

GLOUCESTER & SHARPNESS CANAL

Maximum dimensions

Length: 210'
Beam: 31' 6"
Headroom: 105'

Mileage

SHARPNESS Lock to
Purton: 1½
Saul Junction: 8
GLOUCESTER Lock: 15¼

Locks: 2

Manager

(0452) 25524

RIVER SEVERN

Maximum dimensions

Gloucester to Worcester
Length: 135'
Beam: 21'
Headroom: 24' 6"
Worcester to Stourport
Length: 90'
Beam: 19'
Headroom: 20'

Mileage

GLOUCESTER Lock to
Ashleworth: 5
Haw Bridge: 8¼
TEWKESBURY Junction with River Avon:
13
Upton upon Severn: 19
DIGLIS Junction with Worcester &
Birmingham Canal: 29
Holt Fleet: 36
STOURPORT Junction with Staffs & Worcs
Canal: 42

Locks: 5

The River Severn has always been one of the principal navigations in England. Its great length has made it an important trade artery since the medieval period. With its tributary, the Avon, it cuts deep into the heart of England, linking the iron and coal fields with the Bristol Channel and the British coastal trade. By using the Severn, boats of a considerable size could sail into the Midlands, and into Wales as far as Welshpool. However, the navigation, especially above Worcester, was always difficult, owing to currents, shoals, and the demands of water supply for milling etc.

As boats increased in size, and the cargoes became heavier, the navigational problems increased. The larger boats in common use in the 18thC could rarely sail higher than Bewdley, and so by the end of the century this inland port was beginning to lose its significance. At the same time the sandbanks and shifting shoals in the Gloucester area were seriously affecting the trade on the river

as a whole. In order for the river to survive as a viable trade route, it became necessary for drastic improvements to be made. Various Acts were passed to ensure the maintenance of the towing path, although the Severn maintained its tradition of using gangs of men to bow-haul boats until well into the 19thC. In 1803 over 150 men were still employed in what Telford called 'this barbarous and expensive slave-like office' on the section between Bewdley and Coalbrookdale.

The demands of increasing navigation, and the spread of canals in the West Midlands (the Staffordshire & Worcestershire Canal linking the Severn with Birmingham and the rest of the network was opened in 1772) led to the passing of an Act in 1793 that authorised a canal to be built from Berkeley Pill to Gloucester. Work began on Gloucester Docks in 1794, and over the next few years 5½ miles of canal were cut. Shortage of money then caused work to be stopped, and so the canal remained useless and incomplete. In 1817 Telford was commissioned by the government to report on the feasibility of the canal, with particular reference to the maintenance of navigation on the Severn. He reported in favour of continuing and completing the canal, but recommended that it should run to Sharpness instead of to Berkeley. The government then put up the money for the canal, mainly to relieve acute problems of unemployment, and after considerable delays the Gloucester & Sharpness Canal was opened throughout in 1827.

Some of the structural problems were caused by the decision to build the canal to ship standard. At the time of opening, this was the broadest, deepest canal in the world. But, although it greatly increased the cost, this far-sighted decision has ensured that the canal remains in use, and even today Gloucester and Sharpness Docks are commercial ports.

Once the canal was in use, considerable dredging works and improvements became necessary to maintain the navigation of the upper Severn to Worcester and Stourport. This work, carried out extensively since the formation of the Severn Commission in 1842, included the building of locks and weirs, and the canalisation of parts of the river. The links with the Midlands canal network helped the Severn to flourish, and railway competition increased rather than decreased the traffic both in the docks and on the ship canal. In 1874 Sharpness docks were enlarged and modernised, to handle ships of up to 1000 tons. The same year the Gloucester & Berkeley Canal Company leased the Worcester & Birmingham Canal, to maintain their hold on the trade routes to the Midlands. By 1888 the Severn had a minimum depth of over 6ft, and in most places the depth was 8 to 9ft. Trade continued to thrive, and the recession in the 1920s was soon overcome by the rapidly growing oil traffic, which became the mainstay of the river. Although commercial traffic has declined there are, now and again, signs of a revival.

Natural history

Spring is a good time to visit the River Severn, when the river banks are speckled white with cow parsley and the riverside alders and willows are bearing their catkin flowers, providing valuable nectar and pollen for early moths and bees. In March and April millions of young eels come up-river with the high spring tides after a three-year, 3000-mile journey from their breeding grounds in the western Atlantic. The elvers are followed by twaite shad, a sea fish which migrates into fresh water to spawn, and these provide sport for anglers as the fish try to ascend the weirs at Tewkesbury and Gloucester. Other migrants from the sea include 3ft-long sea lampreys and 9-in river lampreys (which are both parasitic, sucking the blood from other fish), sea trout and salmon. Spring is also the time to listen for nightingales, which sometimes sing in riverside woodlands, and to watch the caddis flies, may flies and stone flies which have newly emerged from their aquatic larvae and now dance across the surface of the water until they have mated, laid their eggs or fallen prey to some surface-feeding fish such as bleak or dace. Other fish found in the Severn include bottom-feeders such as bream, carp, roach, gudgeon, loach and occasionally barbel (which was introduced about 15 years ago), as well as carnivores such as pike, perch and eel.

It is perhaps in August that the river banks look best, with colourful clumps of yellow tansy, purple loosestrife and great willowherb with drooping heads of pink flowers. The recently introduced Himalayan balsam with its handsome pink and white flowers now grows in large clumps at Mythe Bridge near Tewkesbury, Sandhurst near Gloucester and near Gloucester Docks. In marshy areas, riverside pools and withy beds the reedmace grows with brown club-like heads, the common reed with 6ft-high stems and plumed flowerheads, and the greater and lesser pond sedges, which bear separate spikes of male (upper) and female flowers. These areas are the home of the sedge, reed and marsh warbler, although the last-named is rare nowadays.

Very few other birds nest along the Severn, although sand martins and kingfishers sometimes excavate nesting holes where the banks are steep, moorhen and mallard are found in the riverside bushes and two heron colonies are known to inhabit tall trees a little way inland from the tidal part of the river below Gloucester. The best place to look for water birds is undoubtedly the area between Frampton and Slimbridge where the extensive mud flats and sand banks exposed at low tide provide an attractive resting place for spring and autumn passage migrants. This area is especially good for winter visitors such as shoveller, pintail, wigeon, teal, lapwing, golden plover, ringed plover, dunlin, curlew, redshank and turnstone, and holds a roosting colony of about 20,000 common gulls. Two species of geese also come to feed on the riverside pastures in winter: up to 5000 whitefronted geese from Siberia and 100 pink-footed geese from Greenland.

For the most part, the mammals of our rivers are secretive and nocturnal but water vole holes are a common sight in the river banks and the observant walker can sometimes recognise the tracks or other signs of our rare native otter or the accidentally introduced North American mink, a beautifully sleek black animal a little larger than a stoat, which originally escaped from fur farms but is now breeding in the wild along all parts of the Severn which run through Gloucestershire.

Sharpness

The Gloucester & Sharpness Ship Canal,
which was built to bypass the dangerous
winding stretch of the tidal River Severn
between these two places, has its southern
terminus at Sharpness, where there are docks
and a large lock up from the Severn. The
Gloucester & Sharpness Canal is nowadays
the only navigable route between the Severn
estuary and the Severn Navigation above
Gloucester, so all boats heading upstream
must pass through Sharpness Lock and
Docks. It should be noted that the entrance to
the lock dries out completely at low water, so
boats heading in from the estuary should time
their arrival for 3 hours before high water,
notifying Sharpness in advance. The best time
to arrive at the lock is about 2½ hours before
high water when locking down, and about 1
hour before high water when locking up. (The
lock is normally operated 2½ hours before to 1
hour after high water.) BW maintain free
visitor moorings in the docks, which are
available for 48 hours. It is important to give
prior notice of one's intentions to BW at
Dursley on 0453 811644 ex 21 or 36 (or
VHF channel 14). Boatmen wishing to
proceed down the Severn estuary from
Sharpness are advised not to do so without a
pilot. It is important to keep to the marked
channel, and the tide runs extremely fast.
Immediately above the lock are Sharpness
Docks, which handle ships from all over
Europe. The docks are a very busy area and an
important source of revenue to BW's Freight
Services Division. Pleasure boats are
encouraged to move on quickly through the
two swing bridges out of the docks and onto
the ship canal itself. Just north of the two
swing bridges is an arm off to the west: this
leads to a tidal basin which is now,
unfortunately, disused. However the length of
the arm leading to it is used for permanent and
temporary pleasure craft moorings, and there
is a small boatyard at the end of it. It is a
fascinating place to walk round and see the
tidal Severn flowing strongly at the foot of the
stone walls. Across the river is the tree-lined
west bank of the river, only ½ a mile across at
this point. A railway line runs along the
bottom of the hills. However the old 22-
arched railway bridge that used to cross the
river just north of here has been completely
demolished, and only the merest pieces of
some of the stone piers can be seen at low
water. The bridge was badly damaged one
foggy night in November 1959, when a vessel
collided with it; the bridge then stood with a
hole in the middle until it was demolished and
the iron girders sold to – of all places – Chile,
where they now form a road-carrying viaduct.
Along the main line of the canal, the circular
stone structure is all that remains of the
railway's swing bridge over the canal. A mile
from Sharpness Docks, the canal is lined with
trees on each side – an uncharacteristically
river-like stretch that is belied by the
occasional glimpse of the Severn flowing
alongside. Old timber ponds open off the
canal to the right. Timber was stored afloat
here 'in the round'. Then a curve leads to the
little village of Purton and its two swing
bridges. There is only one bridge keeper and
he spends most of his time at the upper swing
bridge (0453 811384). The navigation snakes
through the village, passing the big new
waterworks before settling down to a steady
course of wide, straight reaches. It traverses a
quiet, green and predictably flat landscape
that is well studded with trees and always
bounded to the north by saltings and the mud-
flats of the Severn estuary – which is here
much wider than at Sharpness. At Patch
Bridge (0453 890324) there are two pubs; this
is the best access point to the Slimbridge
Wildfowl Trust (*See over*). There is a water
point by the bridge.

Navigational notes
1 As this is a commercial waterway, moor only
at recognised sites: Old Arm, Sharpness;
Patch Bridge; Fretherne Bridge; Sellars
Bridge; Bakers Quay; Gloucester Docks.

2 The mechanical swing bridges are manned *08.00-18.45 (16.30 winter), lunch break 13.00-13.30,* and are guarded by traffic lights. Proceed only on the green.

3 Bridges and locks operate a listening watch on marine band radio channel 74. It is not necessary to contact each bridge or lock unless you are delayed, or have an emergency.

Shepherd's Patch
Glos. This little settlement existed long before the canal: it used to be where the shepherds watched over their flocks grazing the Severn estuary. There are two pubs here and a youth hostel.

Slimbridge Wildfowl Trust Conveniently situated just ½ mile north west of the canal at Patch Bridge, the Trust is well worth visiting. It is close to the River Severn and apart from containing the largest collection of captive wildfowl (160 kinds) in the world, the Trust's grounds and adjacent water-meadows attract many thousands of migrant birds – white fronted geese, Bewick's swans and all kinds of ducks and waders. Visitors are free to walk all round the Trust's grounds and study the inhabitants, which are fascinating for their variety, quantity and behaviour. The Trust also incorporates an important research establishment that studies all biological aspects of wildfowl, with special reference to ecological trends – it also plays an important role in the defence of the various species from extinction and can already be credited with the rescue of several important species. *Open throughout the year except on Christmas Day.*

Purton
Glos. Tel. A tiny village of lean, modest houses. It derives an unusual charm from being bisected by the Ship Canal. The canal is not particularly wide here, and to have a large German coaster quietly throbbing past the cowering post office seems an incredible distortion of scale. The village has, surprisingly, two pubs – one is on the canal bank, the other is 100yds away on an enviable site beside the Severn estuary. There used to be a ford for cattle across the river nearby – the herdsman had to judge the time to cross the treacherous river to within a few minutes. Just outside Purton, a huge waterworks has been built for the city of Bristol, where up to 24 million gallons of water can be drawn daily from the Ship Canal, purified and pumped through a new 4ft pipe-line down to Bristol for drinking purposes. Small reservoirs have been constructed on the other side of the canal: these will provide a temporary feed if and when a recording device beside the canal nearer Gloucester indicates that the water is too heavily polluted to draw on.

Sharpness
Glos. Tel, bank (Mon, Thu & Fri only). Stores & garage distant. Sharpness exists only for its docks with their tall cranes, old and new warehouses and ever-changing display of foreign ships. It has a strange atmosphere and an interesting situation beside the River Severn. The Severn is wide here, and wild: the tidal range at Sharpness is believed to be the second biggest in the world and the current is very swift, especially when accompanied by the very high winds that often race up the estuary from the sea. Across the water is the hilly Forest of Dean, with a main railway line running almost along the shore. It is only half a mile away, but it could as well be another country, so remote does it seem. In terms of population, Sharpness is very strung out; here and there is a row of terraced cottages, inhabited mainly by dock workers. Along the lockside – the focus of the docks – are the buildings housing the offices of various shipping firms, HM Customs & Excise and BW. The annual tonnage handled here is now approaching the million mark, with cargoes consisting mainly of animal feedstuffs, grain, fertilisers, timber and scrap metal, coming from Ireland, Europe, Russia and Scandinavia. Finnish wooden telegraph poles are also imported at Sharpness. Ships handled here displace up to 5000 tons (the limiting dimensions of the entrance lock are 55ft beam by 21ft 6in draught). An interesting development at Sharpness is the recent conversion of the old Merchant Navy training camp (on the hill by Sharpness Marine) into an outdoor leisure activity centre for the youth of land-locked Birmingham.

BOATYARDS

ⓑ **Sharpness Marine** Floating Yacht Services Store, The Old Dock, Sharpness (0453 811476). Ⓦ Ⓓ Gas, overnight mooring, long-term mooring, chandlery, books and maps, boat building, toilets.
BW Sharpness Office beside Sharpness Lock (0453 811644).

PUBS AND RESTAURANTS

🍺✕ **Tudor Arms** Shepherd's Patch, a few yards from Patch Bridge (0453 890306). Restaurant and bar snacks, children's room.
🍺 **Berkeley Hunt** Purton, by the lower bridge.
🍺 **Berkeley Arms** Purton. 150yds from the lower bridge. Situated beside the river with an excellent view along it.
🍺 **Lammastide Inn** 1 mile east of Sharpness at Brookend. Comfortable pub with 'own brew' beer among others.

An unusual visitor at Sharpness: a Thames Sailing Barge on its way to Gloucester.

Saul Junction

The Shop Canal continues towards Gloucester, with the spacious Severn estuary over to the west. Swing bridges punctuate the canal and at almost every bridge is a bridge keeper's cottage (Junction Bridge – 0452 740444, Cam Bridge – 0453 890272). These cottages are peculiar to the Gloucester & Sharpness Canal and have great charm – they are only small single-storey buildings, but each one has a substantial Classical facade with fluted Doric columns and a pediment. At Cam Bridge is an unnavigable arm that feeds the canal with water from the Cotswolds. At Frampton on Severn the church is passed on the east side, then after a long straight the navigation bends to the north east. Trees encroach here on one side, and several bridges lead past scattered houses to Saul Junction. Over to the east the great Cotswold ridge marches parallel to the canal.

Saul Junction
This unusual waterway 'crossroad' is where the Stroudwater Canal intersects the Gloucester & Sharpness Canal. The former canal was an extension of the Thames & Severn Canal, which used to run from the Thames at Lechlade, through the Cotswolds via the great Sapperton Tunnel and thus to Stroud. Twelve locks brought the Stroudwater Canal down from this point to Saul, where it crossed the Ship Canal and continued to Framilode. Here it locked down into the tidal River Severn. Like the Thames & Severn, the Stroudwater Canal has been disused for many years, and the old lock by Saul Junction is derelict. However a 300yd stretch to the south east from the junction to the first bridge (now lowered) is navigable and in use as a mooring site. At the junction itself is a swing bridge and a cottage (previously the Junction Inn) as well as plenty of boats at the yard. The village of Saul is half a mile to the west. It is worth walking the mile from Saul Junction to the River Severn. The towpath is in good shape and this isolated section of the Stroudwater Canal is still in water. Restoration of both the Stroudwater and the Thames & Severn canals is underway.

Frampton on Severn
Glos. PO, tel, stores, garage. A beautiful linear village notable mainly for its green, which is about 100yds wide and fully half a mile long. All manner of attractive houses attach themselves to the edge of this magnificent expanse of common land, and the occasional cars that drive down the middle of it are kept in their proper scale. Trees and ponds are scattered along it; the gateway that guards the Court is on the east side. The Church of St Mary at the south end of the village, near the canal, is mainly of the 14thC. The stained glass and monuments are worth a look, and the Romanesque lead font is one of only six in Gloucestershire.

Frampton Court Facing the village green is this Georgian mansion (1731-33) whose gardens contain a Gothic Orangery (1745) and an octagonal dovecote. *Visits by written application to the owners in residence only.*

BOATYARDS
Ⓑ **R. W. Davis & Son** Junction Dry Dock, Saul, Gloucester (0452 740233). Ⓡ Ⓢ Ⓦ Ⓓ Pump-out, gas, overnight mooring, long-term mooring, winter storage, crane, dry dock, boat building, boat sales, engine sales and repairs, toilets.

PUBS
🍺 **Bell Inn** Frampton on Severn, ¼ mile south east of Fretherne Bridge.
🍺 **Three Horseshoes** Frampton, halfway along the green.

Hardwicke

On from Saul, the canal continues through
undramatic country, which is slightly wooded.
There are no villages on this section, but
several farms are situated near the canal.
Towards Sellars Bridge (0452 720251), the
navigation enters a cutting for the first time
since Sharpness. There is a pub by this bridge,
and just to the north is an oil wharf for small
ships. This is the furthest (northernmost)
point which the oil traffic reaches on the
Severn Navigation – oil used to be carried
further on past Gloucester and right up to
Stourport in barges, but this is all finished
now. North of Quedgeley Wharf the canal
approaches the River Severn (hidden behind a
flood bank and far narrower up here than
downstream); turning sharply eastward, the
canal reaches Rea Bridge.

Navigational note
The three bridges, Sellars, Rea and Sims (*see
next page*), have a greater headroom (over 7ft)
than the others on the Gloucester & Sharpness
Canal. Boats normally used on the narrow
canals will find no difficulty in getting under
these three bridges without them being
opened, although they do so at their own risk.
Boats should not pass under these bridges
without receiving a green light from the
keeper.

The Severn Bore This famous natural
phenomenon occurs on the section of the river
that is bypassed by the Gloucester &
Sharpness Canal. The Bore is a wave that
travels upstream: it is created by the strong
tidal flow encountering the 'land water' and
chasing it back up the shallow, winding river.
One of the best places from which to see the
Severn Bore is Stonebench, Elmore – only
500yds west of Lower Rea Bridge on the
G & S Canal. (Another good place is
Maisemore Weir, above Gloucester.) A Bore
occurs on the spring tides but a substantial
wave of over 7 to 9ft is a rarer occurrence. SAE
to Area Leisure Officer, BW Dock Office,
Gloucester for annual predictions.

PUBS
⬤ **Pilot** Canalside, at Sellars Bridge.
⬤ **Anchor** Epney (on the river 1½ miles west
of Park End Bridge).

Gloucester

At Rea Bridge the canal enters a cutting and describes a sharp double bend, from which one emerges into a completely different landscape: the quiet countryside has disappeared, its place taken by outlying industrial works on either side of the main road that runs noisily parallel to the navigation. The Ship Canal, strangely enough, plays little part in the generation of wealth that this industry represents, but north of Hempstead Bridge (0452 21880) is a large timber wharf for discharging ships bringing imported wood. Further on is the oil dock, a grain silo and a general cargo quay. Ahead is Gloucester, and the extensive docks that are laid out virtually in the town centre. These are superb docks, for all around are the great warehouses ranged along the quays. Boatmen wishing to moor here – the best place for visiting Gloucester – should go to the office by the lock and seek advice from the BW official. Gloucester Lock (0452 25525) marks the northern end of the Gloucester & Sharpness Canal, and lowers boats back into the River Severn, reminding one that the ship canal is well above the river level. It has to be kept filled with water by pumping up from the river. No boats at the tail of Gloucester Lock should follow the river to the south west, for Llanthony Lock is closed and only a weir awaits them. North of Gloucester Lock, the river is bounded on the town side by a high quay, with moorings more suitable for large vessels than for motor cruisers. Gloucester gaol is nearby. Proceeding upstream, boatmen will find themselves on a dull length of river, narrow and hemmed in by high banks. A sharp bend requires a careful look-out; beyond it are road and rail bridges. The river winds along in its own isolated way, flanked mainly by trees. At one point it approaches a minor road; the former pub here is now a private house. Further upstream is the junction with the big western channel of the Severn, whose separate course between here and Gloucester explains the narrowness of the navigation channel. There is in fact a lock (Maisemore Lock, now closed) just 300yds along the western channel of the Severn. This is a relic of the days before the Ship Canal was built; it used to give access from the upper Severn to the Herefordshire & Gloucestershire Canal (now derelict), which joined the Severn near Gloucester.

Navigational notes
1 As with all river navigations, the Severn must be treated with respect, especially after periods of prolonged rain, when the current increases. If you are in any doubt regarding your safety on the river, moor up out of the main stream and seek *expert* advice.
2 All locks on the River Severn are manned. They are open: *08.00-19.15 summer, 08.00-16.30 winter. Meal breaks 13.00-13.30, 17.00-17.30.* Do not enter a lock unless the green light is showing.

Gloucester
MD: street market Sat, cattle market Mon and Thur. All services. Now a busy manufacturing town, commerical centre and port, Gloucester was once the Roman colony of Glevum. The town was laid out in a cross plan, with north, south, east and west gates. This geography still survives, if only in name. Traces of Roman habitation are much more difficult to find than in other Roman towns in Britain, but when the Bell Hotel was being demolished in recent years, excavations revealed 1000 sq ft of paved courtyard, believed to be the site of the Roman forum. There are a few interesting old buildings in the town centre, notably the 12thC Fleece Hotel and numbers 11-15 Southgate, but otherwise the town centre is of less interest than one might expect. However the glorious cathedral provides an oasis of peace and beauty in the town. The other area of real interest is the docks.

Gloucester Cathedral Founded as an abbey in 1089 by Abbot Serlo, this splendid building is essentially Norman, but extensive remodelling of the choir and transepts between 1330 and 1370 shows fine examples of early Perpendicular architecture. These alterations were authorised by King Edward III, whose father Edward II was murdered at Berkeley (2 miles south of Sharpness). Gloucester Cathedral was the only place that would offer him burial in consecrated ground, and his tomb here became the object of pilgrimage. The new king showed his gratitude to the then Abbot of Gloucester with financial assistance. The great east window is particularly fine – the glass dates almost entirely from 1350, when the window was built, and is one of the first examples of a church window depicting rows of people. But perhaps the most interesting part of the present building is the adjacent cloisters: they feature the earliest known fan-vaulting (mid-14thC). It is still in good condition and is delightfully ornate.

City Museum & Art Gallery Brunswick Road. Exhibits of furniture, glass, silver, costumes and coins; also local archaeology, geology and natural history. *Open weekdays.*

Folklife and Regimental Museum 99-103 Westgate Street. Housed in three Tudor timber-framed buildings known as Bishop Hooper's Lodging and scheduled as an ancient monument. Fine collection of local history and bygones: there is a whole section on the River Severn, its vessels and the salmon and eel fishing industries that it once supported. Relics of the siege of Gloucester (1643) are here, also the collection of the Gloucester Regiment. *Open weekdays.*

Gloucester Docks These extensive docks close to the centre of Gloucester are, to many people, really much more interesting than the town itself. They are at the north end of the Gloucester & Sharpness Ship Canal, where it locks down into the Severn and were built around 1827. Imported timber and grain are two of the main cargoes brought up here – they arrive mostly in big barges from ports down the Bristol Channel, for nowadays only a few coasters a week navigate the length of the canal. One may be sure that if the canal had not the generous dimensions that it has, Gloucester Docks would be disused by now, like the wharves up-river at Worcester and Stourport. The seven-storey dock warehouses are magnificent. Many of the original buildings still stand, lining the waterside-like block houses and concealing it from the town. The docks have now gained an interesting new feature, for the old Llanthony swing bridge carrying a road across the docks has been recently replaced by an elegant steel bascule

bridge, which carries heavier traffic and is faster to operate than the old one. Gloucester Docks add up to a fascinating scene and are now the subject of an extensive restoration scheme, which includes the establishment of the National Waterways Museum in the Llanthony Warehouse (*see below*).

The National Waterways Museum Llanthony Warehouse, Gloucester Docks, Gloucester (0452 318054). Entered through a replica lock chamber, this listed building houses two floors of exhibits illustrating the history of navigation, presented in a lively and interesting way. There are audio-visual displays; historic craft moored outside – including a steam dredger dating from 1925 and the narrowboat *Oak*; a working 'Seagull' vertical compound steam narrowboat engine and demonstrations of traditional canal crafts. Shop, cafe. *Open 10.00-18.00 every day during British Summer Time (closed 17.00 during winter).* Charge.

Museum of Advertising & Packaging Albert Warehouse, Gloucester Docks. Gloucester (0452 302309). Contains the fascinating Robert Opie collection, with soap powder and cereal boxes, coffee tins and household cleaners to stir memories of childhood in all who see them. There are also television commercials from the 1950s and 60s, and a wealth of old advertisements. *Open 10.00-18.00, closed Mon.* Charge.

Tourist Information Centre St Michael's Tower, The Cross, Gloucester (0452 504273) and at the National Waterways Museum (0452 330152).

BOATYARDS

Ⓑ **A & D Marine Services** Hempstead Dry Dock, 338 Bristol Road (0452 307674). Ⓦ Boat sales, engine repairs, dry dock, books and maps

BW Regional Office Llanthony Warehouse, Gloucester Docks, Gloucester (0452 25524).

PUBS

Walk east from the docks to find these pubs.
🍺 **Cross Keys** Cross Keys Lane, Southgate Street, Gloucester. Whitbread and Flowers real ale in a historic old pub. *Lunchtime* food, family room, garden and regular live music.
🍺 **County Tavern** Southgate Street, Gloucester. Comfortable hotel with a good choice of real ale, including Eldridge Pope, Ushers and Wadworth. Food *lunchtime and evenings.*
🍺 **Crown & Thistle** 99-101 Eastgate Street, Gloucester. *Lunchtime* food and a good range of real ale in this busy city centre pub.

The National Waterways Museum, Gloucester. *British Waterways.*

Ashleworth

Leaving the junction (known as the 'Upper Parting') of the east and west channels of the River Severn, the river from this point northwards is predictably wider. Its character changes very little in all its journey to Stourport – most of the way it is lined by trees and high banks. The surrounding countryside that accompanies the river is quite pretty but because of the banks, the boater will see little beyond except for the occasional hills. The walker along the banks is luckier, in having good views of the river and the surrounding countryside; but the towpath has mostly been eroded away. Away from the centre the river is often extremely shallow; there are anyway few mooring places, so access to the villages on either side is severely limited. After a series of long reaches, the spire of Ashleworth Church appears on the left side as the river bends to the east towards the hills that rise steeply from the river bank. Unfortunately, access to Ashleworth from the river is poor. The main hill here is Wainlode Hill, which reaches a height of almost 300ft.

Navigational note
Because of Wainlode Hill's susceptibility to erosion by the river, old barges have been sunk in the river near the east bank, in order to protect it. All boats should keep to the north side of the river to avoid the hulks. The area is marked by posts.

Ashleworth Quay
Glos. PO, tel, stores. Behind the tiny isolated pub is a fascinating group of 15thC buildings, all virtually intact. Ashleworth Court, a long, low, stone building, was completed in 1460 and stands next to the church. (*Open only to parties on written application to the owner in residence.*) The church, with its pretty spire, is nearby; but of greater interest is the big stone tithe barn (125ft by 25ft). This is owned by the National Trust but is still used as a working barn by the farmer – *open daily during daylight hours.* Ashleworth Manor and the rest of the village are set well back from the river. The Manor is contemporary with the Court, and is of timber-framed construction. (*It is open only by written appointment to the owner in residence.*)

PUBS
🍺 **Boat** Ashleworth. A delightfully isolated pub on the river.
🍺 **Queen's Arms** Village Green, Ashleworth.

Haw Bridge

The towering mass of Wainlode Hill slowly recedes as the tree-lined river curves round to the north west. The silted-up lock on the east bank is the entrance to the former Coombe Hill Canal, now partly restored, but land-locked. The modern bridge to the north is Haw Bridge. There are pubs and good moorings. Navigators should keep away from the east bank near this bridge – there is a submerged obstruction. The river winds through an S-bend, passing a riverside pub and a line of hills to the east; then it straightens out somewhat as it heads for Tewkesbury. Another riverside pub, the Yew Tree Inn, is passed – a sailing club is based here. Opposite is Odda's chapel, but access is bad because of the rocky banks.

Deerhurst
Glos. Tel, stores. The most important feature of this small village is the beautiful Church of St Mary, parts of which date back to the year 804. The font with its trumpet-spiral motif dates from the late 9thC and for some time the bowl was used as a wash tub in a farm. It was discovered and reunited with the stem in the late 19thC, and is now thought to be one of the best preserved Saxon fonts in England. The church contains some interesting brasses and 15thC stained glass. Access is bad from the river, as the banks are rocky.
Odda's Chapel About 200yds south west of the church. This Anglo-Saxon chapel dates from 1056; for years part of a farmhouse, it was rediscovered for what it is during repairs in 1885. *Open at any reasonable time.*
Haw Bridge The old cast-iron bridge, built in 1824, was knocked down accidentally by a barge in December 1958, when the river was in spate. The replacement bridge was opened in 1961, a few yards downstream of the old one. There are two pubs at the bridge, but little else. The villages of Tirley and Hasfield are a mile to the north west.
Coombe Hill Canal This short canal, running eastwards from the Severn for 2¾ miles, was built in 1796 to facilitate the carriage of coal to Cheltenham. There were two locks. Despite high tolls, the canal never made any money, and changed hands several times during the 19thC. In 1875 the lock gates were swept away by floods, and the canal was formally abandoned the following year. Having lain derelict for many years, it was purchased by the Severn & Canal Carrying Company for £35,000 (seven times the original company's capital). The canal and wharf manager's house, near the basin, have now been restored, and a museum and trips along the canal were planned before the company went into liquidation. It has now been purchased by the Gloucestershire Trust as an important wildlife habitat, and is scheduled as a site of special scientific interest.

PUBS AND RESTAURANTS
🍺✖ **Yew Tree Inn** On west bank of river, opposite Deerhurst (045 278 333). Large pub at the end of a lane. Sailing club based here; food always available. Reasonable temporary moorings. The quiet village of Chaceley (*PO, tel.*) is a mile up the lane.
🍺✖ **Coal House** On east bank of river near Apperley (045 278 211). Moorings not brilliant, but food is available.
🍺 **New Inn** Haw Bridge.
🍺 **Haw Bridge Inn** at Haw Bridge. Moorings. Skittle room.

Mythe Bridge

The river now passes another pub, facing a sailing club. There is a private ferry between them; access to the pub is difficult because of shallow water. One of the two channels of the Warwickshire Avon enters here from Tewkesbury: the Battle of Tewkesbury was fought just to the east of here in 1471. Marked by the abbey, Tewkesbury can be seen to the north east, but the Severn sweeps round to the west of the town, leaving an enormous expanse of flat, empty meadow between them. The big lock (0684 293138) is well concealed on a corner between the weir and a backwater. (The weir is, incidentally, the highest point to which normal spring tides flow.) Upstream of the lock is a junction with the main (navigable) course of the River Avon – boats heading for the Lower and Upper Avon navigations should turn east here, as should boats intending to visit Tewkesbury. Beware of the shallow spit projecting south west from the tip of the junction. Continuing up the Severn, one reaches the single 170ft-span of the cast iron Mythe Bridge over the river, built by Thomas Telford in 1828. Steep wooded hills rise on the east bank by this bridge, but the river bears off to the north west and soon leaves them behind. Its character remains virtually unchanged – it is lined by high banks and trees, untouched by villages or towns, and seemingly isolated from the countryside that its wide course divides so effectively.

The River Avon in Tewkesbury It is certainly worth turning off the Severn into the River Avon – this is the way to Tewkesbury, Evesham and Stratford-upon-Avon. Boaters not wishing to buy the short-term pass on to the Lower Avon Navigation may tie up just below the big Healing's Mill to visit Tewkesbury, but those who decide to go through the pretty Avon Lock (operated by a lock keeper) will find it a worthwhile diversion. *See page 16* and the River Avon section for all details and boatyard services in the town.

PUBS

🍺 **Lower Lode** ¼ mile below Tewkesbury Lock. 15thC inn with excellent moorings. Bar meals *lunchtime and evenings*, morning coffee and afternoon teas.

Upton bridge

10½M 1L
Worcester

Tewkesbury
6M 0L

Upton upon Severn

Saxon's Lode

Ripple Ferry

Ripple

M50 motorway

River Severn (non-tidal)

Windmill Tump

Upton upon Severn

The River Severn continues on its predictable,
undramatic course northwards, flanked by
wooded banks that prevent any views of the
countryside. There are few signs of habitation
or human activity apart from boats and
anglers. The big steel viaduct carrying the
M50 motorway provides a rare feature of
interest. The significant-looking pipes sticking
out of the ground on the east bank at this point
betray the existence of an old underground oil
depot, but it is now disused. A mile further on,
things improve as the old church tower at
Upton upon Severn comes into view, followed
by the graceful modern bridge and interesting
waterfront of this very attractive small town.
Plenty of boats are moored here – there are
temporary public moorings on the west bank,
just downstream of the bridge.

Upton upon Severn
*Hereford & Worcs. EC Thur. PO, tel, stores,
garage, banks.* This delightful town is well
provided with fascinating old timbered and
early Georgian buildings, and it is doubly
welcome for being situated on the river bank.
The best area is nearest the river, where
various pubs and venerable hotels beckon;
nearby is the prominent 13thC tower with its
18thC copper-covered cupola, all that remains
of the church that was demolished in 1937.
The tower and the former churchyard have
recently been restored as a public garden. The
'new' Church of SS Peter and Paul was built
in 1878, on the edge of the town – a good
place for it. There are good shops in Upton,
including a delicatessen, and it is the best
place along the Severn (apart from Worcester)
to forsake a boat for a trip to the famous
Malvern Hills, which rise to the west. Great
Malvern is under 6 miles to the north west,
and the hills are visible from the Severn.
Ripple
Hereford & Worcs. PO, tel, stores. Although set
back from the river, Ripple is well worth a
visit. It is a pretty village, the houses scattered
irregularly along the road. The large church is
very fine and dates almost entirely from the
late 12thC. Only the chancel is late 13thC.
The central tower at one time had a spire.
Inside are 15thC choir stalls, carved with
astrological symbols.

BOATYARDS

Ⓑ **Upton Marina** Upton upon Severn (0684
593111). Ⓡ Ⓢ Ⓦ Ⓟ Ⓓ Pump-out, gas,
overnight mooring, long-term mooring, winter
storage, slipway, crane, dry dock, chandlery,
books and maps, boat building, boat sales,
engine sales and repairs, toilets, showers.
Starline Narrowboats is based here (0684
593443).

PUBS AND RESTAURANTS

The only riverside pubs on this section are in
Upton upon Severn.
🍺 **Plough** Riverside, near the bridge. Upton
upon Severn. A nicely situated pub, where
Marston's real ale is available. Bar meals
lunchtime and evenings.
🍺 **Ye Olde Anchor Inn** High Street, Upton
upon Severn. This pub is dated 1601, and is
now run as a home-brew house, also offering
Uley and Hook Norton real ale. Once the
haunt of body snatchers, it now provides
meals *lunchtime and evenings*, and has a
children's room and garden.
🍺✕ **Swan Inn** Waterside, Upton upon
Severn (0684 592118). Wadworth and
Butcombe real ale, bar snacks and restaurant
meals (*L & D*). No dogs.

Hanley Castle

Leaving Upton, the river resumes its high-banked course through the countryside. On the west bank, but hardly visible from a boat, is the village of Hanley Castle. Further up, on the east bank, is a wooded ridge with a curious turreted house projecting from the trees. The village of Severn Stoke is to the east; it is reached by a lane from a jetty on the river. West of here is an enjoyably romantic stretch of river, where tall, steep red cliffs rise sharply from the water to over 100ft. Trees and shrubs struggle to grow from this treacherous slope, and somewhere hidden at the top is Rhydd Court. The steep hill recedes, allowing a large caravan site to nestle by the river. A scattering of bungalows appears; then the river leaves houses and hills and wanders off north east. Distantly, to the west, can be seen the grey lumps of the Malvern Hills.

Severn Stoke
Hereford & Worcs. Tel. The village is scattered along the main road, and has no real centre. The best part is near the pretty half-timbered pub with its rose garden. Nearby is the church with its curious 14thC side tower.

Hanley Castle
Hereford & Worcs. Tel. The early 13thC castle, built by King John, has now vanished, leaving only its moat as a memorial. But the village that grew up around it still thrives. It is extremely pretty, with a good collection of half-timbered and brick cottages around the little green. Overlooking the green is the church, set in an attractive churchyard. It is a curious building, half 14thC stone, half 17thC brick, with a squat brick tower. Nearby are the 17thC almshouses and grammar school, the whole group a remarkable indication of village life long ago. A lane leads to the village from the river, but mooring is difficult. It is not too far to walk from Upton.

PUBS

🍺 **Rose & Crown** Severn Stoke. Off the main road near the church.
🍺 **Three Kings** Hanley Castle. In the village centre. Food, garden.

Kempsey

The river winds past the hamlet of Pixham, then the bold tower of Kempsey church appears on the east bank, and a line of moored boats betrays the presence of a boatyard. There are temporary moorings along here for visitors to the village. Upstream, the river straightens out as it makes for Worcester. The Malvern Hills may be glimpsed occasionally, forming the western horizon. Soon the Severn narrows somewhat as a wooded ridge encroaches from the east. The Severn Motor Yacht Club is based here – it is well-named, for the cruisers moored along here are lavish and grand. There is a pub up among the trees near the club. The Battle of Worcester was fought in 1651 near where the little River Teme joins the Severn. Above here is the pair of Diglis Locks (0905 358758), on the outskirts of Worcester. There is a BW maintenance yard and a large freight depot above the locks, so dredgers and tugs are often seen.

Battle of Worcester, 3 September 1651 On 22 August 1651 the young Charles Stuart (later Charles II), having been proclaimed king by the rebels at Scone, reached Worcester with his Scottish army of 17,000. The Roundhead General Lambert was sent off in pursuit with his northern cavalry, and captured the Severn Bridge at Upton upon Severn, cutting off Charles' retreat. Meanwhile another army of 28,000 under Cromwell advanced on Worcester from Nottingham. Charles, realising that he would have to fight at Worcester, organised his defences around the rivers Severn and Teme. After receiving further reinforcements from Banbury, the Roundhead armies advanced across the Severn, using a pontoon made of boats; meanwhile their cavalry crossed by a ford south of Powick Bridge, on the Teme. Heavy fighting broke out, and Charles' Scottish infantry, taken by surprise, were soon driven back. Charles tried to redeem the battle by leading a brave charge out of the east gate of Worcester; supported by cavalry this would have succeeded, but by this time the Scottish cavalry had fled. Cromwell held his ground and forced the Royalists back into the town, killing many in the narrow streets. This Roundhead victory ended the Royalist hopes; Charles fled with a few followers, and after the famous Boscobel Oak episode he made his way back to France.

Kempsey
Hereford & Worcs. PO, tel, stores. A dull village in which acres of new housing have swamped the old. One or two beautiful thatched cottages have survived to defy the invasion of modernity; but it is the church that should be visited, for the enormous scale of this building is matched by interior grandeur. It was constructed to cater for the Bishop of Worcester and his huge retinue – the Bishop's Palace used to stand just a few yards west of the church. Hence the generous proportions of, especially, the chancel and sanctuary. Note the medieval glass in the chancel.

BOATYARDS

BW Diglis Maintenance Yard Diglis Lock (0905 356204).
Ⓑ ⛟ ✕ **Seaborn Yacht Company** Court Meadow, Kempsey, Worcester (0905 820295). Ⓡ Ⓢ Ⓦ Ⓓ Ⓔ Pump-out, gas, overnight mooring, long-term mooring, winter storage, slipway, crane, books and maps, boat building, boat sales, engine repairs, toilets, showers, licensed club house, restaurant.

PUBS

⛟ **Anchor** Kempsey. A popular main road hostelry dispensing Ansells real ale and Gaymers real cider. Food *lunchtime and evenings.*
⛟ **Farmers Arms** Kempsey Common. Banks's real ale, meals *lunchtime and evenings*, garden with play area and skittle alley.

Worcester

Just above Diglis Locks is the terminal basin where the oil tankers used to come to unload before the traffic finished some years ago. A few hundred yards on are the disused wharves and the two locks that lead into Diglis Basin, the Worcester & Birmingham Canal. (*See page 183.*) Worcester Cathedral is well in view now; the big square tower commands the town and the riverside. Two other church towers contribute to the scene, and the unspoilt nature of the west bank makes Worcester's riverside a pretty one. Anglers fish from a path along the east bank, seemingly just below the great west window of the cathedral, while 'fours' and 'eights' appear from rowing clubs. There are two bridges over the river in Worcester – a five-arched stone road bridge and, just north of it, a curious iron railway bridge. The best temporary moorings are north of the railway bridge. The west bank is built up while the east bank is green and tree-lined, with the racecourse right by the river. At its northern end is a busy waterworks, contrasting with the bijou houses which adjoin it. North of here the river moves out into pleasantly wooded country; the only trace of civilisation is the glimpse of the occasional farm and a pretty, secluded riverside pub with good moorings. There is a field of hops nearby.

Worcester
Hereford & Worcs. EC Thur. MD Sat. Two stations. All services. The 'Faithful City', Worcester has shown loyalty and devotion to the Crown for the last 900 years. Hence the name of Royal Worcester Porcelain, which is still one of the biggest firms in the town. Other industries include glove manufacturing and the making of a certain brown sauce. Worcester has plenty to offer the visitor, although one's enjoyment is lessened by the constant flow of heavy traffic through the town. Foregate Street has many irregular Georgian buildings with attractive pediments. A railway bridges the street, but does not intrude, for the girders are suitably decorated and trains are infrequent. However the best area is around Friar Street, and of course the cathedral.
Worcester Cathedral An imposing building that dates from 1074 (when Bishop Wulstan started to rebuild the Saxon church), but has work representative of the five subsequent centuries. There is a wealth of stained glass and monuments to see – including the tomb of King John, which lies in the chancel. Carved out of Purbeck marble in 1216, this is the oldest royal effigy in England. When he was dying at Newark, King John demanded to be buried at Worcester Cathedral between two saints: but the saints have gone now. The best way into the cathedral is from the Close with its immaculate lawns and houses, passing through the cloisters where one may inspect five of the cathedral's old bells. (Two of these were cast in 1374.) The gardens at the west end of the building look over the Severn and over to the Malvern Hills – a particularly fine sight at sunset. The Three Choirs Festival is held annually in rotation at the cathedrals of Worcester, Gloucester and Hereford, during the last week in *Aug.* This famous festival has inspired some fine music, one notable composer being Vaughan Williams. For further information about the festival, contact the Town Clerk in any of the three cities.
The Commandery By Kings Head Lock, on the Worcester & Birmingham Canal. This was founded as a small hospital by Bishop Wulstan in 1085, but the present timbered building dates from the reign of Henry VII in the 15thC. It served as Charles Stuart's headquarters before the Battle of Worcester in 1651. The glory of the building is the superb galleried hall with its ancient windows and the Elizabethan staircase. Teas. *Open Mon-Sat and Sun afternoons.*
Tudor House Folk Museum Friar Street. A new museum of local antiquities, furniture and porcelain housed in traditional Elizabethan buildings (the wattle and daub that make up the walls can be clearly seen in

places). Amongst other exhibits are a modern copy of a traditional coracle, a tiny fishing craft used for thousands of years on the River Severn, and a painting of the Waterman's Church in Worcester – a chapel on a floating barge, last used in the 1870s, when it was taken ashore and set up on dry land. *Closed Thur and Sun.*

The Dyson Perrins Museum of Worcester Porcelain The Royal Porcelain Works, Severn Street (0905 23221). Here, where it should be, is the most comprehensive collection of Worcester porcelain in the world, from 1751 to the present day. *Open Mon-Sat. Tours of the porcelain works can be arranged.*

The Guildhall High Street. Built in 1721-23 by a local architect, Thomas White, this building has a splendidly elaborate facade with statues of Charles I and Charles II on either side of the doorway and of Queen Anne on the pediment. It contains a very fine assembly room.

City Museum and Art Gallery Foregate Street. Collections of folk life material and natural history illustrating man and his environment in the Severn valley. In the Art Gallery are a permanent collection and loan exhibitions. Also museum of the Worcestershire Regiment. *Closed Thur and Sun.*

The Greyfriars Friar Street. *NT property.* Dating from 1480, this was once part of a Franciscan priory and is one of the finest half-timbered houses in the country. Charles II

escaped from this house after the Battle of Worcester on 3 September 1651. It is an antique shop now.

Tourist Information Centre The Guildhall, High Street (0905 723471).

BOATYARDS

Ⓑ **Grist Mill Boatyard** Diglis Basin, Worcester (0905 350814). Craftsmen boatbuilders and fitters, engine repairs.
Ⓑ **Mick Wade** Diglis Basin, Worcester (0905 763249). Marine engineer.

PUBS

🍺 **Camp House Inn** Camp Lane, Grimley. An isolated riverside pub below Bevere Lock. Flowers real ale, Bulmers real cider and excellent bar food *lunchtime and evenings.*
🍺 **Wheatsheaf Inn** Henwick Road, Worcester. Marston's real ale and bar food *lunchtime and evenings* in a pleasant pub overlooking the racecourse and the river.
🍺 **Crown & Anchor** Hylton Road, Worcester. Lively pub with a skittle alley. Marston's real ale and Bulmers real cider. *Lunchtime bar meals and snacks.*
🍺 **Severn View Hotel** Newport Street, Worcester. Marston's, Wadworth and Banks's real ale in a comfortable riverside hotel. Meals *lunchtime and evenings.*

DIGLIS BASIN
Enlargement from map page165

The River Severn at Worcester. *Derek Pratt.*

Holt Castle

Just upstream of the Camp House Inn is Bevere Lock (0905 640275), which is certainly one of the prettiest on the Severn. There is a delightful rose garden, tended by the lock keeper and his wife. The island adjoining the lock is connected to the land on the far side by a graceful iron footbridge. Continuing upstream of the lock, the river is approached by wooded hills on its east bank, while on the other side the plain green fields continue, edged by high banks and trees. At one point the little River Salwarpe and the disused Droitwich Canal enter together from the east. The Salwarpe is navigable for craft up to 35ft as far as Judge's Boatyard at Hawford, but there are no visitors' moorings. The canal has yet to be restored. The village of Grimley is at the end of a lane leading up from the river, but it is difficult to distinguish this track, and there are no moorings. The river continues north west now, until Holt Castle is reached, a curious composite building overlooking the river. Beside it is the discreet tower of a small church. Further on is the delicate iron span of Holt Fleet Bridge, and beyond it a steep wooded hillside, with pubs and caravans nearby. Above Holt Lock (0905 620218), the steep wooded hills continue, rising straight up from the river bank. It is a pleasant scene, and there is a riverside pub nearby. The next few miles form an attractive reach, with steep wooded hills rising from the river bank on one side, then on the other. There is a riverside pub close by.

Holt
Hereford & Worcs. Tel, stores. Holt is a scattering of assorted settlements, around the river. The elegant narrow bridge here was built by Telford in 1828. Holt Fleet exploits the river in a most unattractive fashion, being composed of a large sprawling caravan site, whose television aerials and wires swamp the riverside. There are two large pubs. Holt Castle is up on the hill, overlooking the river. The 'castle' is a 14thC tower, for the rest of the building is a 19thC battlemented mansion. Nearby, set among the fruit fields, is the church, a fine late Norman building with interesting carving around the doorways, and rich in interior ornamentation.
Grimley
Hereford & Worcs. Tel. A small farming village close to, but hidden from, the river. The well-placed church has some Norman work, but has been heavily restored; it has a curious outside staircase by the river. Access from the river is not easy.
The Droitwich Canal This attractive rural waterway, which leaves the Severn ½ mile north east of Bevere Lock, used to go to Droitwich – 5¼ miles and eight locks away. It was then joined by the Droitwich Junction Canal, whose seven locks led it a further 1½ miles to terminate in a junction with the Worcester & Birmingham Canal at Hanbury Wharf (*see page 185*). Both the Droitwich canals have been derelict for most of this century, but they are now reviving. Wychavon District Council and the Droitwich Canals Trust are implementing a scheme to open up the Droitwich Canal from the town to the River Severn, and it is hoped later to extend the restoration to the Junction Canal. When this happens, it will restore a 22-mile ring of cruising waterways.

BOATYARDS
ⓑ **George Judge** Mill House, Hawford (0905 51283). Just east of the A449 bridge on the River Salwarpe. Ⓦ Gas, boat sales and repairs, chandlery, provisions, cafe. camping and caravan site, long-term mooring. Visitor mooring is very restricted, and craft over 35ft *cannot turn.*

PUBS AND RESTAURANTS
🍺 **Lenchford** Holt. Riverside, upstream of Holt Lock.
🍺 **Holt Fleet** Holt Fleet, by the bridge.
🍺 **Wharf Hotel** Holt Fleet, north bank by caravan site.
🍺✕ **Waggon Wheel** Grimley (0905 640340).

The Burf

The reach from Lenchford to Stourport is one
of the most pleasant on the Severn. Unlike
much of its journey further downstream, the
river runs here through a well-defined valley,
with steep wooded hills never far away from
either bank. The hills on the west bank are the
more impressive and the more thickly
wooded, although the old church at Shrawley
can sometimes be seen peering over the
woods. Roads keep their distance, but at the
site of Hampstall Ferry (The Burf) there is a
small village and a riverside pub, with good
moorings. From here very steep hills encroach
on the east bank of the river, almost hanging
over it at Lincomb Lock (029 93 2887). This
pretty lock is now the northernmost on the
river, for signs of Stourport soon come into
view. On the opposite side of the river, at the
foot of a cliff, is the Redstone Rock – an
unexpected outcrop of crumbling red
sandstone. There was once a hermitage in
caves here. On towards Stourport, there is a
modest restaurant on the east bank and,
beyond it, Stourport Power Station. The River
Stour flows in here.

The Burf
An isolated riverside settlement, comprised
mainly of new housing for retired persons.

PUBS AND RESTAURANTS
⚓ **Hamstall Inn** The Burf, overlooking the
river. Good moorings. Food.

Stourport-on-Severn

At Stourport Power Station the River Stour
flows in from the east, and just to the north the
Staffordshire & Worcestershire Canal drops
down into the Severn from the unseen basins.
There are two sets of locks – narrow canal
boats should use the upstream set. Just above
these locks is Stourport Bridge, a heavy iron
structure built in 1870. The River Severn is
not officially navigable for more than a couple
of hundred yards above Stourport Bridge, at
which point BW's jurisdiction as navigation
authority ends. However, in suitable
conditions small boats not drawing more than
1ft 9in can penetrate upstream to within a mile
of Bewdley Bridge. A shoal across the river
impedes further progress, and boatmen must
tie up or wade ashore when they reach the
shoal. Bradshaw's *Canals and Navigable
Rivers, 1904* states that a few craft, in times of
full water, proceed as far as Arley Quarry, 5
miles above Bewdley, although the trade is
very small. There is a road into Bewdley on
either side of the river (the B4194 on the west
bank being the most direct). Alternatively, one
can avoid all this by leaving the boat in
Stourport and taking a bus to Bewdley, an
excursion well worth the effort.

River Severn above Bewdley
In the 19thC the Severn was fully navigable
for a long way past Stourport: it used to be a
vital trade artery right up into Wales, through
Bridgnorth, Shrewsbury and Newtown. It
used to connect with the Montgomery Canal
at Shrewsbury, and the Shropshire Canal at
Hay. It is unfortunate that this upper section is
unnavigable, for the river is much prettier than
further south: it runs along a narrow valley,
hemmed in by steep and wooded hills.
However, there is a public right of way along
one or both banks up to Bridgnorth and
beyond, and this can form an interesting walk.
Another attraction north of Bewdley is the
Severn Valley Railway, a private railway which
runs a summer service of steam trains between
Bridgnorth, Bewdley and Kidderminster
(0299 403816 for details).

Bewdley
*Hereford & Worcs. EC Wed. PO, tel, stores,
garage, bank.* Bewdley is a magnificent small
18thC riverside town, still remarkably intact.
It is blessed with a fine river frontage and
elegant bridge that make the most of the wide
Severn, and a handsome main street that leads
away from the river to terminate at the church.
The scale of the whole town is very pleasing, a
comfortable mixture of old timber-framed
buildings and plainer, more elegant 17th and
18thC structures. Most of the town is on the
west bank, and so Telford's three-arch stone
bridge, built in 1798 to replace an earlier
medieval structure, forms a fitting entrance to
Bewdley.

Stourport-on-Severn
*Hereford & Worcs. EC WEd. PO, tel, stores,
garage, bank.* When the engineer James
Brindley surveyed the line for the
Staffordshire & Worcestershire Canal in the
early 1760s, he intended to meet the River
Severn at Bewdley, which was already an
established river port. But the residents there
objected to his plans, and so he chose instead
the hamlet of Lower Mitton, 4 miles
downstream, where the little River Stour
flowed into the Severn. Basins and locks were
built for the boats, warehouses for the cargoes
and cottages for the workmen. The canal
company even built in 1788 the great Tontine
Hotel beside the locks. The hamlet soon
earned the name of Stourport, becoming a
busy and wealthy town. The two basins were
expanded to five (one has since been filled in)
and the locks were duplicated. Nowadays,
plenty remains of Stourport's former glory, for
the basins are always full of boats (there is a
boat club and boatyards). The delightful clock
tower still functions, a canal maintenance yard
carries on in the old workshops by the locks,
and the Tontine Hotel still has a licence. Mart
Lane (on the north east side of the basins) is
worth a look – the original 18thC terrace of
workmen's cottages still stands. Numbers 2, 3
and 4 are listed as ancient monuments. In

contrast with the basin area, the town of Stourport is not interesting, and although it was built on account of the canal, the town has no relationship at all with the basins now.

BOATYARDS

ⓑ **BW Stourport Yard** Stourport Basin, Stourport (029 93 77661). Ⓡ Ⓢ Ⓦ Dry dock.
ⓑ **Severn Valley Cruisers** York Street Boatyard, Stourport (029 93 71165). Ⓡ Ⓢ Ⓦ Ⓓ Pump-out, gas, narrowboat hire, overnight mooring, long-term mooring, winter storage, slipway, crane, dry dock, chandlery, books and maps, boat building, boat sales, engine sales and repairs, toilets. Boat shop in Mart Lane.

BOAT TRIPS

Severn Steamboat Company Stourport (029 93 71177). 40-minute river trips from the bridge *Sun & B. Hols in season.* Also public day trip to Worcester and return *Wed in Jul & Aug.* Two 199-passenger boats available for private charter (with disco).

PUBS AND RESTAURANTS

Bewdley is a town with many fine pubs, including:
🍺 **Black Boy** Wyre Hill. (*Not the* Black Boy *Hotel*). Although this locals' pub is ½ mile from the river, up a steep hill, the well kept Banks's real ale is a just reward for your efforts. *Lunchtime* food, garden.

🍺 **Cock & Magpie** Severnside North, Bewdley. Right in the town centre, on the old quay, this quiet local dispenses Banks's real ale and bar snacks.
🍺 **Little Pack Horse** High Street, Bewdley. A low-beamed traditional pub offering a select range of real ales, and good food *lunchtime and evenings.* Open fire on cold days.
🍺 **Rising Sun** Kidderminster Road, Wribbenhall, Garden.
🍺 **Horn and Trumpet** Welchgate, Bewdley. Busy pub just a short walk from the river. Regular jazz and folk evenings, Courage and John Smith's real ale, and food at *lunchtime.* Open fire.
🍺 **Bird in Hand** Stourport. Canalside, south of the railway bridge. Whitbread real ale, garden.
🍺 **Black Star** Stourport. Canalside, by bridge 5. Marston's real ale, snacks.
✕ ❢ **Lock, Stock & Barrel** By bridge 5 (029 93 6014). Intimate restaurant. *Closed Sun.*
🍺 **Lord Nelson** York Street, Stourport. M & B real ale.
🍺 **Bell** Stourport, by York Street Lock. Hanson's real ale, food, garden.
🍺 **Tontine Hotel** Stourport Basin. Banks's real ale and food (*lunchtime Mon-Sat*) in a very large pub built by the canal company in 1788.
🍺 **Old Crown** Stourport, by the Severn Bridge. Banks's real ale.
✕ ❢ **Severn Tandoori Restaurant** 11 Bridge Street, Stourport (029 93 3090). Excellent yet reasonably priced. Take-away service. *L & D.*

STOURPORT BASINS

Stourport. *Derek Pratt.*

STRATFORD-ON-AVON

Maximum dimensions

King's Norton to Kingswood
Length: 70'
Beam: 7'
Headroom: 7' 3"
Kingswood to Stratford
Length: 70'
Beam: 6' 10"
Headroom: 6'

Manager

(0926) 492192

Mileage

KING'S NORTON JUNCTION to
Hockley Heath: 9¾
LAPWORTH Junction with Grand Union
Canal: 12½
Preston Bagot: 16¼
Wootton Wawen Basin: 18½
Wilmcote: 22
STRATFORD-ON-AVON Junction with
River Avon: 25½

Locks: 54

The opening of the Oxford Canal in 1790 and of the Coventry Canal throughout shortly afterwards opened up a continuous waterway from London to the rapidly developing industrial area based on Birmingham. It also gave access, via the Trent & Mersey Canal, to the expanding pottery industry based on Stoke-on-Trent, to the Mersey, and to the East Midland coalfield. When the Warwick & Birmingham and Warwick & Napton Canals were projected to pass within 8 miles of Stratford-on-Avon, the business interests of that town realised that the prosperity being generated by these new trade arteries would pass them by unless Stratford acquired direct access to the network. And so, after the usual preliminaries, on the 28th of March 1793 an Act of Parliament was passed for the construction of the Stratford-on-Avon Canal, to start at King's Norton on the Worcester & Birmingham Canal (itself a long way from completion at that time). The junction was to be less than 3 miles from the junction of the Worcester & Birmingham with the Dudley Canal, and would thus provide a direct route to a major coal producing area without passing through Birmingham.

Progress was rapid at first; but almost the total estimated cost of the complete canal was spent in the first three years, on cutting the 9¾ lock-free miles to Hockley Heath. It took another four years, more negotiations, a revision of the route and another Act of Parliament to get things going again. By 1803 the canal was open from King's Norton Junction to its junction with the Warwick & Birmingham Canal (now part of the Grand Union main line) near Lapworth, with through traffic along the whole of this northern section. Even more delays now followed, with little enthusiasm on the part of private investors to put up more money.

Cutting re-commenced in 1812, the route being revised yet again in 1815 to include the present junction with the River Avon at Stratford. (From here, the Avon was navigable down to the Severn at Tewkesbury.)

In its most prosperous period, the canal's annual traffic exceeded 180,000 tons, including 50,000 tons of coal through the complete canal, down to Stratford. By 1835 the canal was suffering from railway competition. This grew so rapidly that in 1845 the Canal Company decided to sell out to the Great Western Railway. There was opposition, however, and it was not until 1st January 1856 that the sale was considered complete. Thus the canal has been in full, independent operation for less than 40 years. Traffic was not immediately suppressed by the new owners, but long-distance haulage was the first to suffer as it was a more direct threat to the railway. In 1890 the tonnage carried was still a quarter of what it had been 50 years before, but the fall in ton-miles was much greater.

This pattern of decline continued in the 20thC, and by the 1950s only an occasional working boat was using the northern section; the southern section (Lapworth to Stratford) was badly silted, some locks were unusable and some of the short pounds below Wilmcote were dry. It is believed that the last boat to reach Stratford did so in the early 1930s, but there is evidence that a pleasure cruiser reached Wilmcote during the Easter holiday of 1947.

After the 1939-45 war interest began to grow in boating as a recreation. In 1955 a Board of Survey had recommended sweeping canal closures, including the southern section of the Stratford Canal. Public protest was such that a Committee of Enquiry was set up in 1958, and this prompted the start of a massive campaign to save the canal. The campaign was successful: the decision not to abandon the canal was announced by the Ministry on the 22nd of May 1959. On October 16th of the same year the National Trust announced that it had agreed a lease from the British Transport Commission under which the Trust would assume responsibility for restoring and maintaining the southern section. The transfer took place on the 29th September 1960 and restoration work began in earnest in March of the following year. The terms of the arrangement included a contribution towards the cost of restoration but a very substantial sum was provided by the Trust, which maintained the southern section at its own expense.

The reopening ceremony was performed by Queen Elizabeth the Queen Mother on the 11th of July 1964, after more than four years of hard work by prison labourers, canal enthusiasts, Army units and a handful of National Trust staff. On the 1st April 1988 control of the southern section of the Stratford-on-Avon canal was passed to the British Waterways Board (now British Waterways), finally relieving canal users of the necessity to purchase a separate licence, and the National Trust of a property which, with the best will in the world, it was not ideally qualified to care for.

Natural history

Between the green tunnel of trees near King's Norton and the lily-covered basin at Stratford, there is great scope for seeing the wildlife and plants that frequent this delightful Warwickshire canal. After passing through Shirley, the canal enters the old Forest of Arden and for miles the banks are bordered by sturdy oaks and hazel bushes, which are a great attraction to grey squirrels. Here, the harsh calls of jays and the rattle of magpies are familiar sounds. It is worth making a halt at Earlswood, for it is only a few minutes' walk to the feeder reservoirs which attract naturalists from all over the Midlands. Here, at any time of the year, several pairs of great crested grebes can be seen carrying out their curious courtship ritual; the birds face each other, shake their heads from side to side, then dive and present offerings of weed. In early summer the young grebes can sometimes be seen riding on the parents' backs.

East of the open fields of Hockley Heath, the canal descends through the Lapworth flight. The locks and bridges are interesting as the walls are often covered with a profusion of plant life, including the small ferns of the spleenwort family. Further down, in the southern section past lock 29, there is a magnificent display of hartstongue ferns growing near a demolished railway bridge. Past lock 27, the western bank is lined with large alders and pollarded willows, the haunt of tits and warblers. During late summer these trees provide a roosting place for countless swallows.

At Yarningale, the canal crosses a tributary of the River Alne, which flows parallel for several miles. The dipper, which is rather like a blackbird but with a white breast, is sometimes seen around here, skimming over the water or perched on a stone. It is unique in being able to 'fly' underwater, as well as walk on the stream bed in search of insects. From Preston Bagot to Bishopton, the canal passes through one of the richest parts of Warwickshire as far as wildlife is concerned. Badgers are very common in the area and can sometimes be observed from the canal several hours before sunset; with luck, weasels can be seen hunting on the banks. These animals can be observed only when the boat is moored and quiet. It is worth a pause at bridge 51 and a walk up the bridle path to Austy Wood. Apart from numerous warblers, this wood houses a large number of great spotted woodpeckers, whose drumming can be heard during spring. In this area, Canada geese and several species of ducks frequently fly over to Wootton Pool. The harsh 'kwark' of the heron is a familiar sound, for there is a small heronry at the Pool and the birds are busy at their nests from March until August. At least four pairs of kingfisher have their homes on the Stratford Canal, and they may occasionally be seen perched on lock gates as they watch for rising fish. Another interesting bird, which can be heard singing during late afternoon and evening, is the grasshopper warbler; it sounds just like a grasshopper or a fisherman's reel. The moorhen is the most common water-bird on the canal; 57 have been counted in the 5 mile stretch between Lowsonford and Wilmcote. The moorhen nests from early spring to late September, so great care should be taken to avoid clumps of reeds in which a nest may be concealed. Many nests are easy to spot from a boat and, as a rule, they are limited to one side of the canal – opposite the towpath. Moorhens feed on almost anything; they can be seen pecking at blackberries, pulling leaves off plants or foraging in the fields amongst cows. At night they frequently roost in the alder trees lining the bank.

Wild flowers of the canal are too numerous to list. Purple loosestrife is one of the most showy flowers but is not found above Wootton Wawen. It is one of the food plants of the elephant hawkmoth caterpillar, a creature some 3in long with a pair of conspicuous eye spots near the front of its body. The arrowhead is generally considered to be quite rare in the British Isles, but towards Stratford its peculiar arrow-shaped leaves and spikes of white flowers are abundant in summer. The flowering rush is fairly common throughout the canal. Anyone particularly interested in pond life should dip his net at the winding holes where all manner of aquatic insects are to be found among the pink spikes of bistort.

King's Norton

The west end of this delightful canal is at
King's Norton, just outside Birmingham. As
may be guessed from the map, the first 5 miles
of the navigation pass entirely through
residential outskirts of the Birmingham
conurbation. The canal veteran might expect
this to be a dull or scruffy stretch, but he
would be wrong: in fact the Stratford Canal is
bordered all the way with dense but varied
vegetation and, thus protected from the
inroads of the suburbs, forms a quiet, winding
ribbon of green all the way through to the real
countryside. In conjunction with the northern
section of the Worcester & Birmingham
Canal, this is a far more scenically interesting
route between Lapworth and Birmingham
than via the Grand Union Canal. Leaving the
Worcester & Birmingham (*see page 189*) at
King's Norton Junction, the Stratford-on-
Avon Canal proceeds straight to the well-
known King's Norton Stop Lock. In the days
of the private canal companies, stop locks
were common at junctions, as one canal
sought to protect its water supply from any
newcomer; but King's Norton Stop Lock is
unusual in having two wooden guillotine gates
mounted in iron frames balanced by chains
and counterweights. The machinery is now
seized up, and boats pass under the two gates
without stopping. The next bridge is a small
swing bridge, then round the corner is
Brandwood Tunnel. Further east is a beautiful
tree-lined cutting, then a bridge with a pub
beside it (*petrol and telephone nearby*) and the
remains of an old arm just beyond it. A water
point is outside a cottage near bridge 5. The
canal continues through pleasant wooded
cuttings – access is bad at most of the bridges,
so the seclusion is virtually complete.

The Patrick Collection Motor Museum
180 Lifford Lane, adjacent to King's Norton
Stop Lock (021-459 9111). Cars from 1913 to
the present day. Picnic area, souvenir shop,
refreshments, outdoor play area for children
including radio-controlled cars and electronic
games. *Open weekday afternoons and weekends
Easter-Oct.*
Brandwood Tunnel 352yds long, this tunnel
has no towpath. Horse-drawn boats had to be
hauled through by means of an iron hand-rail
on the side. Lengths of this rail can still be
seen in the tunnel.

BOATYARDS
ⓑ **Lyons Boatyard** Canal Bank, Limekiln
Lane, Warstock (021-474 4977). At bridge 3
on the Stratford-on-Avon Canal. S W D
Pump-out, gas, overnight mooring, long-term
mooring, 7 ton crane, chandlery, groceries
nearby, books and maps, small boat sales,
engine sales and repairs, toilets, showers,
laundry, gifts.

PUBS
🍺 **Horse Shoe** Canalside, at bridge 3. Food.
Telephone and petrol nearby.

Earlswood

Passing over a small aqueduct, the canal
reaches a steel lift bridge, which has to be
raised and lowered with a windlass. (There are
two more of these bridges nearer Lapworth.)
Passing under a railway bridge, the canal
sheds all traces of the suburbs but maintains
its twisting course in wooded cuttings through
quiet countryside. The bridges over the
navigation are mostly the generous brick
arched bridges typical of the canal between
King's Norton and Lapworth Locks (in
contrast to the much smaller bridges further
south), but few roads of any significance come
near the canal. At bridge 16 the canal emerges
from a long cutting and is joined by a feeder
from the nearby Earlswood reservoirs. Several
boats are moored along it, for at the junction
there is the Earlswood Motor Yacht Club.
There are no villages along this rural stretch of
canal, but at Salter Street there is a modern
school and a strange Victorian church.

Navigational note
Bridge 8 operates hydraulically, using a lock
windlass.

Earlswood Reservoir Half a mile south of
bridge 16 is this canal-feeding reservoir,
surrounded by trees and divided into three
lakes: Windmill Pool, Engine Pool and Terry's
Pool.

BOATYARDS
Ⓑ **Stephen Golsbrough Boats** Warings
Green Wharf, Lime Kiln Lane, Hockley Heath
(0564 778210). Ⓡ Ⓢ Ⓦ Ⓓ Pump-out, gas,
long-term mooring.
Ⓑ ⬤ **Earlswood Marine Services** Lady
Lane, Earlswood (056 46 2552). By the
Earlswood feeder. Ⓡ Ⓢ Ⓦ Ⓔ Overnight
mooring, long-term mooring, winter storage,
slipway, dry dock, licensed club house. Base of
the Earlswood Yacht Motor Club: visitors
welcome.

PUBS
⬤ **Blue Bell** Canalside, at bridge 19. Good
mooring jetty.
⬤ **Bull's Head** ¼ mile south of bridge 17.
Old country pub serving Ansells and Ind
Coope (Burton) real ale and Coates real cider.
Food *lunchtime and evenings (not Sun).* Live
music on *Fri.*
⬤ **Red Lion** 500yds south of bridge 16, near
Earlswood Reservoir.
⬤ **Drawbridge** By bridge 8. Davenports and
Flowers real ale, *lunchtime and evenings* food,
canalside patio. Also sells Westons real cider.

Lapworth Locks

The canal continues to wind gently south
eastwards through the quiet countryside,
sometimes in minor cuttings and often flanked
by trees. To begin with, there are no locks, and
the bridges – especially those in the cuttings –
are still the big brick arches worthy of a
broader canal. At Hockley Heath (bridge 25)
there is a tiny arm that once served a coal
wharf. Nearby the Wharf Inn overlooks the
canal. East of here things change dramatically,
for the first of the 55 narrow locks down to
Stratford is reached. (The top lock is
numbered 2, the old stop lock at King's
Norton being number 1.) The surroundings of
the top lock are indeed pleasant: a white house
surrounded by walls and hemmed in by trees
stands beside the lock, while a cottage with a
delightful garden faces the towpath just below.
To the south west can be seen the spire of
Lapworth church. After the first four locks is a
½-mile breathing space, then the Lapworth
flight begins in earnest, with each of the next
nine locks spaced only a few yards from its
neighbour. There is a useful shop by lock 13
selling groceries, home-made bread and cakes,
brassware and gifts. The short intervening
pounds have been enlarged to provide a bigger
working reservoir of water, so that one side of
each lock is virtually an isthmus. The locks
have double bottom gates and are not heavy
going. They are interspersed with the old cast-
iron split bridges that are such a charming
feature of the Stratford-on-Avon Canal. These
bridges are built in two halves, separated by a
1 in gap so that the towing line between a
horse and a boat could be dropped through
the gap without having to disconnect the
horse. Below lock 19 is Kingswood Junction:
boats heading for Stratford should keep right
here. A short branch to the left through lock
20 leads under the railway line to the Grand
Union Canal.

Navigational notes
1 *See note 3, on page 177,* regarding lock 15.
2 Bridges 26 and 28 operate hydraulically,
using a lock windlass.

Lapworth
Warwicks. PO, tel, stores, garage, station.
Indivisible from Kingswood, this is more a
residential area than a village. Two canals pass
through Lapworth: the heavily locked
Stratford-on-Avon Canal and, to the east, the
main line of the Grand Union Canal. These
two waterways, and the short spur that
connects them, are easily the most interesting
aspect of Lapworth. The canalside buildings
are attractive and there are two small
reservoirs at the junction. The mostly 15thC
church is quite separate from the village and is
1½ miles west of the junction; it contains an
interesting monument by Eric Gill, 1928.
Packwood House *NT Property*. Lapworth.
(0564 782024). ½-mile north of the B4439
road bridge. A 16thC timber-framed house,
enlarged in the 17thC by John Fetherstone, it
was he who created the clipped yew garden
that is held to represent the Sermon on the
Mount. The house contains collections of
tapestry, needlework and furniture. *Open
afternoons only Easter-Sep, Wed-Sun & B. Hols.
Also open all day Wed-Sun in Oct.* Charge.
Hockley Heath
Warwicks. PO, tel, stores, garage.

BOATYARDS
Ⓑ **Swallow Cruisers** Wharf Lane, Hockley
Heath (0564 783442). Ⓡ Ⓢ Ⓦ Ⓓ Ⓔ (by
arrangement). Pump-out, gas, day hire craft,
winter storage, slipway, groceries, chandlery,
books and maps, boat sales, outboard engine
sales and repairs, toilets, off-licence.

PUBS
🍺 **Navigation** Lapworth. Canalside, on
Grand Union Canal at bridge 65.
🍺 **Boot Inn** Lapworth, near lock 14.
🍺 **Wharf Tavern** Hockley Heath. Canalside,
with garden, at bridge 25. Smart pub offering
Marston's real ale, *lunchtime* snacks and
evening meals (*no food Sun*). Children's room.

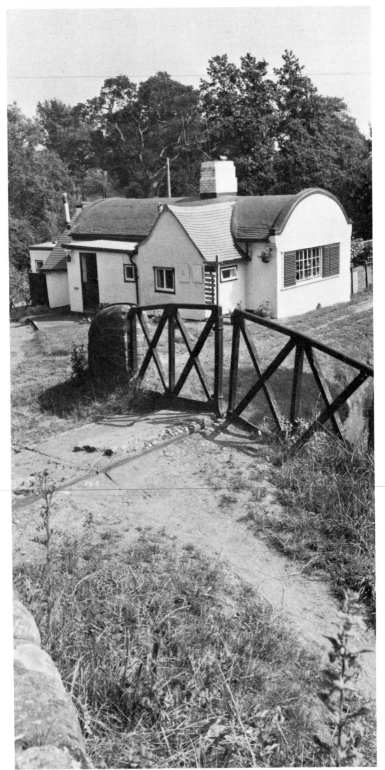

A barrel-roofed cottage and split bridge, both typical of the Stratford-on-Avon Canal. *Derek Pratt.*

Preston Bagot

At Kingswood Junction the Stratford Canal continues south, locking steadily downward. Good moorings are provided by lock 25. These locks have single gates and very small paddles, so they are slow to fill and empty. At some of them are the little iron split bridges over the lock-tail; and at intervals may be seen the delightful barrel-roofed lock cottages which are just as much a hallmark of this canal as are the bridges. Most of these cottages are inhabited and well cared for – a great contrast to many on the canal system. However, the canal itself, and many of its structures, appear fragile and overgrown. It is this, and the fact that its course is secreted amongst folds of pretty wooded countryside, that gives it such great charm (but see navigational notes). At Lowsonford is a pub where boats may moor in among the weeping willows of the garden; at Yarningale the canal, having followed a small stream for several miles, crosses it on a tiny aqueduct adjoining lock 34. Look out for kingfishers at Preston Bagot.

Navigational notes
1 The water level in the pound above lock 22 can drop dramatically when the lock is being filled.
2 Bank erosion is a serious problem on all canals, and especially so on this one. *Please go slowly* to minimise your wash.
3 Due to rebuilding, the chamber of lock 15 on the Lapworth flight is now over 2ft shorter than the other locks. Those in full length boats should take extra care when descending.

Preston Bagot
Warwicks. A small, scattered settlement with attractive, ancient houses here and there, including the 16thC manor. The Church of All Saints has a Norman nave and other Norman details, with Victorian additions.
Lowsonford
Warwicks. EC Thur. Tel. Another small and scattered hamlet, tucked away by the canal.

PUBS AND RESTAURANTS

Crab Mill Inn Preston Bagot. Comfortable country pub, charging top prices for Hook Norton, Wadworth, Marston's and Flowers real ale. Bar meals *lunchtime and evenings*, garden with children's playthings.
Haven Tea Rooms & Restaurant By lock 38 (0926 84 2420). Lunches, grills, salads, snacks and cream teas. Garden. *Open 10.30-18.00, closed Mon and Tue.*
Fleur-de-Lys Lowsonford, by canal north of lock 31. Ancient beamy pub with a large garden. Flowers and one guest real ale (changed monthly). Bar meals *lunchtime and evenings*.
Tom o'the Wood Finwood Road, Rowington. Canalside on the Grand Union. 16thC pub named after one of the three windmills which used to stand in the village. Flowers and Whitbread real ale, bar meals *lunchtime and evenings*, garden, family room.

Wilmcote

Lock 38 at Preston Bagot introduces two long pounds, which are welcome on such a heavily locked canal. The canal continues through delightfully quiet country, passing a newly rebuilt split bridge (number 50) and a farm as the big Austy Wood looms up on the hill to the east. (The low stone hall is Austy Manor.) Beyond bridge 53 the canal widens into a basin – a boatyard and a pub are here – and then crosses the A34 road on a cast iron aqueduct. Soon it enters a slight cutting – rare on the southern section of this canal – and then straightens out at lock 39 – known as the Odd Lock. Further south the canal rises on an embankment and is then carried across the water-meadows, a road and a railway by the splendid Edstone Aqueduct. At the south end is a very pretty cottage and garden. The navigation now winds along a secluded course to Wilmcote. Just north of the village are the remains of a bridge – this used to carry a horse tramway that served nearby quarries. The winding hole and the cottages on the towpath at this point were built for the quarry trade. Wilmcote is close to the canal, and you must moor north of bridge 59.

Wilmcote
Warwicks. PO, tel, stores, off-licence, garage. A small and attractive village, typical of this part of the world. A beautiful lime tree on the green is the centre of the village: nearby are a fine old pub, a residential hotel and the most well-known building in the village – Mary Arden's Cottage. The school and a vicarage by the church were built by William Butterfield c1848. The little railway station is to the east of the canal: with its trim roses and well-painted structures it is kept very much in the old tradition.

Mary Arden's Cottage Wilmcote. This was the home of Shakespeare's mother, and is a beautiful 15thC timbered farmhouse. The long, low house crouches behind luxurious and well-tended flower beds, and contains a museum of agricultural implements and local rural bygones. It is owned by the Shakespeare Birthplace Trust. *Open daily (closed Sun in winter)*.

Edstone (or Bearley) Aqueduct This major aqueduct, approaching 200yds in length, consists of a narrow cast-iron trough carried on brick piers across a shallow valley. As with the two other – but much smaller – iron aqueducts on this canal (at Yarningale and Wootton Wawen) the towpath runs along the level of the bottom of the tank, so that towing horses and pedestrians get a duck's eye view of passing boats. This feature makes the aqueducts on this canal very unusual.

Wootton Wawen
Warwicks. PO, tel, stores, garage, station, farm shop to the west of the basin. This scattered but very pretty village is half a mile west of the basin. The village has been designated a conservation area. There are plenty of timbered houses and the late 17thC Hall looks superb across the parkland and pond; but the chief glory is the Church of St Peter on its rise overlooking the whole village. This church should certainly be visited. Its unusual building history has given it a pleasantly disorderly external appearance, but inside there are really rare and fascinating things to see. The church is the only one in Warwickshire that derives from Saxon times, and the original sanctuary in the centre of the 11thC church survives intact, still the focus of the church after over 900 years. The nave is conspicuously Norman, the chancel is bare but large, with a superb 14thC east window. The Lady Chapel is probably the oddest part of the whole building – it is like a barn in more ways than one. It is enormous, with a primitive tiled roof and a completely irregular brick floor. Birds are often to be found, enjoying the shelter it provides. All around the walls is a medley of monuments. It all adds up to an intriguing building.

Wootton Wawen Basin This wide, embanked basin was built when construction of the canal was halted here for a while. A boat hire base – one of the few on this canal – has been built here, and was in 1972 awarded a Civic Trust commendation for its design. With a nearby pub and petrol station, the wharf is a popular halt with both boaters and motorists. A cast iron aqueduct carries the canal over the A34 by the basin. This aqueduct has often been damaged by lorries hitting the underside, so now a triangular road sign warning motorists of the headroom is mounted on the aqueduct. Unfortunately this sign has been positioned so that it almost completely obscures the original iron plaque that commemorates the opening of the aqueduct in 1813. Just down the hill from the aqueduct is a fine brick watermill, in good repair. This dates from the late 18thC.

BOATYARDS
Ⓑ **Anglo Welsh Narrowboats** The Wharf, Wootton Wawen (0564 793427) Ⓡ Ⓢ Ⓦ Ⓟ Ⓓ Ⓔ Pump-out, gas, narrowboat hire, overnight mooring, long-term mooring, books and maps, groceries nearby, slipway, boat building, boat sales, engine repairs. *Closed winter weekends.* Farm shop to the west, at Yew Tree Farm.

PUBS AND RESTAURANTS
🍺✕ **Swan House Hotel** Wilmcote. Comfortable small hotel near Mary Arden's cottage. Hook Norton, Everards, Wadworth and guest real ales, meals *lunchtime and evenings,* terrace and accommodation.
🍺 **Masons Arms** Aston Cantlow Road, Wilmcote. Turn right at the Swan House Hotel. A fine stone-built pub with comfortable bars and a dining room. Flowers real ale and excellent bar meals *lunchtime and evenings.*
🍺 **Golden Cross** Bearley Cross. Flowers real ale and food *lunchtime and evenings.*
🍺 **Navigation Inn** Wootton Wawen, at the basin. Flowers real ale and meals *lunchtime and evenings.*

Mary Arden's cottage at Wilmcote. *David Perrott.*

Map labels (left):

Stratford-upon-Avon

A422

B4086

N

Stratford lock

Theatre
(wide lock)

river Avon
see page 25

B

56

Kingswood Jnc
13M   36L

68

A46

55

54

67

53

66   65

station

52

W

A439(T)

A422

64

Stratford on Avon canal

A34

51

Bishopton

WR

63

62A

Copham's
Hill

50

49

48

47

46

45

40–50 Wilmcote locks

44

43

42

41

40

60

Wilmcote station

wharf

3¾M   16L
Stratford Bsn

Kingswood Jnc
9¼M   19L

59

Wilm
cote

Stratford-upon-Avon

South of Wilmcote, the two long pounds from Preston Bagot are terminated by a dense flight of locks – there are 11 in the Wilmcote flight, in groups of 3, 5 and 3. They are, in the main set in pleasant open country, in which Stratford can occasionally be seen to the east although a rather smelly rubbish tip cannot be ignored by locks 45 to 47. Meanwhile the countryside seems flatter, even though there are more locks to come. At bridge 64, a slight bend suddenly reveals the nether regions – gas holders and industrial works – of Stratford. Past two railway bridges, a grassy wharf on the right is a boatyard, by an engineering works. At the next bridge is a winding hole, petrol station and telephone box; then the canal disappears down its own private and inaccessible corridor towards the River Avon. It drops steeply through several locks, accompanied by the little-used towpath; then the towpath disappears altogether, the canal passes through the lowest bridge since Lapworth and one suddenly emerges at the splendid great basin in the middle of the riverside parkland beside the Shakespeare Memorial Theatre. The contrast is astonishing – here is an unwalled, public and attractive basin, constantly surrounded by the famous Stratford tourists, while only a few yards away the canal is completely shut away in a world of its own, forgotten by all except boaters. If all the moorings in the basin are taken, a place can usually be found on the river above Stratford Lock.

Navigational notes

1. The bridges on the approach to Stratford Basin are very low. Take care.
2. It may be a good idea to fill up with water before arriving at the basin.

Stratford-upon-Avon
See page 25 for details

BOATYARDS

Ⓑ **Stratford-upon-Avon Marina** Clopton Bridge, Stratford-upon-Avon (0789 69669). Ⓡ Ⓢ Ⓦ Ⓓ Ⓔ Pump-out, gas, narrowboat hire, day boat hire, overnight mooring, long-term mooring, winter storage, slipway, chandlery, provisions, books and maps, boat building, boat and engine sales and repairs, toilet, showers. *Closed Sat afternoon & Sun in winter.*

PUBS

None on the canal. Plenty in Stratford – *see page 26.*

WORCESTER & BIRMINGHAM

Maximum dimensions

Length: 71' 6"
Beam: 7'
Headroom: 8'

Manager

(0527) 72572

Mileage

WORCESTER, Diglis Basin to
Tibberton: 5¾
Dunhampstead: 7½
Hanbury Wharf: 9¼
Stoke Wharf: 12¾
Tardebigge Top Lock: 15½
Bittell Reservoirs: 20½
KING'S NORTON JUNCTION: 24½
BIRMINGHAM Gas Street Basin: 30

Locks: 58

The Bill for the Worcester & Birmingham Canal was passed in 1791 in spite of fierce opposition from the Staffordshire & Worcestershire Canal proprietors, who saw trade on their route to the Severn threatened. The supporters of the Bill claimed that the route from Birmingham and the Black Country towns would be much shorter, enabling traffic to avoid the then notorious shallows in the Severn below Stourport. The Birmingham Canal Company also opposed the Bill and succeeded in obtaining a clause preventing the new navigation from approaching within 7ft of their water. This resulted in the famous Worcester Bar separating the two canals in the centre of Birmingham.

Construction of the canal began at the Birmingham end following the line originally surveyed by John Snape and Josiah Clowes. Even at this early stage difficulties with water supply were encountered. The company was obliged by the Act authorising the canal to safeguard water supplies to the mills on the streams south of Birmingham. To do this, and to supply water for the summit level, 10 reservoirs were planned or constructed. The high cost of these engineering works led to a change of policy: instead of building a broad canal, the company decided to build it with narrow locks, in order to save money in construction and water in operation.

Work in King's Norton Tunnel, described at the time as 'a stupendous undertaking', began in 1794; by 1807 boats could get from Birmingham to Tardebigge Wharf. Here work came to a standstill for several years while the company considered alternative cheaper ways of completing the line down to the Severn. Work eventually started again under a new engineer, John Woodhouse, a great exponent of boat lifts. He proposed reducing the number of locks down to Worcester from 76 to 12, using lifts

to descend most of the fall. The company were less enthusiastic and limited his enterprises to one experimental lift at Tardebigge. This seems to have worked reasonably well but the company were still sceptical. They called in the famous canal engineer John Rennie, who decided that the mechanism would not withstand the rough treatment that it would doubtless receive from the boatmen. Consequently locks were built but reduced in number to 58. The site of the lift became the top lock of the Tardebigge flight – which accounts for its unusual depth.

After this, work progressed steadily and the canal was completed in 1815. In the same year an agreement with the Birmingham Canal proprietors permitted the cutting of a stop lock through Worcester Bar. The canal had cost £610,000, exceeding its original estimate by many thousands of pounds. Industrial goods and coal were carried down to Worcester, often for onward shipping to Bristol, while grain, timber and agricultural produce were returned to the growing towns of the Midlands. The canal basins in Worcester became important warehousing and transhipment points: Diglis Basin had warehousing for general merchandise, grain and wine, and Lowesmoor Basin specialised in coal and timber. Prosperous businesses were conducted from these wharves and they were an important port of call for the main canal carriers. However the opening of railways in the area in the 1840s and 1850s reduced this traffic considerably and had a profound effect on the fortunes of the canal.

In an attempt to win back salt carrying, the canal company cut the Droitwich Junction Canal in 1852 to connect the Droitwich Barge Canal and the town of Droitwich with their main line at Hanbury Wharf. Toll income and profits continued their relentless decline, however, and after 1864, the company was unable to pay a dividend. In 1874 the canal was bought by the Sharpness New Docks Company. (The words 'Sharpness New Docks and Gloucester & Birmingham Navigation Company' can still be seen on old notices on some of the bridges.) The new management commenced a programme of works to improve the canal in the hope of attracting trade but, in effect, the canal was subsidised by the Gloucester & Berkeley Ship Canal for the rest of its working life.

The animals that used to draw the boats along the Worcester & Birmingham Canal were mainly donkeys worked in pairs instead of the more usual horse. Why this should have been so is not recorded but both horse and donkey were unsatisfactory on the summit level with its four tunnels, for only the short Edgbaston Tunnel has a towpath through it. To overcome the delays caused by the need to 'leg' boats through the other tunnels, steam tugs were introduced in the 1870s and successfully hauled trains of boats through the tunnels for many years.

By the early 1900s the commercial future of the canal was uncertain, although the works were in much better condition than on many other canals. Schemes to enlarge the navigation as part of a Bristol–Birmingham route came to nothing. Commercial carrying continued until about 1964, the traffic being mostly between the two Cadbury factories of Bournville and Blackpole, and to Frampton on the Gloucester & Sharpness Canal. After nationalisation, several proposals were made to abandon the canal, but the 1960s brought a dramatic increase in the number of pleasure boats using the waterway, thus securing its future use. Now it is part of the popular cruising circuits comprising the River Severn, the Staffordshire & Worcestershire Canal and part of the Birmingham Canal Navigations, and the rivers Severn and Avon and Stratford-on-Avon route.

Natural history

The Worcester & Birmingham Canal has a rich variety of plant, bird and insect life throughout its length. Apart from its general interest it provides material for more serious study since it flows past extensive salt deposits left by an ancient sea of the Triassic period; consequently the water is quite brackish in some localities. After emerging from the gloom of the West Hill Tunnel, it is worth pausing at the exit not only to admire the tree-covered avenue but to examine the variety of ferns and liverworts which grow on the dripping clay of the high banks. A mile or so downstream, a mooring at Bittell is a must, for the reservoirs are among the best-known bird haunts in this part of the country, particularly for wild duck. One large reservoir (Bittell Lower) lies im-mediately against the west bank of the canal. There are always great crested grebe and mallard here, but the commonest waterbird is the coot.

The Tardebigge flight of locks gives splendid views over open meadowland where the song of the skylark is usually heard in summer. Here clumps of great willowherb and orange balsam line the banks. The orange balsam was introduced from America, being first recorded in Surrey in 1822; it has now spread along the river and canal system to most of England. When touched, the pods shoot out their seeds to a distance of several feet.

Where the vegetation is dense the harsh scolding of the sedge warbler can be heard; it is particularly frequent in this reach of the canal where caddis flies and other insects are abundant. Two common dragonflies are the large yellow aeshna and the delicate damselfly *ischura elegans*, which has a vivid blue spot on the abdomen. When the locks are emptied the walls can be seen to be covered with thousands of aquatic snails (limnaea). With such an abundance of aquatic organisms it is not surprising that the Worcester & Birmingham Canal is a favourite among anglers.

The calls of redshank and common sandpiper are not unfamiliar at Tardebigge for these waders often fly over on their way to Tardebigge reservoir, which is beside the locks. In addition to waders and waterbirds, herons are usually to be seen feeding in the shallows. In late summer varieties such as the wood sandpiper and the black tern may be occasionally seen at both the Bittell and Tardebigge reservoirs.

At Stoke Prior a subtle change comes over the canal, for the water becomes rather brackish. One interesting waterweed is the enteromorpha – a kind of alga which looks like floating transparent tubes about ½in across. Although the canal is enclosed by brick walls for a short distance, a mass of rosebay willowherb clothes the industrial scars in summer and parts of the waterway are covered with yellow water lilies.

From the Astwood flight to past Hanbury there are many beds of phragmites (reeds) on the west bank. Reed warblers are common in this area as they can only weave their suspended nests in the stems of these plants. Moorhens are common throughout the canal and, in places where bushes and trees hang into the water, families of mallard can usually be seen. Where the bank is low, a grass snake may sometimes be observed swimming in the water hunting for frogs or small fish. The water vole is common everywhere. Being rather short-sighted and slightly deaf it can sometimes be watched from a distance of 3ft for, like many creatures of the canal, it expects intruders only from the towpath.

Worcester

The Worcester & Birmingham Canal begins at
Diglis, on the south side of Worcester. It
leaves the River Severn a few hundred yards
north of the Diglis Locks, climbs two wide
(18ft) locks and opens out into one of the two
Diglis Basins, where a large number of
pleasure boats are moored, several of them
sea-going; a couple of boatyards and other
boating facilities are available here. Past the
basin, the canal becomes hemmed in by the
town as it enters the first of many deep,
narrow locks up to Birmingham. By Sidbury
Lock is the Commandery (*see below*). The
canal curves round the east side of Worcester,
between the town and Shrub Hill station. At
one point, near the railway viaduct that leads
to Foregate station and the west, the towpath
rises over the entrance to the Lowesmoore
Basin and wharves. Fish and chips are
available in Southfield Street, beyond the
viaduct. A series of four locks lifts the canal up
and away from the outskirts, then it is crossed
by a railway line, with an isolated industrial
estate beside it. Worcester is well behind, and
the canal is in open country, but the A449
runs parallel. Hindlip Park is to the north.

Worcester
For notes on Worcester, *see page 165.*
Diglis Basin This is a fascinating terminus at
the junction of the River Severn and the
Worcester & Birmingham Canal. It consists of
basins, boatyards, old warehouses and a dry
dock. Commercial craft have been entirely
replaced by a mixture of pleasure boats
designed for narrow canals, rivers and the sea.
There are plenty of facilities, a boatyard, and
the usual BW services. Permission to use the
dry dock should be sought from the BW basin
attendant (0905 358758), whose house is at
the top of the two locks down into the river.
The locks will take boats up to 72ft by 18ft
6in, although obviously only narrowboats can
proceed along the canal beyond the first lock.
The locks are under the supervision of the
basin attendant, who is available *from 08.00-
19.30 (16.00 winter) with breaks for meals.*
Craft are not permitted to use the locks
outside of these times. The locks incorporate a
side pond to save water; and near the second
lock is a small pump-house that raises water
from the river to maintain the level in the
basin.
The Commandery By Sidbury Lock.
Founded as a small hospital by Bishop
Wulstan in 1085, the present timbered
building dates from the reign of Henry VII in
the 15thC. It served as Charles Stuart's
headquarters before the Battle of Worcester in
1651. The glory of the building is the superb
galleried hall with its ancient windows and the
Elizabethan staircase. Teas. *Open Tue-Sat and
Sun afternoons.*

BOATYARDS
ⓑ **Viking Afloat** Lowesmoor Basin,
Lowesmoor Terrace, Worcester (0905
612707). Ⓡ Ⓢ Ⓦ Ⓓ Pump-out, gas,
narrowboat hire, overnight mooring, long-
term mooring, boat sales, toilets, gifts.

PUBS
🍺 **Cavalier Tavern** Worcester. Canalside, at
bridge 12. Comfortable modern pub serving
Flowers real ale and *lunchtime* food. Garden.
🍺 **Bridge Inn** Lowesmoor Wharf. A pleasant
local serving M & B real ale and *lunchtime*
snacks.
🍺 **Bricklayers Arms** Blockhouse Lock.
Unspoilt backstreet local. Banks's real ale.
🍺 **King's Head Inn** Near Sidbury Lock.
Comfortable hotel with a skittle alley. Banks's
real ale, regular live music.
🍺 **Red Lion Inn** Adjacent to Sidbury Lock.
Marston's real ale and *lunchtime* snacks in a
busy local.
🍺 **Potters Wheel** Severn Street. 200 yards
from Sidbury Lock, opposite the Royal
Worcester Factory. Excellent pub food.
🍺 **Anchor Inn** Diglis Road, just outside the
basin. Banks's real ale and *lunchtime* snacks.

Dunhampstead

This is a very pleasant stretch of rural canal entirely typical of the Worcester & Birmingham. Having left the outskirts of Worcester, and accompanied by a minor road, the canal now goes under the A449 and ascends the six Offerton locks, which are set in pleasant pasture land with a pretty cottage at lock 15. The M5 motorway crosses on its skewed steel bridge; it vanishes immediately as the canal enters a short, curving cutting that brings one to the village of Tibberton. There are two pubs nearby, and fruit trees remind one of Worcestershire's orchards. The canal moves towards a ridge of hills to the east, but a railway line intercedes to prevent the canal reaching the side of the valley. This is the main Bristol–Birmingham line, which carries many fast passenger trains, but the only station near the canal is at Bromsgrove. At Oddingley there is a little church and a timbered farm that look out together over the canal; further on are the crowded moorings at Dunhampstead Wharf (popular pub nearby). A wooded cutting leads to Dunhampstead Tunnel, the first of five between here and Birmingham. There is no towpath in the tunnel; horses used to walk over the hill while boatmen pulled the boats through by the handrail (still in place) along each side of the tunnel. It is 230yds long.

Dunhampstead
Hereford & Worcs. Tel. A hamlet consisting of no more than five buildings, including the railway signal box. The only life in the area, apart from the trains that roar past the woods, is provided by the canal and the nearby pub. To the north is the tunnel.
Tibberton
Hereford & Worcs. PO, tel, stores (all to the south of the pub). A small but expanding canalside village, of little interest. There is a fine old rectory by the Victorian church. Milk is sold by bridge 25.

BOATYARDS

Ⓑ **Brook Line** Dunhampstead Wharf, Oddingley (0905 773889). Ⓦ Ⓓ Pump-out, gas, narrowboat hire, boat building. Gift shop nearby.

PUBS

🍺 **Fir Tree Inn** Dunhampstead. Very smart and comfortable pub near the canal. M & B, Banks's and Bass real ale, and meals *lunchtime and evenings.*
🍺 **Bridge Inn** Tibberton. Handsome village local serving Banks's real ale. Lots of toys in the garden for the children.
🍺 **Speed the Plough** Tibberton. Attractive cottagey pub with a small garden. Banks's real ale, food *Mon-Sat.*

Hanbury Wharf

Leaving Dunhampstead Tunnel, the canal enters flatter countryside as the hills recede to the east. The pretty, residential settlement of Shernal Green flanks the canal, while Hadzor House (late 18thC in the Classical tradition) is visible in the trees on the west side of the canal. This straight stretch is terminated by the very busy area of Hanbury Wharf, where an old arm and a new building comprise a boatyard for small pleasure boats. There is a pub by the main road bridge – the Droitwich Junction Canal (unnavigable but undergoing restoration) joins here. North of here the ridge of hills approaches again from the east. Navigators should relish this 5½-mile level – it is easily the longest pound between Worcester and Tardebigge Top Lock. But as the canal passes under the railway to take up an uninterrupted position on its east side, the ridge of hills nears again, accompanied by attractive parkland. Ahead are the six locks in the Astwood flight, set in pleasant open pastureland. Near the top is a pub, beside the railway line; and beyond the cottages at Astwood Bridge is a semi built-up area – a minor road joins the canal, lined by workmen's terraced cottages. To the north of this settlement is the reason for its existence – a huge industrial chemical works. The canal goes through the middle of this works, much of which is now changing use.

Stoke Works Now closed, this establishment was built in 1828 to pump brine (salt) from underground sources for industrial uses, and provided much of the canal's trade (later gained by the railways). Now an industrial estate, where the housing fronts the tree-lined canal, and all is very tidy.
Hanbury Hall (0527 821214). *NT property. (Access via the public footpath leading south east from lock 17.)* Set in spacious and well-wooded park, this is a Wren-style red-brick house built in 1701 and little altered since then. On show are the long room and main staircase with painted ceilings by Thornhill. *Open Wed and Sat afternoons Apr-Sep.*
Hanbury Wharf An interesting canal settlement at the junction of the Droitwich Junction and Worcester & Birmingham Canals. A short arm leads to the original wharf, but the old canal cottages here are now overshadowed by the big new shed that houses a busy modern boatyard.

BOAT TRIPS

The Droitwich Canal Trust 1 Hampton Road, Droitwich (0905 774225). *Sabrina* is available for charter for up to 50 persons. Buffet, bar, music.

PUBS

☛ **Butchers Arms** Shaw Lane, Stoke Works. Small village local, with unique decor in the bar. Davenports real ale.
☛ **Boat & Railway** Canalside, just south of Bridge 42. Traditional pub with a terrace on to the canal. Hanson's real ale, food and skittle alley. ☛ **Bowling Green** Beside railway bridge, 200yds south west of bridge 41. Small, attractive and peaceful pub serving Banks's real ale and food. Garden, bowling green.
☛ **Eagle & Sun** Hanbury Wharf. Canalside, at bridge 35. Comfortable, with several cosy rooms. Excellent food, with *lunchtime* cold buffet during the summer. Bass real ale.

Tardebigge Locks

Approaching Stoke Wharf from the old works, boaters will note the hills to the north east with some misgiving. At Stoke Wharf is the first lock for over a mile; beyond is a crowded mooring site, and then more locks, flanked by trees and pastureland. These locks (numbers 23-28) form the Stoke flight, but in fact there is only a short breathing space of a few hundred yards, with a well-placed pub, before the first of the 30 Tardebigge locks is reached. Forward progress becomes a crawl as this great flight is climbed, but the pleasures of the surroundings make the effort worthwhile. The locks wind up through pretty, folding countryside, leaving the busy railway behind in the west. There are attractive, well-cared-for cottages scattered along the flight, generally near the bridges; their gardens overlook the canal. The locks themselves have great charm, being equipped throughout with traditional wooden gates and balance beams. Large paddles speed up locking, and so a reasonably well co-ordinated crew of two can work through a lock every five minutes. Regrettably, there is no pub at the top, the next being well beyond Shortwood Tunnel. The remote rural course of the canal takes it well wide of Bromsgrove, but Bromsgrove station is only a mile north west of bridge 51. Between locks 50 and 54 Tardebigge reservoir can be seen behind an embankment on the east bank. This feeder reservoir is particularly popular with fishermen. As the reservoir is about 50ft below the summit level, a steam engine was installed to pump water up the hill. The engine-house still stands near the canal, now converted into a restaurant/disco. Tardebigge Top Lock has a fall of 14ft, one of the deepest narrow locks in the country. When the canal was built, there was a vertical boat lift here. Technical problems caused the lift to be replaced by the deep lock, and there is little trace of it now. Above the lock is Tardebigge Wharf, overlooked by the elegant spire of Tardebigge church, up on the hill to the east. At the wharf is an attractive BW maintenance yard, and a large mooring site. Leaving the wharf and its cottages behind, the canal vanishes into a tunnel, passing under a main road (A448) at the tunnel mouth.

Tardebigge

Hereford & Worcs. Stores (on A448, 10 mins' walk from south end of Tardebigge Tunnel). A small farming village flanking the main road. Apart from the settlement near the canal, the best part of the village is up on the hill, around the fine 18thC church with its delicate spire. At the top of the locks a plaque commemorates the founding of the Inland Waterways Association in 1946 by L. T. C. Rolt and Robert Aickman, aboard the narrowboat *Cressy*, moored at this spot.
Stoke Wharf A pretty canal settlement in the best tradition – a lock, a wharf and warehouse, and a pleasant line of houses facing the canal, now housing a boatyard. Stoke Wharf is the only compact element of Stoke Prior – perhaps the heart of the village was drawn to the canal when the latter was built, and has remained there ever since. Stoke Prior church, which is mainly of the 12thC, stands by itself ½ a mile north of the wharf, the other side of the busy railway junction. Stoke Prior is not a good place for shopping: it is better to victual up at the settlement near bridge 42. However there is a pub near the wharf.
Avoncroft Museum of Buildings, Stoke Prior. *1 mile north of Stoke Wharf, off B4091.* Old buildings rescued from demolition are re-erected and displayed here. Exhibits include an 18thC post mill, a local nail and chain works, a 15thC timber-framed house from Bromsgrove, and the 14thC roof of Guesten Hall, Worcester. There is also a reconstruction of an Iron Age hut. *Open mid Mar-mid Oct, Tue-Sun.*

BOATYARDS

Ⓑ **Grist Mill Boatyard** Diglis Basin, Worcester (0905 350814). Craftsmen boatbuilders and fitters, engine repairs.

ⓑ **Mick Wade** Diglis Basin, Worcester (0905 763249). Marine engineer.
ⓑ **BW Tardebigge Yard** Tardebigge Top Lock (0527 72572). Ⓡ Ⓢ Ⓦ Overnight mooring, long-term mooring, toilets. Dry dock available.
ⓑ **Black Prince Holidays** Stoke Wharf (0527 575115). Ⓡ Ⓢ Ⓦ Ⓓ Pump-out, narrowboat hire, overnight mooring, long-term mooring, winter storage, books and maps, wet dock, boat and engine sales, engine repairs, toilets, gifts.

PUBS AND RESTAURANTS

✕ ❗ **Engine House** Tardebigge, by lock 57. (0527 35238). Restaurant, bar and disco, which welcomes boaters by offering them their own special menu. *Open Fri and Sat evenings.*
🍺 **Queen's Head** Canalside at bridge 48. Busy pub with good food *lunchtime and evenings*, and Banks's, Samuel Smith and Marston's real ale. Terrace by the water.
🍺 **Navigation** Behind Stoke Wharf. A fine spacious pub with a neat smoke room, serving Davenports real ale.

DIGLIS BASIN
Enlargement from map page 183

The long haul up Tardebigge Locks. *Derek Pratt.*

Alvechurch

This is a most delightful stretch of canal that winds through the hilly Worcestershire countryside. The flat Severn valley seems very distant as the canal plunges first into Tardebigge and then Shortwood Tunnel. There is a boatyard between the tunnels. East of Shortwood Tunnel and the surrounding fruit plantations, the canal emerges high up on the side of a low wooded hill, overlooking the modest valley of the River Arrow. The canal continues northward, winding steadily through this tranquil landscape until the small town of Alvechurch is reached. The town is set below the canal in a hollow, its church up on a hill; the canal winds tortuously along the steep hills round the outskirts, passing a boatyard, a station and a charming canal pub. Then the canal turns abruptly north; ahead in the distance is the ridge of hills that is pierced by King's Norton Tunnel. Unexpectedly, an aqueduct carries the canal over a little lane that leads to Barnt Green and its station (a mile to the west). Past the aqueduct and through bridge 65, Lower Bittell reservoir comes into view, beside and below the navigation. The canal crosses the valley on an embankment; at the north end of this is a very pretty cottage, which stands at the point where the feeder from Upper Bittell reservoir enters the canal. With these on two sides and an overflow weir and the lower reservoir on the third, the house seems to be virtually surrounded by water.

Bittell reservoirs
These two reservoirs were built by the canal company, the upper to feed the canal, the lower being a compensation to local mill owners for the loss of water resulting from construction of the canal. The reservoirs are popular among anglers and bird watchers.

Alvechurch
Hereford & Worcs. PO, tel, stores, garage, bank, station. A pleasant little town with some fine half-timbered houses, Alvechurch is situated at the bottom of a hollow and surrounded by folds of green hills. The church stands alone on a hill; it is of Norman origin but was largely rebuilt by Butterfield in 1861. There are some interesting monuments. There are shops about ¼ mile east of bridge 61.

Shortwood and Tardebigge Tunnels
613yds long and 580yds long respectively, these are two out of the four tunnels on the 14-mile summit level of the Worcester & Birmingham Canal. Neither contains a towpath, and until the turn of the century a company tug used to pull all boats through Tardebigge, Shortwood and the great King's Norton Tunnel. Navigators will find Shortwood Tunnel extremely wet.

BOATYARDS
Ⓑ **Alvechurch Boat Centre** Scarfield Wharf, Alvechurch (021-445 2909). At bridge 60. Ⓡ Ⓢ Ⓦ Ⓓ Pump-out, narrowboat hire, gas, overnight mooring, long-term mooring, slipway, books and maps, boat building and sales, toilets, showers.
Ⓑ **Dartline** Old Wharf, Tardebigge (0527 73898) Ⓡ Ⓦ Ⓓ Pump-out, gas, narrowboat hire, day hire craft, overnight mooring, long-term mooring, winter storage, books and maps, boat sales, engine sales and repairs, toilets.

BOAT TRIPS
Midlander available for private charter. 42 persons. Ring 0527 73898.

PUBS
🍺 **Crown** Alvechurch. Canalside, at bridge 61. Pleasant country pub serving M & B and Springfield real ale. Seats outside amongst geraniums.
🍺 **Swan Hotel** Swan Street, Alvechurch.

King's Norton Tunnel

Leaving the reservoirs, the canal curves
through a slight cutting to Hopwood, where
there is a pub, a boatyard and a busy main
road crossing. North of here the canal enters a
cutting that leads to King's Norton Tunnel.
The ridge of hills that this tunnel penetrates
serves as an important geographical
boundary: to the south of it is the rolling open
countryside of rural Worcestershire, while
north of the tunnel is Warwickshire, and the
southernmost indications of Black Country
industrial development. The built-up area is
revealed as soon as the canal leaves the cutting
at the north end of the tunnel: to the west is
King's Norton, while all around are new
houses and light industries. At bridge 71 (the
best access point for the village and its shops)
is the main mooring site of the local boat club;
just past it is the old canal cottage at King's
Norton Junction. Here the Stratford-on-Avon
Canal enters at right angles – the guillotine
mechanism of the celebrated King's Norton
Stop Lock can be seen a few hundred yards
along it. Boats heading for the south east
should turn off down the Stratford Canal here
(*see page 173*). (*see page 173*). Meanwhile the Worcester &
Birmingham Canal continues towards
Birmingham, under a roving bridge at the
junction, then under an inelegant steel bridge
that connects a canalside factory with its car
park. Another turnover bridge (73) is
encountered: there is a telephone box near it
and a further industrial stretch just beyond.

King's Norton
*West Midlands. PO, tel, stores, garage, bank,
station.* The village has done well to survive as
a recognisable entity, for the suburbs of
Birmingham have now extended all around it,
and the amount of urban traffic passing
through the village leaves one gasping. But it *is*
still a village, and the small village green, the
old grammar school buildings and the soaring
spire of the church ensure that it will remain
so. The church is set back a little from the
green in an attractive churchyard, and is
mainly of the 14thC, although two Norman
windows can still be seen. The grammar
school is even older – it was probably founded
by King Edward III in 1344. An interesting
puzzle is that the upper storey is apparently
older than the ground floor. . . . The school
declined during the last century and was
closed in 1875. Now restored it is an ancient
monument.
King's Norton Tunnel
Otherwise known as
Wast Hill or West Hill Tunnel, this 2726yd
bore is one of the longest in the country. It is
usually difficult to see right through the
tunnel, and there are plenty of drips from the
roof in even the driest weather. A steam-
powered – and later a diesel – tunnel tug
service used to operate in the days of horse-
drawn boats (there is no towpath). The old
iron brackets and insulators that still line the
roof were installed to carry telegraph lines
through the tunnel. Grandiose bridges (nos
69 and 70) span the cutting at either end.
Hopwood
West Midlands. Tel, garage. Provisions
available at mobile home site, 200yds north
west of bridge 67. More a name than a village,
Hopwood is merely a small settlement. There
are buildings near the canal which may be
useful to canal travellers; a pub, a boatyard, a
petrol station. A fast main road bisects the
area.

PUBS
🍺 **Navigation Inn** King's Norton, 100yds
west of bridge 71
🍺 **Hopwood House** Hopwood. Canalside, at
bridge 67. Food *Mon-Sat.*

Map labels (left column):

Botanical Gardens
N
Edgbaston tunnel
83
Edgbaston
82
A38
Birmingham University
81

3M	0L
Gas St Basin	
King's Norton	
2½M	0L

80 Selly Oak station
Selly Oak
79
78
A441
Cadbury's Works
Bournville
Bournville station
77
A4040
75
74
A441
Stratford-on-Avon Canal
see page 173
72
Kings Norton Junction
pipe bridge

Edgbaston

Just north of King's Norton Junction, the canal enters an industrial area. Canal veterans will recognise this as typical of an approach to the great city of Birmingham and will doubtless resign themselves to 10 miles of this kind of scenery. But, thankfully, it does not last, for the canal seems to hold the industries at bay on one side, while a railway line (the main line from Worcester and the south west to Birmingham) draws alongside on its west flank. Canal and railway together drive through the middle of Cadbury's Bournville works, which is interesting rather than oppressive. There is an exhibition, 'Cadbury World', in Linden Road, near the factory, which explains the history of this place. Beyond it is Bournville station, followed by a cutting. Soon the railway vanishes briefly behind the buildings of Selly Oak; the canal goes through this suburb, but access is closed off at the road bridge (80). Between this and the next, skewed, railway bridge is the site of the junction with the Dudley Canal, but no trace remains here now of either the junction or the canal itself. North of here the canal and railway together shrug off industry and town, and head off on an embankment towards Birmingham in splendid isolation and attractive surroundings. Below on either side is the green spaciousness of residential Edgbaston, its botanical gardens and woods. A hospital is on the west side. The University of Birmingham is on the east side; among its many large buildings the most conspicuous is the Chamberlain campanile tower, which was erected in 1900. At one of the bridges near the University, two Roman forts used to stand; but most evidence of them was obliterated by the building of the canal and railway. Only a reconstructed part of the larger fort exists now. Past the University's moorings, canal and railway enter a cutting, in which their enjoyable seclusion from the neighbourhood is complete; the charming old bridges are high, with no access possible, while the cutting is steep, and always lined by overhanging foliage. It is a remarkable approach to Birmingham. The railway is the canal's almost constant companion, dipping away here and there to reappear a short distance further on; but trains are not too frequent, and in a way their occasional appearance heightens the remoteness that attaches to this length of canal. At one stage the two routes pass through short tunnels side by side: the canal's tunnel is the northernmost of the five on this canal and the only one with a towpath through it. It is a mere 105yds long.

Edgbaston
West Midlands. A desirable residential suburb of Birmingham, Edgbaston is bisected but unnoticed by the canal, and there is little contact between them. However, for those who contrive to be on the 'landward' side of Edgbaston, there are several places worthy of exploration.
Cannon Hill Park Edgbaston, about 1½ miles east of the University. Formal gardens including a Japanese Garden of Contemplation; tropical and sub-tropical plants adjacent. Birmingham Zoo is now housed here.
Cannon Hill Museum Pershore Road, Edgbaston. Designed primarily for children. Illustrated leisure-time pursuits including bird-watching, bee-keeping, fishing and pets. Safari hut around which the sounds, sights and smells of the African bush are recreated. *Open daily. Closed Sun morning.*
Geological Department Museum The University, Edgbaston (021-472 1301). Collection of palaeontology, stratigraphy, petrology, mineralogy and physical geology, including the Holcroft collection of fossils and the Lapworth collection of grapholites. *Open daily by arrangement.*
Botanical Gardens Edgbaston. Founded over 100 years ago. Alpine Garden, lily pond and a collection of tropical birds. *Open daily.*

Perrott's Folly Monument Road, Edgbaston. Seven-storey tower built in 1758 by John Perrott. One theory as to its origin is that Mr Perrott could, from its height, gaze on his late wife's grave 10 miles away. Since the late 1800s it has been used as an observatory.

The Dudley Canal This canal used to join the Worcester & Birmingham at Selly Oak, thus providing a southern 'bypass' round Birmingham. The eastern end of the canal has been closed for many years, and will certainly remain so. The tremendously long (3795yds) Lappal Tunnel (now collapsed) emerged 2 miles from Selly Oak. This bore was more like a drain pipe than a navigable tunnel, as it was only 7ft 9in wide, a few inches wider than the boats that used it, and headroom was limited to a scant 6ft. Boats were assisted through by a pumping engine flushing water along the tunnel, but it must still have been a nightmarishly claustrophobic trip for the boatmen.

Bournville Garden Factory The creation of the Cadbury family, who moved their cocoa and chocolate manufacturing business south from the centre of Birmingham. The Bournville estate was begun in the late 1800s and is an interesting example of controlled suburban development. The old canal wharves can be clearly seen, but nowadays most of the ingredients travel by rail – the shunting engines are painted in the familiar Cadbury's livery.

Cadbury World Linden Road (by the factory) (021-458 2000 ex 2843). The story of chocolate. Audio visual, a jungle, and Victorian Birmingham. *Open 10.00–17.30 Mon-Sat, 12.00–18.00 Sun.* Admission charge.

Selly Manor and **Minworth Greaves** Bournville. Two half-timbered Birmingham houses of the 13th and early 14thC re-erected in the 1920s and 1930s in Bournville. They contain a collection of old furniture and domestic equipment. *Open Tue, Wed, Fri afternoons.* Enquiries to the Curator, 44 Mulberry Road, Bournville, Birmingham B30 1TA. *The nearest point of access from the canal is at Bournville station: walk west to the Cadbury's entrance. There is a public right of way (Birdcage Walk) through the works: bear right at the fork, then turn right at the village green. The two houses are close by, on the left.*

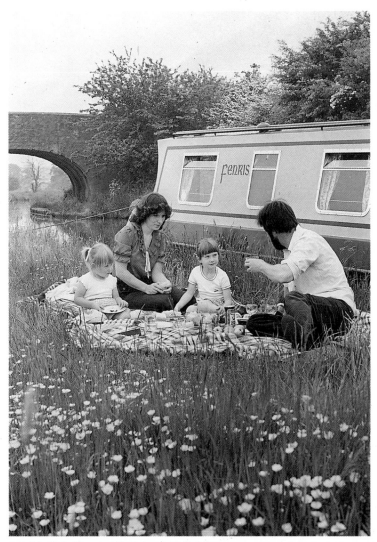

A picnic beside the Worcester & Birmingham Canal. *Derek Pratt.*

Birmingham

The Worcester & Birmingham Canal now
completes its delightful approach to
Birmingham, and in only the last few hundred
yards to Gas Street Basin does it assume the
appearance of a typical Birmingham
waterway. The railway disappears underneath
in a tunnel to New Street station, while the
canal suddenly makes a 90-degree turn left to
the basin. The terminus of the Worcester &
Birmingham Canal is the former stop lock;
this is known as Worcester Bar, for originally
there was a physical barrier here between the
Worcester & Birmingham Canal and the
much older Birmingham Canal. The latter
refused to allow a junction, and for several
years goods had to be transhipped at this point
from one canal to the other. This absurd
situation was remedied by an Act of
Parliament in 1815, by which the last stop lock
was allowed to be inserted to connect the two
canals. Nowadays the stop gates are kept open
and one can pass straight through, on to the
Birmingham Canal. This canal goes under a
short tunnel (or a long bridge) with a church
on top of it, to Farmer's Bridge Junction.
From here the Birmingham Canal aims off
north west towards the body of the
Birmingham Canal Navigations network (*see
book 2*).

*The route described below is the Birmingham &
Fazeley Canal from Farmer's Bridge to Salford
Junction, where it links up with the canals
described in book 2 of this series.*

Turning north east off the main line of the
Birmingham Canal, one arrives shortly at
Cambrian Wharf, a pub, sanitary station and
moorings all overlooked by four big blocks of
flats. There are some well-painted locks too,
for from this point the superb Farmer's Bridge
flight of 13 locks descends steeply into the
heart of Birmingham. Many of the locks were
built very close together and so the intervening
pounds were expanded as much as possible in
every direction. This results in one side of
each lock becoming like a peninsula, flanked
by water. The course of the flight is mainly
dark and mysterious, for over the years the
canal has become frequently crossed by
bridges, and even roofed over by vast
buildings, but much recent work has
transformed this once forgotten area into a
tidy and exciting environment, a popular
walking and jogging route for the city dwellers.
After passing the base of Birmingham's Post
Office Tower and under the great arch of the
now closed Snow Hill station, the canal levels
out as the locks come to an end. But soon
comes Aston Junction, marked by the old iron
turnover bridge, on which is cast 'Horseley
Iron Works Staffordshire 1828'. Here there is
an intriguing mixture of old canal
architecture, green open space and the hi-tech
buildings of the University Science Park. To
the north east is the main line of the
Birmingham & Fazeley, falling through the 11
Aston locks to Salford Junction. At the second
lock from the bottom is a lock-keeper's
cottage: its gate onto the road gives access to a
small grocery, a petrol station and a pub.
Towards Salford Junction itself, the buildings
become fewer and lower as the canal creeps
quietly under a tangle of motorways which
comprise Gravelly Hill, otherwise known as
Spaghetti Junction.

Salford Junction At this unusual junction
the Birmingham & Fazeley arrives from
Birmingham, crossing the River Tame on an
aqueduct and bearing half right (east) towards
Minworth and Fazeley. Meanwhile the short
Birmingham & Warwick Junction Canal
appears from the Grand Union Canal to the
south, also crossing the River Tame on a low
aqueduct. The straight canal entering the
junction from the north west is the Tame
Valley Canal, part of the BCN system.
However, this intersection of waterways is of
little significance compared to what is going
on overhead, for this is the site of the
notorious Gravelly Hill interchange – the most
elaborate urban road junction in Britain. So

the whole area of Salford Junction is completely overpowered by the mass of concrete pillars and decking carrying the lines of unseen vehicles in all directions. The sky is truly filled with roads, while the canals creep along underneath. The noise is a little disheartening, but it is a fascinating way to see this remarkably lavish piece of civil engineering.

The Digbeth Branch This leaves the Birmingham & Fazeley main line at Aston Junction, and descends through six locks to Bordesley Basin, now disused, where it meets the former Warwick & Birmingham Canal, which became part of the Grand Union Canal when the GUC Company was formed in 1929. There was a stop lock – called Warwick Bar – at the junction by Bordesley Basin. One of the lesser-known tunnels on the canal system is on the Digbeth Branch – Ashted Tunnel. There is a narrow towpath through it, protected by railings and with a corrugated surface for the towing horses to get a good grip on.

Cambrian Wharf The winner of a Civic Trust award in 1970, it is now looking the worse for wear. The construction of four new tower blocks of flats near Farmer's Bridge (very close to the centre of Birmingham) provided the incentive for BWB to dredge out and restore the basins at the beginning of the former Newhall branch canal; for Birmingham City Council to make a pleasing canalside walk and restore two 18thC terraces of cottages in the nearby Kingston Row; and for a local brewery company to build a new canal pub. There are moorings available here. For walkers, it is impossible to go by canal from Cambrian Wharf to Gas Street Basin (*see below*), since the towpath is sealed off at Cambrian Wharf. One must therefore go through the streets, and the route is as follows: Cambrian Wharf, Kingston Row, St Martin's Place, Cambridge Street, straight across Broad Street, down Gas Street and turn left through a small opening. This leads down onto the towpath at the Basin.

Gas Street or Worcester Bar Basin Before the demolition of the surrounding warehouses, this basin had a unique atmosphere. It is still full of colourful narrowboats, but the new buildings are uninspiring. The basin is shaped like a flat triangle, with a causeway across the middle. *See page 192 for an explanation of the 'Worcester Bar'.*

BOATYARDS

Ⓑ **Sherborne Wharf** (Brummagem Boats) Sherborne Street Wharf, Oozell's Street Loop west of Farmer's Bridge Junction (021-455 6163). Ⓡ Ⓢ Ⓦ Ⓓ Pump-out, gas, wet dock, overnight mooring, winter storage, books and maps, boat building, boat sales and repairs. Toilet.

BOAT TRIPS

Second City Canal Cruises (021-643 4384). Trips from Gas Street Basin to the Black Country Museum and around the BCN *each weekend*. Also trips *some weekday lunchtimes (phone for details)*. Private charter, gift shop, museum.
Sherborne Wharf Trips for parties of up to 48 people. Details from 021-455 6163.

PUBS

🍺 **Duke of Wellington** near the second lock from Salford Junction, on the Birmingham & Fazeley Canal. The only pub easily accessible from the canal between Farmer's Bridge and Salford.
🍺 **James Brindley** Gas Street Basin. A noisy modern pub offering seafood *lunchtime and early evenings (Mon-Sat)*.
🍺 **Flapper and Firkin** Cambrian Wharf. Canalside, near the top lock. Ansells real ale, food.
🍺 **Prince of Wales** Cambridge Street, 2 minutes from Farmer's Bridge Junction. A fine unspoilt local serving Ansells, Tetley's and Ind Coope (Burton) real ale. Snacks at *lunchtime and early evenings.*

Cambrian Wharf, Birmingham. *Derek Pratt.*

A BRIEF HISTORY OF BRITISH CANALS

River navigations, that is rivers widened and deepened to take large boats, had existed in England since the Middle Ages: some can even be traced back to Roman times. In 1600 there were 700 miles of navigable river in England, and by 1760, the dawn of the canal age, this number had been increased to 1300 miles. This extensive network had prompted many developments later used by the canal engineers, for example, the lock system. But there were severe limitations: generally the routes were determined by the rivers and the features of the landscape and so were rarely direct. Also there were no east-west or north-south connections.

Thus the demand for a direct inland waterway system increased steadily through the first half of the 18thC with the expansion of internal trade. Road improvements could not cope with this expansion, and so engineers and merchants turned to canals, which were used extensively on the continent.

One of the earliest pure canals, cut independently of existing rivers, was opened in 1745, at Newry in Northern Ireland, although some authorities consider the Fossdyke, cut by the Romans to link the Rivers Trent and Witham, to be the first. However, the Newry is more important because it established the cardinal rule of all canals, the maintenance of an adequate water supply, a feature too often ignored by later engineers. The Newry Canal established the principle of a long summit level, fed by a reservoir to keep the locks at either end well supplied. Ten years later, in England, the Duke of Bridgewater decided to build a canal to provide an outlet for his coal mines at Worsley. He employed the self-taught James Brindley as his engineer, and John Gilbert as surveyor, and launched the canal age in England. The Bridgewater Canal was opened in 1761. Its route, all on one level, was independent of all rivers; its scale of operations reflected the new power of engineering, and the foresight of its creators. Although there were no locks, the engineering problems were huge; an aqueduct was built over the River Irwell at Barton, preceded by an embankment 900yds long; 15 miles of canal were built underground, so that boats could approach the coal face for loading (eventually there were 42 miles underground, including an inclined plane), and the puddled clay method was used by Brindley to make the canal bed watertight. Perhaps most important of all, the canal was a success financially. Bridgewater invested the equivalent of £3 million of his own money in the project, and still made a profit.

Having shown that canals were both practical and financially sound, the Bridgewater aroused great interest throughout Britain. Plans were drawn up for a trunk canal, to link the four major rivers of England: the Thames, Severn, Mersey and Trent. This plan was eventually brought to fruition, but many years later than its sponsors imagined. Brindley was employed as engineer for the scheme, his reputation ensuring that he would always have more work than he could handle. The Trent & Mersey, and the Staffordshire & Worcestershire Canals, received the Royal Assent in 1766, and the canal age began in earnest.

Canals, like the railways which followed, were built entirely by hand. Gangs of itinerant workmen were gathered together, drawn by the comparatively high pay. Once formed, these armies of 'navigators' - hence 'navvies' - moved through the countryside as the canal was built, in many cases living off the land. All engineering problems had to be solved by manpower alone, aided by the horse and occasional steam pump. Embankments, tunnels, aqueducts, all were built by these labouring armies kept under control only by the power of the section engineers and contractors.

The Staffordshire & Worcestershire Canal opened in 1770. In its design Brindley determined the size of the standard Midlands canal, which of course had direct influence on the rest of the English system as it was built. He chose a narrow canal, with locks 72ft 7in by 7ft 6in, partly for reasons of economy, and partly because he understood that the problems of an adequate water supply were far greater than most canal sponsors realised. This standard, which was also adopted for the Trent & Mersey, prompted the development of a special vessel, the narrowboat, with its 30-ton payload. Ironically, this decision by Brindley in 1766 ensured the failure of the canals as a commercial venture 200 years later, for by the middle of the 20thC a 30-ton payload could no longer be worked economically.

The Trent & Mersey was opened in 1777; 93 miles long, the canal included five tunnels, the original one at Harecastle taking 11 years to build. In 1790 Oxford was finally reached and the junction with the Thames brought the four great rivers together. From the very start English canal companies were characterised by their intense rivalries; water supplies were jealously guarded, and constant wars were waged over toll prices. Many canals receiving the Royal Assent were never built, while others staggered towards conclusion, hampered by doubtful engineering, inaccurate estimates, and loans that they could never hope to pay off. Yet for a period canal mania gripped British speculators, as railway mania was to grip them 50 years later. The peak of British canal development came between 1791 and 1794, a period that gave rise to the opening of the major routes, the rise of the great canal engineers, Telford, Rennie and Jessop, and the greatest prosperity of those companies already operating. At this time the canal system had an effective monopoly over inland transport: the old trunk roads could not compete, coastal traffic was uncertain and hazardous, and the railways were still a future dream. This period also saw some of the greatest feats of engineering.

An early photograph of the Foxton 'staircase'.

A contemporary view of canal promoters. *Eric de Maré.*

The turn of the century saw the opening of the last major cross-country routes; the Pennines were crossed by the Leeds & Liverpool Canal between 1770 and 1816, while the Kennet & Avon (opened in 1810) linked London and Bristol via the Thames. These two canals were built as broad navigations: already the realisation was dawning on canal operators that the limits imposed by the Brindley standard were too restrictive, a suspicion that was to be brutally confirmed by the coming of the railways. The Kennet & Avon, along with its rival the Thames & Severn, also marks the introduction of fine architecture to canals. Up until then canal architecture had been functional, often impressive, but clearly conceived by engineers. As a result the Kennet & Avon has an architectural unity lacking in earlier canals. The appearance of architectural quality was matched by another significant change: canals became straighter, their engineers choosing as direct a route as possible, arguing that greater construction costs could be outweighed by smoother, quicker operation, whereas the early canals had followed the landscape. The Oxford is the prime example of a contour canal, meandering across the Midlands as though there were all the time in the world. It looks beautiful, its close marriage with the landscape now makes it ideal as a pleasure waterway, but it was commercial folly.

The shortcomings of the early canals were exploited all too easily by the new railways. At first there was sharp competition by canals. Tolls were lowered, money was poured into route improvements; 14 miles of the Oxford's windings were cut out between 1829 and 1834; schemes were prepared to widen the narrow canals; the Harecastle Tunnel was doubled in 1827, the new tunnel taking three years to build (as opposed to 11 years for the old). But the race was lost from the start. The 19thC marks the rise of the railways and the decline of the canals. With the exception of the Manchester Ship Canal, the last major canal was the Birmingham & Liverpool Junction, opened in 1835. The system survived until this century, but the 1914-18 war brought the first closures, and through the 1930s the canal map adopted the shape it has today. Effective commercial carrying on narrow canals ceased in the early 1960s, although a few companies managed to survive until recently. However, with the end of commercial operation, a new role was seen for the waterways, as a pleasure amenity, a 'linear national park 2000 miles long'.

Water supply has always been the cardinal element in both the running and the survival of any canal system. Locks need a constant supply of water - every boat passing through a wide lock on the Grand Union uses 96,000

The rudimentary tools of the early 'navvies'. *Hugh McKnight.*

Worcester and Birmingham Canal Company toll ticket dated 1816. Hugh McKnight.

gallons of water. Generally two methods of supply were used: direct feed by rivers and streams, and feed by reservoirs sited along the summit level. The first suffered greatly from silting, and meant that the canal was dependent on the level of water in the river; the regular floods from the River Soar that overtake the Grand Union's Leicester line show the dangers of this. The second was more reliable, but many engineers were short-sighted in their provision of an adequate summit level. The otherwise well-planned Kennet & Avon always suffered from water shortage. Where shortages occurred, steam pumping engines were used to pump water taken down locks back up to the summit level. The Kennet & Avon was dependent upon pumped supplies, while the Birmingham Canal Navigations were fed by six reservoirs and 17 pumping engines. Some companies adopted side ponds alongside locks to save water, but this put the onus on the boatman and so had limited success. Likewise the stop locks still to be seen at junctions are a good example of 18thC company rivalry; an established canal would ensure that any proposed canal wishing to join it would have to lock *down* into the older canal, which thus gained a lock of water each time a boat passed through.

Where long flights or staircase locks existed there was always great wastage of water, and so throughout canal history alternative mechanical means of raising boats have been tried out. The inclined plane or the vertical lift were the favoured forms. Both worked on the counterbalance principle, the weight of the descending boat helping to raise the ascending. The first inclined plane was built at Ketley in 1788, and they were a feature of the West Country Bude and Chard Canals. The most famous plane was built at Foxton, and operated from 1900-10. Mechanical failure and excessive running costs ended the application of the inclined plane in England, although modern examples work very efficiently on the continent. The vertical lift was more unusual, although there were eight on the Grand Western Canal. The most famous,

built at Anderton in 1875 (and currently being rebuilt), stands as a monument to the ingenuity shown in the attempts to overcome the problems of water shortage.

Engineering features are the greatest legacy of the canal age, and of these, tunnels are some of the most impressive. The longest is at Standedge, on the Huddersfield Narrow Canal (not navigable throughout, but restored in part). This tunnel runs for 5716yds through the Pennines, at times 638ft below the surface. It is also on the highest summit level, 644ft above sea level. The longest navigable tunnel is the Dudley Tunnel, at 3154yds long (but internal combustion engines must not be used, due to inadequate ventilation). Others of interest include: Blisworth, at 3056yds long; the twin Harecastle Tunnels on the Trent and Mersey Canal – the first 2897yds long and now disused, the second 2919yds and still in use; Sapperton, which carried the Thames & Severn Canal through the Cotswolds, and Netherton on the Birmingham Canal Navigations. This last, built 1855-58, was the last significant tunnel to be built in England, and was lit throughout by gas lights, and at a later date by electricity.

Netherton Tunnel was built wide enough to allow for a towing path on both sides. Most tunnels have no towing path at all, and so boats had to be 'legged', or walked through.

The slowness and relative danger of legging in tunnels led to various attempts at mechanical propulsion. An endless rope pulled by a stationary steam engine at the tunnel mouth was tried out at Blisworth and Braunston between 1869 and 1871. Steam tugs were employed, an early application of mechanical power to canal boats, but their performance was greatly limited by lack of ventilation, not to mention the danger of suffocating the crew.

An electric tug was used at Harecastle from 1914 to 1954. The diesel engine made tunnel tug services much more practical, but diesel-powered narrowboats soon put the tugs out of business: by the 1930s most tunnels had to be navigated by whatever means the

Islington Tunnel during construction. *Hugh McKnight.*

boatman chose to use. Legging continued at Crick, Husbands Bosworth and Saddington until 1939.

Aqueducts contribute significantly to the excitement of the canal system, with Telford's elegant structure at Pontcysyllte on the Llangollen Canal standing head and shoulders above all others. It crosses the River Dee at a height of 120 feet, using a cast iron trough mounted on slim stone pillars. Taking ten years to build, it opened in 1805. A couple of miles away, on the same canal, the sturdy stone built aqueduct at Chirk would seem impressive, were it not for the magnificence of its close neighbour. Amongst many others, Sir Edward Leader Williams' swing aqueduct at Barton is particularly interesting, as it crosses the Manchester Ship Canal with a 234-ft 800-ton section which swings at right angles to let ships through.

Until the coming of the diesel boats, the horse reigned supreme as a source of canal power. The first canals had used gangs of men to bow-haul the boats, a left-over from the river navigations where 50-80 men, or 12 horses, would pull a 200-ton barge. By 1800 the horse had taken over, and was used throughout the heyday of the canal system. In fact horse towage survived as long as large-scale commercial operation. Generally one horse or mule was used per boat, a system unmatched for cheapness and simplicity. The towing path was carried from one side of the canal to the other by turnover bridges, a common feature that reveals the total dominance of the horse. Attempts to introduce self-propelled canal boats date from 1793, although most early experiments concerned tugs towing dumb barges. Development was limited by the damage caused by wash, a problem that still applies today, and the first fleets of self-propelled steam narrowboats were not in service until the last quarter of the 19thC. Fellows, Morton & Clayton, and the Leeds & Liverpool Carrying Co. ran large fleets of steam boats between 1880 and 1931, by which time most had been converted to diesel operation. With the coming of mechanical power

the butty boat principle was developed: a powered narrowboat would tow a dumb 'butty' boat, thereby doubling the load without doubling the running costs. This system became standard until the virtual ending by the late 1960s of carrying on the narrow canals. Before the coming of railways, passenger services were run on the canals; packet boats, specially built narrowboats with passenger accommodation, ran express services, commanding the best horses and the unquestioned right of way over all other traffic. Although the railways killed this traffic, the last scheduled passenger service survived on the Gloucester and Berkeley Canal until 1935.

The traditional narrowboat with its colourful decoration and meticulous interior has become a symbol of English canals. However, this was in fact a late development. The shape of the narrowboat was determined by Brindley's original narrow canal specification, but until the late 19thC boats were unpainted, and carried all male crews. Wages were sufficient for the crews to maintain their families at home. The increase in railway competition brought a reduction in wages, and so bit by bit the crews were forced to take their families with them, becoming a kind of water gipsy. The confines of a narrowboat cabin presented the same problems as a gipsy caravan, and so the families found a similar answer. Their eternally wandering home achieved individuality by extravagant and colourful decoration, and the traditional narrowboat painting was born. The extensive symbolic vocabulary available to the painters produced a sign language that only these families could understand, and the canal world became far more enclosed, although outwardly it was more decorative.

As the canals have turned from commerce to pleasure, so the traditions of the families have died out, and the families themselves have faded away. But their language survives, although its meaning has mostly vanished with them. This survival gives the canals their characteristic decorative qualities, which make them so attractive to the pleasure boater and the casual visitor.

FISHING

Many anglers start their fishing careers on the canals and navigable rivers. Most of these cross-country waterways have natural reed-fringed and grassy banks, and in addition to the delightful surroundings the fishing is generally good. In most areas there has been a steady improvement in canal fishing in recent years, and in many places new stocks of fish have been introduced. The popular quarry are roach, perch and bream, but the canals also hold dace, tench, chub and carp. There are also pike and other species in particular areas.

Canals afford good hunting grounds for those seeking specimen fish (that is, fish above average size), and these are liable to be encountered on almost any water. The canals also make good venues for competition fishing, and in most places nowadays matches are held regularly at weekends throughout the season.

The statutory close season for coarse fish is March 15 to June 15 inclusive, but in some areas the close season is from February 28 to May 31, and there may be a special close season for pike from March 15 to September 30.

Permits and fishing rights

Most parts of the waterways system are available to anglers. The big angling associations - eg the London AA, Birmingham AA, Reading & District AA, Coventry & District AA, Nottingham AA plus many smaller clubs - rent fishing rights over extensive areas on the system. In most cases, day tickets are available.

On arrival at the waterside it is essential to make enquiries as to who holds the fishing rights, and to obtain a permit if one is required *before* starting to fish. Remember, also, that a National River Authority rod licence is usually required in addition to a fishing permit. It is essential to obtain these *before* starting to fish. Some fishing permits and licences are issued by bailiffs along the bank, and local enquiry will help to determine this.

A canalside pub or a local fishing tackle shop are good places to enquire if permission or day tickets are required for a particular stretch of water. Canal lock keepers are usually knowledgeable about the fishing rights in the immediate locality, and often a lock keeper may be found who issues day tickets on behalf of an angling association, or owner. It is likely that he will also know some of the better fishing areas, as well as local methods and baits which may be considered most successful.

The fishing rights on most canals are owned by British Waterways, and many miles of good fishing are leased to clubs and angling associations. They also issue day tickets on certain lengths, so it is worth enquiring at the local British Waterways Office (addresses in this book) when planning a trip. Special arrangements are made for fishing from boats - again, enquire with BW locally.

'Private fishing' notices should *not* be ignored. If the owner's name and address is on the board, then application can be made for permission for a future occasion. Once permission has been obtained it would be advisable to find out if there are any restrictions imposed, since some clubs and associations ban certain baits, or have restrictions on live-baiting for pike: and on some fisheries pike fishing is not allowed before a specified date.

Other restrictions may concern size-limits of fish, and this certainly applies to the London AA canal fisheries. Some by-laws prohibit the retention of under-sized fish in keep nets. A local club holding the fishing rights may have imposed their own size-limits in order to protect certain species. Such restrictions are generally printed on permits and licences.

Tackle

In the slow moving and sluggish waters of canals float tackle needs to be light, and lines fine, in order to catch fish. When fishing for roach and dace lines of 1½lb to 2lb breaking strain are the maximum strength normally needed in order to get the fish to take a bait - particularly when the water is clear, or on the popular reaches that are 'hard-fished'.

Fine tackle also means small hooks, sizes 16 and 18 - or even as small as 22 at times. Such light gear is also effective when fishing for the smaller species, such as gudgeon and bleak. This tackle will require a well-balanced float to show the slightest indication of a bite.

Bait

Baits should be small, and maggots, casters (maggot chrysalis), hempseed, wheat, tiny cubes of bread crust, or a small pinch of flake (the white crumb of a new loaf) may take fish. It always pays to experiment with baits; bait that is effective on one occasion will not necessarily prove to be as effective on the next. With slight variations, similar fishing methods can be used effectively on the majority of waterways.

Northern anglers who regularly compete in contests on canals use bloodworms as bait. They have become extremely skilful in using this tiny bait and often take fish on bloodworms when all other baits fail. Bloodworms are the larvae of a midge, and are a perfectly natural bait, gathered from the mud. After a wash in clean water, they are ready for use.

The basis of most groundbaits is bread, and many other materials may be added, although stodgy mixtures should be avoided, as canals do not respond to heavy groundbaiting tactics. It is far better to use a cloudbait, and this can be purchased ready for use. Some anglers wet their cloudbait with milk instead of water to increase its effectiveness.

Barbel

Bleak

Common Bream

Bullhead

Common Carp

Chub

Dace

Freshwater Eel

Gudgeon

River Lamprey

Perch

Minnow

Roach

Pike

Ruffe

Rudd

Stickleback

Tench

Brown Trout

Methods

Once the swim - that is the area of water to be fished - has been decided upon, and the tackle set up, use a plummet to find the depth and adjust the float, but be cautious when doing so in clear waters. At times it may be best to find the depth by trial and error. Often most fish will be caught around mid-water level, but always be prepared to move the float further up the line in order to present the bait closer to the bottom, where the bigger fish are usually to be found. At frequent intervals toss a few samples of the hook-bait into the top of the swim to keep the fish interested.

Fish in different waters may vary in the way they take a bait, and this creates a different bite registration. It may be found that fish take the hook-bait quickly, causing the float to dip sharply or dive under the surface. The strike should be made instantly, on the downward movement. On some canals the fish are even quicker - and perhaps gentler - not taking the float under at all, and in this case the strike should be made at the slightest unusual movement of the float.

Roach and dace abound in many lengths and, although working the float tackle down with a flow of water takes most fish, better quality fish - including bream - are usually to be taken by fishing a laying-on style, with the bait lying on the bottom. This method can often be best when fishing areas where there is no flow at all. The float tackle should be adjusted to make the distance from float to hook greater than the depth of water, so that when the float is at the surface the bait and lower length of line are lying on the bottom.

An alternative method of fishing the bottom is by legering, using a weight, but no float. Without a float a bite is registered at the rod-tip where, if need be, a quiver-tip or swing-tip may be fitted. Legering is a method often used where barbel and chub are found. These species grow to good sizes in canal waters - chub up to 7lb and barbel up to 14lb have been taken, but these are exceptional and the average run of fish would be well below those weights. Nevertheless, both species are big fish and big baits and hooks may be used when fishing for them.

Many bigger than average fish - of all species - have been taken by fishing the bait on the bottom. Whatever the style of leger fishing, always choose the lightest possible weight, and position it some 12 to 18in up from the hook. There are no hard and fast rules governing the distance between weight and hook, so it pays to experiment to find the best to suit the conditions.

Anglers who regularly fish the Northern and Midland canals invariably use tiny size 20 and 22 hooks, tied to a mere ¾lb breaking strain line, and when float-fishing use a tiny quill float - porcupine or crow quill. A piece of peacock quill is useful because it can be cut with scissors to make it suit prevailing conditions. Such small floats only need tiny weights to balance them correctly, and usually the angler positions these on the line just under the float, so that the bait is presented naturally. Once the tackle has been cast out, the bait falls slowly through the water along with hook-bait samples, which are thrown in at the same time. This is called 'fishing on the drop'. A fine cloudbait is also used with this style.

Canals which have luxuriant weed growth harbour many small fish, which are preyed upon by perch. These move in shoals, and invariably the perch in a shoal are of a similar size. Usually the really big perch are solitary, so it pays to rove the canal and search for them. They are to be caught from almost any canal and, although they are susceptible to various angling methods, the most effective is usually float-fishing. The fishing depth can vary according to conditions, time of year, and actual depth of the canal, so it pays to vary your approach. The usual baits for perch are worms, small live-baits (minnows etc) and maggots. Close by wooden lock gates is a favourite haunt of large perch.

In certain places canals and rivers come together and take on the characteristics of the river (ie with an increased flow) and different methods are needed. These places are often noted for splendid chub (and sometimes barbel) in addition to roach and other species. Trotting the stream is a popular and effective fishing style.

Weather

Weather conditions have to be taken into consideration. Canals often run through open country and catch the slightest breeze. Even a moderate wind will pull and bob the float, which in turn will agitate the baited hook. If bites are not forthcoming under such conditions then it may be best to remove the float and try a straightforward leger arrangement.

When legering, the effects of the wind can be avoided by keeping the rod top down to within an inch or two of the water level - or even by sinking the rod-tip below the surface. Nevertheless, in some circumstances a slight wind can be helpful because it will put a ripple on the water, and this can be of assistance when fishing in clear waters.

Where to fish

Most canals are narrow and this makes it possible to position the tackle towards the far bank, where fish may have moved because they had been disturbed from the near bank. Disturbance will send the fish up or downstream and often well away from the fishing area. So always approach the water quietly, and remember to move cautiously at all times. When making up the tackle to start fishing it is advisable to do so as far back from the water as possible to avoid scaring the fish. It pays to move slowly, to keep as far from the bank as possible, and to avoid clumping around in heavy rubber boots. If there is cover along the bank - shrubs, bushes, tall reeds and clumps of yellow flag iris - the wise angler will make full use of it.

There are some canals that are no longer navigable, and these are generally weedy. At certain times in the season the surface of the water disappears under a green mantle of floating duckweed, which affords cover and security for the fish. It is possible to find the best sport by fishing in the pockets of clear water that are to be found.

Some canals have prolific growths of water lilies in places, and are particularly attractive for angling. They always look ideal haunts for tench, but they can also be rather difficult places from which to land good fish. Tench are more or less evenly distributed throughout the canals and the best are found where weed growth is profuse. It may be best to fish small areas of clear water between the weeds. Groundbait can encourage tench to leave the weed beds, and to feed once they are out. Sometimes it is an advantage to clear a swim by dragging out weeds or raking the bottom. This form of natural groundbaiting stirs the silt, which clouds the water and disturbs aquatic creatures on which the fish feed.

Bream seem to do well in canals and some fairly good fish up to 5lb may be taken. Any deep pools or winding holes (shown on the maps) are good places to try, particularly when fishing a canal for the first time.

Other places worth fishing are 'cattle drinks' regularly used by farm animals. These make useful places to fish for bream, roach and dace. The frequent use of these drinking holes colours the water, as the animals stir up the mud, and disturb various water creatures. The coloured water draws fish into the area - on the downstream side of the cattle drink when there is the slightest flow.

Pike are to be found in every canal in the country - they are predators, feeding on small fish (which gives a sure indication of the most effective baits). Any small live fish presented on float tackle may take pike. The best places to fish are near weed beds and boats that have been moored for a long time.

The great majority of canals are cut through pleasant and peaceful countryside, and this enables anglers to spend many delightful hours along the banks - and always with the chance of making a good catch. As a general rule, never fish in locks on navigable canals, or anywhere that could obstruct the free passage of boats. Remember that you will inconvenience yourself as well as the boatman if you have to move in a hurry, or risk a broken line.

Don't obstruct the towpath, or make life difficult for walkers, cyclists or disabled people. Never leave discarded line or weights on the bank, and never throw these items into the water. Waterfowl may become entangled in the line. Use non-lead weights only. All responsible anglers take their spoilt tackle and litter home with them, and dispose of it properly. An irresponsible minority don't, and get the rest a bad name.

British Waterways produce a 'Waterways Code for Anglers', which can be obtained from British Waterways Offices, the addresses of which are given in this book. All who intend to fish on BW's waterways are strongly advised to obtain a copy, as it contains information regarding safety, health and pollution.

BRITISH WATERWAYS OFFICES

CUSTOMER SERVICES
British Waterways, Willow Grange, Church Road, Watford, Hertfordshire WD1 3QA (0923 226422).

AREA OFFICES

Will deal with enquiries regarding stoppages, long-term moorings and specific problems on a particular canal. The canal manager's telephone number is given on the introductory page for each waterway.

Birmingham Area British Waterways, Peels Wharf, Lichfield Street, Fazeley, Staffordshire B78 3QZ (0827 252000).
Grand Union Canal (north of Napton)
Stratford-on-Avon Canal
Worcester & Birmingham Canal

Gloucester Area British Waterways, Llanthony Warehouse, The Docks, Gloucester GL1 2EJ (0452 525524).
Kennet & Avon Canal
Monmouthshire & Brecon Canal
Gloucester & Sharpness Canal
River Severn

South East Area British Waterways, Brindley House, Corner Hall, Lawn Lane, Hemel Hempstead, Hertfordshire HP3 9YT (0442 235400).
Grand Union Canal (south of Braunston)
Lee & Stort Rivers
Oxford Canal

For assistance from operational staff outside normal office hours, and at weekends, dial 100 and ask for **FREEPHONE CANALS.** *Vodaphone* and *Cellnet* users should call 0384 240948.

Other navigation authorities are listed in the appropriate place in the text.

Lock mechanism, Worcester & Birmingham Canal. *Derek Pratt.*

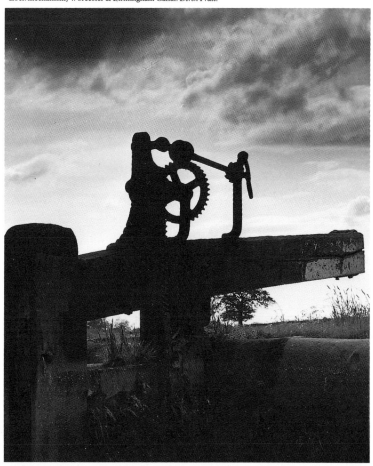

INDEX